FAMILY LAW AND POLITICS WITH BIOLOGY AND ROYALTY IN AFRICA AND NORTH AMERICA

PETER ATEH-AFAC FOSSUNGU

Edited by Tendai Rinos Mwanaka

Mwanaka Media and Publishing Pvt Ltd,
Chitungwiza Zimbabwe
*
Creativity, Wisdom and Beauty

i

Publisher: Mmap
Mwanaka Media and Publishing Pvt Ltd
24 Svosve Road, Zengeza 1
Chitungwiza Zimbabwe
mwanaka@yahoo.com
www.africanbookscollective.com/publishers/mwanaka-media-and-publishing
https://facebook.com/MwanakaMediaAndPublishing/

Distributed in and outside N. America by African Books Collective
orders@africanbookscollective.com
www.africanbookscollective.com

ISBN: 978-1-77929-595-8
EAN: 9781779295958

© Peter Ateh-Afac Fossungu 2021

DISCLAIMER
All views expressed in this publication are those of the author and do not necessarily
reflect the views of *Mmap*.

Dedicated To Getting Africa Into Africa

Table of Contents

INTRODUCTION

I believe firmly that education has failed Africa woefully because we Africans persist in sheepishly following or copying others rather than innovating or reinventing; not paying the required attention to our proper existential conditions. All this holding because the brand of teaching as well as its mode of delivery we have so far been exposed to would give us the idea that intellectuals are only those who can read and write a language that is not even ours; that these intellectuals are to be found only within the formal academy, etc. wearing suit and tie even under hot African sun. This book (like most of my other writings) comes to reverse the "abstract learning" trend by relating education and living to the reality of the people concerned. Intercontinental as it is, this narrative revolves around the Bangwa generally but Nwangong Fondom especially. According to some experts, "the Nwangong Royal Family Politics can be so complexly informative, hurtful and enjoyable – all at once. That, I think, is the logical price and beauty of multitude and diversity: the more interestingly so when truthfully exposed" (Fossungu, 2015: 107). Such truthful exposure is one of the hallmarks of this book which is geared toward educating and entertaining as well as also provoking a rethinking in the circles of family law and politics, in the spheres of unity and of poverty reduction discourses, and of development generally.

Truth, they say, is constant and always prevails eventually. Africa is thus gladly bringing some to North America (and the rest of the world), hoping that the latter would be open enough to straightforwardly embrace and learn. That is, especially from Momany who is said to be "exceptional in the domain and [the world must] thus valuably learn something from his moving love and understanding experiences" (Fossungu, 2014: 119). I would want to immediately give so many thanks (in advance) to all the Bangwa Fons, Chiefs, and other title holders who are here to enormously aid in impacting on our understanding of some family law and politics topical issues relating to solidarity and progress, and therefore children's welfare and community advancement: given that these children are generally considered to be the future of a nation or country. It is helpful here to pose some fundamental queries drawn from the Just Lecturer's reprimanding/counselling statement to the sensible and humble visiting city teacher:

Do most of us claiming intellectualism in this country or continent even know what we don't know? Do we believe our villages could be places to get instruction from? Has time not proven those old Bangwa village women right? Can most of us, Africans, now be able to distinguish the fox in goat-skin? Have we really reached this stage? In other words, have we already learnt the lessons that have all this while been cut off our present textbooks [which are even written by lielistical non-Africans, for that matter]? (Fossungu, 1998: 10)

The square-bracketed information is leaning on Mawere and van Stam (2015: 198) who have pertinently theorised that "many of the texts on Africa are written by foreigners who, from their experiences as researchers, visitors or travellers, write 'about Africa'.

Meanwhile lielistical (from lielisticalism (Fossungu, 2015c: 73)) is anchored on their incapability to tell it as it is. For instance, take the majesty of Great Zimbabwe National Monument about which some Great Zimbabwe University scholars have competently theorized that early scholars such as Carl Mauch and Theodore Bent, among several others, completely rejected the indigenous origins of the site. Sadly, several scholars – including the local ones – years later and even to date, followed the same erroneous approaches of interpreting the monument using borrowed Western-biased scientific lenses, regardless of the fact that some of them do not fit in context. These lenses have ultimately presented people with an incomplete story of Great Zimbabwe National Monument (Mubaya, Mawere and Chikozho, 2015: 316).

All that, I must emphasize, must necessarily invite a very persisting and clear call for Frantalkism (see Fossungu, 2016) which is obviously the backbone of the Immaculate Freedom, Unity and Development Theory. Its handmaiden is Crisebacology which involves a lot of separating-cooperating and balancing of different matters of love, family, and academics at the same time. But it can very briefly be seen here as the science of critical balancing in whatever we do or talk about (see Fossungu, 2014: 25-29); with some experts equating or analogising it to "The Value of Balanced Critique" (Fossungu, 2015a: 104-126). In pursuit of such balanced critique, therefore, Dr Folefac Fidelis has energetically argued in the ill-famed Postponementolodramacracy in the Cameroon Goodwill Association of Montreal (CGAM) that "differences in ideas, reasoning and understanding should not be considered personality conflict. It is this type of reasoning or interpretation in the reverse direction that is driving us behind" (cited in Fossungu, 2018: 81). The science of crisebacology obviously has no problem with his postulation. In said discipline, when there is an imbalance, the crisebacologist (or balanced critical thinker) has to attempt equalising by either (1) taking off some of the (unnecessary) stuff from one side or (2) adding stuff to the other side (matter that was not there and thus creating the imbalance). I am inclined to think that it is more helpful and sensible to engage in alternative two than one, especially when star-like corner-kickers (or traitors) are involved, as they certainly are in the family cohesion and progress tango under review that is inestimably affecting blameless children adversely.

Children are so important to society that their upbringing and education must be critical to any community that desires to be united and progressive.

Isn't their importance being endlessly sung in the 'future leaders of tomorrow' cliché? This maliciously ambiguous value could even also be deduced from some self-centred American politicians "when they present their descendants as the best proof of their investment in the future" (Bruni, 2016). But do they actually put these children's future in the priority position of what they do? Some experts have responded to this central query by seeing in the 'future leaders of tomorrow' cliché only the use of children as "the new excuse for everything" (Selick, 1996a: 46). Thus, according to Maitre Karen Selick, Human beings, generally speaking, are fond of children. We can't help it – we're hard-wired that way. Maybe millions of years ago a branch of our evolutionary tree had members who detested children; but it would have quickly died out, for obvious reasons. Unfortunately, this fondness makes us vulnerable to manipulation and skullduggery. Just as kidnappers use children to extort money from distraught parents, other scoundrels in philanthropists' clothing invoke our affection for kids to inveigle us into all sorts of dubious deals (Selick, 1996a: 46, paragraghing altered).

You are invited to read on then to the end and decide what grade to accord to this experienced Canadian family lawyer (and others still to come) for theorizing as she does (they do) in this untraditional book whose driving force unmistakably is "fossungupalogy (that is, the science of straightforwardness, necessitating the fearless looking at truth in the eye)" (Fossungu, 2015a: xi). With four Chapters, the first explores the relationship between biology, gender, 'modern' education, and unity in the context of African family law and politics in order to provide some answers and solutions to the nagging problems of unity and progress in both family and the larger community. The second Chapter studies children wellbeing politics as well as the philosophies behind the names given to them, learnedly breaking down some hard-to-comprehend African cultural and philosophical theories to easily digestible bits to both non-Africans and Africans themselves. The third Chapter, still within the confines of the family, demonstrates how to get Africa into Africa by employing the expibasketical science in accentuating the critical importance of Four-Eyesism or seething intellectualism; making it clear that authentic lessons in Four-Eyesism could really be what Africa really needs for its liberation, protection and development, not Africa-bashing postcolonial education. The fourth Chapter advocates a rethinking in the circles of unity conversation, poverty and illiteracy elimination discourses, and development communication; eruditely charting the much needed re-direction while also greatly enhancing our comprehension of the ineffectiveness of the little-known Illiteracy and Poverty Eradication Projects that are hinged on the studied family to demonstrate how substituting *Africa* in place of *family* in it can give one a near perfect explanation of why the continent (like the family in question) remains behind the others. The concluding part reinforces the importance of eschewing unnecessary categorizations, two-facedness and one-sidedness in family and other relationships

CHAPTER 1

BIOLOGY, GENDER, AND UNITY IN AFRICAN FAMILY LAW AND POLITICS: DISAPPOINTING THE MARSIAN EXPLORER IN CANADA

Two-facedness is unhealthy for progress and this contribution is all about the truth which is known to seriously hurt a lot of its haters. Anyone sensible enough will thus not fail to agree with Dr Fidelis Folefac, a Bangwa title holder – Nkem – based in Montreal, Canada, who posited in August 2006 (during the aforementioned CGAM Debates) that "if we must grow as a family, then we need to act without fear or favour" (cited in Fossungu, 2018: 89). An expert has expibasketically theorised in support that

You cannot know yourself until you can confront the truth about yourself and also about those you deal with. If you are not afraid of your own truth, you will hardly be scared of someone else's truth. Those who tell the truth about themselves do not do so to get pity and/or praise; only those who tell lies do (Fossungu, 2013: 1).

Truth can never be logical to liars, just as truth-tellers would not accept or embrace lies: unless you untruthfully make lies and truth synonyms rather than the antonyms that they truthfully are. That is not to truthfully say though that truth-tellers should cease from 'Texas-Massachusettsly Hammering' the truth home at all times, with 'Africa Keenly Watching' (Fossungu, 2015: chapter 5).

This chapter thus explores the relationship between biology, gender, 'modern' education, and unity in the context of African family law and politics in order to provide some answers and solutions to the nagging problems of unity and progress not only relating to the studied Royal Family but the world community at large. In other words, the question of why unity and progress are such headaches in the Nwangong Royal House is dug into by examining the relationship between biology, gender, postcolonial education, and unity in the context of African notions of

1

family and community. It is aligned on the two interlocking concepts of trouble and of division, notions which are hardly bedfellows of the peace and harmony and progress that would appear to have dominated the life of Chief Formbuehndia (aka Emmanuel Nguajong Fosungu) who is seen in Figure #1. The philosophy of unity is therefore studied through *Formbuehndialization*, using the estate and other similar family disasters to sustain the case against divisive categorisation of a household's children – a discrimination which is better known as *Mamiteelization*.

Figure #1: Chief Formbuehndia Nguajong & HRM Fon David Foncha Fossungu in 1993
Source: Photo Dave, Yaoundé

The job of this chapter is handled under three major parts. The first schools readers on the family background and unity issues of the central family in the Nwangong Royal House, before the second troubles the metrics of *Mamiteelization* (or the biological discrimination of children) in the context of the estate cataclysm and the unique succession formula that the Fondom appears to be proudly and confusedly holding out to the entire world for emulation! The third part is devoted to studying the disillusionment of the visiting explorer from Mars to Canada, a disappointment provoked by the moneyintrigusit comportment of African biological mothers which is highly sustained by that country's faulty children welfare policies.

Polishing Up the Troublesome and Divisive Biography and Uncovering the Grand Family-Unity Philosophy

A better understanding of the unity-and-development arguments of this book would obviously benefit from a little knowledge at this point on the farsighted Bangwa Chief called Chief Formbuehndia. A smooth comprehension of the issues would require that I first polish up the Chief's troublesome and divisive biography that brings in the grand wisdom acquired. As noted already, this Chapter is aligned on the two interlocking concepts of trouble and of division which are hardly bedfellows of the peace and harmony and progress that would seem to have dominated Chief Formbuehndia's life. I will thus first study the said notions through *Formbuehndialization* in the course of which the kicking against divisive categorisations of a household's children will be attained. To that end, I have to make great use of biographical information from royal burial and funeral programmes, including particularly that of Mamie Regina, to fortify the grand family-unity theory. The second part of the chapter is devoted to a study of the consequences of family disunity and distrust, eventually leading to the Chief Formbuehndia unique succession formula and estate disaster.

Figure #2: Chief Foletia (aka Vincent Aghegndia. Sixtus Fossungu) in October 2002
Source: Benji Photo-Video, Dschang

Why unity and progress are such problems in the Nwangong Royal House is something that I will simply let the biographies and death programmes of some Nwangong Royals lead readers to the land of discovery, beginning with the biography of Chief Formbuehndia himself which was presented by Chief Foletia Vincent (his brother who is seen in Figure #2) at the funeral ceremony on 19 October 2002. That presentation during his burial-funeral event indicated that Chief Formbuehndia Nguajong was born in 1931 in Nwangong Fondom, Alou Sub-Division in Lebialem Division of Debundschazone of Cameroon. The Chief attended Catholic School Bota in Victoria (now Limbe), N.A.

School Tali in Mamfe, and Technical High School Enugu in Nigeria. Upon graduation from Enugu as an engineer, he returned to West Cameroon and worked for Powercam Bota in Victoria, and then became station manager of Powercam Yoke and Kumba, respectively, from 1968 to 1974. From 1974 to 1990 when he went on retirement, he served as the provincial head of statistics for SONEL (French acronym for the national electricity corporation) Limbe. He left behind eight children and twelve grandchildren.

That was a portion of the biography, as given at the *attehttah* (ceremony ground), with the said children being made up of many girls and just two boys; namely, Joseph Njumo Fosungu and Bernard Mbancho Fosungu "who is followed, in order, by Beatrice Nguikem Fosungu; Annastasia Chamo Fosungu; Maureen Nkengafac Fosungu; Gladys Mazano Fosungu; Quinta Alonche Fosungu; and Justine Mamefat Fosungu. Justine was born almost at the same time with Delphine Fosungu from papa's other younger wife, Julie Fosungu" (Fossungu, 2013: 7). From these further details, two family unity issues can immediately be raised: (1) why Julie Fosungu and her daughter, Delphine Fosungu, never featured in Chief Formbuehndia Mbancho's call in November 2016 for the Combined Death Celebration (studied below); and (2) it would appear like Chief Foletia's talk of eight children above is faulty or that Chief Foletia (like Bernard – used most of the times in this book simply to avoid confusing the living and dead Chief Formbuehndia) was just referring to only the children of Thecla Anangfac Fosungu (Mamie Thecla – the woman behind *Mamiteelization* or the biological discrimination of children) because both Julie Fosungu and Delphine Fosungu in Figure #3 died long ago.

But the same death-science logic would still seem to fault the given number because Gladys Mazanue Fosungu in Figure #4 also died before their dad. The information is correct though since Therese Nkengafac Fosungu, the lone child from their dad's very first wife (who "had attempted to poison papa at the instigation of her *njumba*, a Nigerian man" (Fossungu, 2013: 40)) was still alive then and present at the burial

5

too, being the controversial *Asoba* in the new Chief Formbuehndia Royal Cabinet.

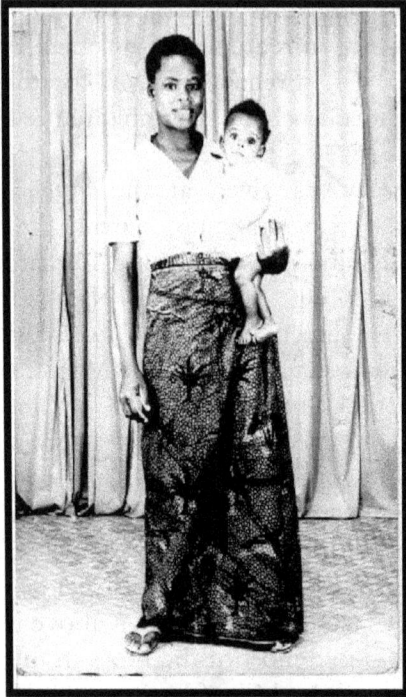

Figure #3: Julie Fosungu and daughter, Delphine Fosungu
Source: Julie Fosungu

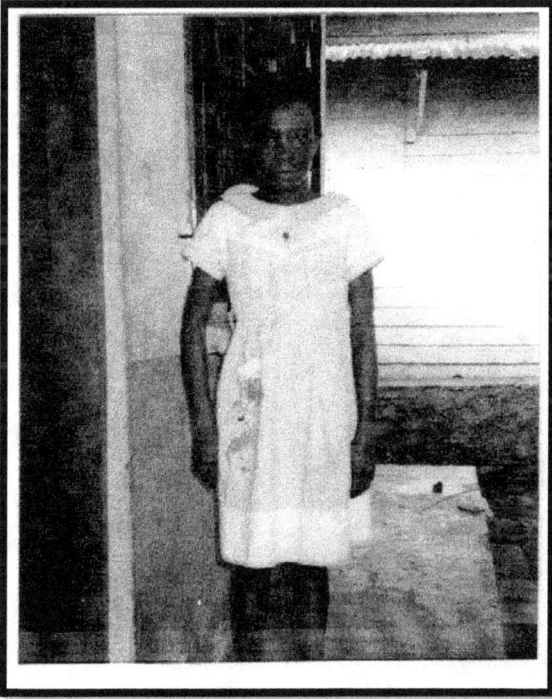

Figure #4: Gladys Mazanue Fosungu in the 80s
Source: Photos taken by Momany Fossungu

Biological Numerics and Interesting Unity Lessons from Mamie Regina's Biography
The biological problem though would seem to resonate around Josephine Forzi Fosungu in Figure #5, one of "the few older children in the household at the time I arrived there" (Fossungu, 2013: 7). Must she not be added to the list of surviving children? This query may appear especially fitting, since Chief Formbuehndia's 8-paragraph Will (titled 'THE WILL OF PA CHIEF FORMBUEHNDIA E.N. FOSUNGU', done and signed in Yoke Village, Muyuka by Pa Fosungu E.N. Formbuehndia) also provided in her regard in Paragraph 6: "…The administrator, Fosungu Anastasia, should always give 25.000 francs after every cocoa season to Madam Josephine and 25.000 francs to Madam

7

Beatrice." (The Will administrator is seen in Figure #6 with the other beneficiary in Figure #7). By the Will-providing reasoning, Marie-Claire Efuelancha Afueh (née Fossungu) and Peter Ateh-Afac Fossungu (aka Momany) both of whom are also named in Paragraph 2 of the Will would also fault the figure: "The plot at Letia (Nwangong Village) should be used by the entire family including Afueh Marie-Claire and Fossungu Peter Ateafac to be crowned Nkem. The plot at Mile I – Limbe should be built and used by the whole family accordingly."

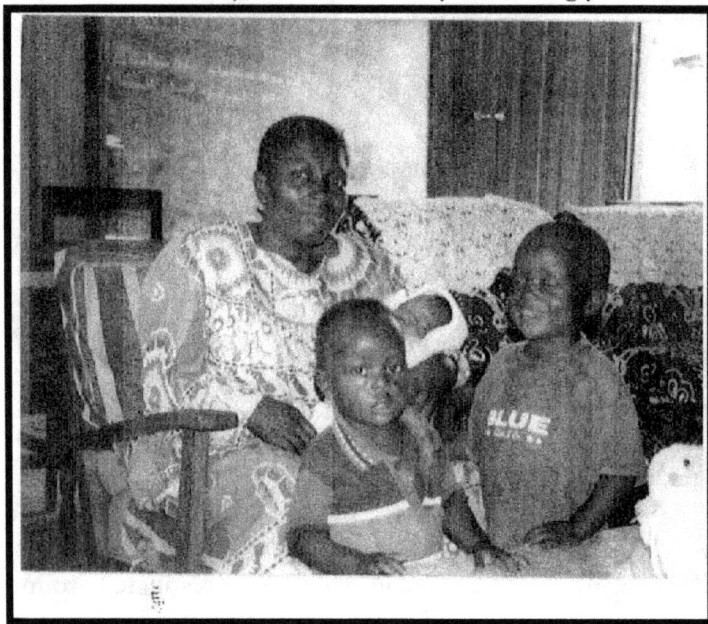

Figure #5: Josephine Forzi Fosungu and her grandchildren in Yoke in 2002
Source: Photo taken by Momany Fossungu

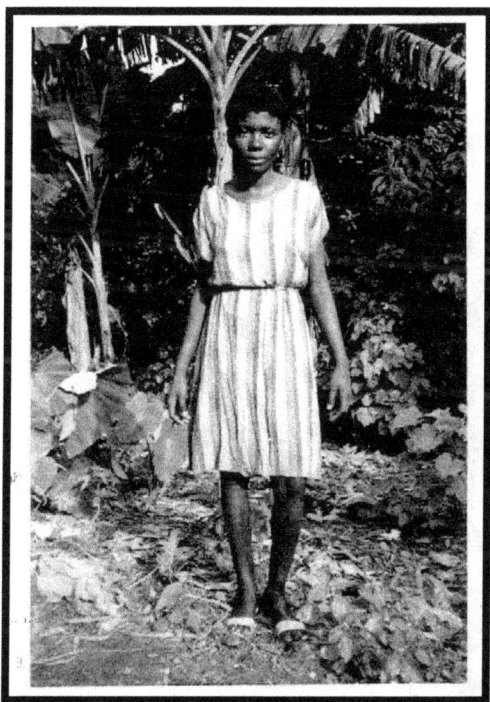

Figure #6: Anastasia Chamo Fosungu in the 80s
Source: Photo taken by Momany Fossungu

Figure #7: Beatrice Nguika Fosungu (carrying her daughter, Minette) in the 80s
Source: Photo taken by Momany Fossungu

The figure given by Chief Foletia is somewhat numerically good though in view of the fact that the detailed reading and exposition of the biography by Chief Foletia did make a clear distinction between Chief Formbuehndia's surviving biological children and those others that he raised (see Fossungu, 2013: 162). *Momanyism* would appear to stiffly question that distinction between a Household's children, this being based essentially on the "great wisdom that I have gained over the years; and would next be sharing with you through my large extended royal family generally but particularly my two sets of parents" (Fossungu, 2013: 2). Readers would correctly understand this Grand Family-Unity Philosophy especially within a study of the burial and funeral programmes relating to the Nwangong Royal House, including that of Mamie Regina – Momany's biological mother. Her burial and funeral programme and others may have to be described in this study to also strengthen the comprehension of unity and development in Africa (and elsewhere), which should be devoid of unhelpful discrimination. Let's then continue 'expibasketising' and 'crisebacologising' on the grand family-unity philosophy from the biography portion of the burial and funeral programme of Mamie Regina who is seen in Figure #8.

Figure #8: Mafor Regina Akiefac Fossungu in Nwangong Fondom in June 2004
Source: Photo taken by Momany Fossungu

An email got to Canada from Fon Nicasius Nguazong Fossungu, he being the one who could speedily get to Momany through email: since the main organizers (Nkemanang and his wife, and Mafor Fotale'eh Esther), awkwardly, don't use that medium – an issue of great concern that Chapter 4 further details out. The Fon's email was informing and asking Momany's views on what they had put up as programme for the burial and funeral of his birth mother. After reviewing everything and taking into consideration his tentative travel plans, on Monday, 23 June 2014, Momany sent out an email titled "Funeral Update" to the 8th Fon of Nwangong, also copying those others that he could reach through email with the following message:

HRM, Chiefs: Here is what the programme for mom's funeral briefly looks like. *Friday 18 July 2014*: Corpse leaves mortuary, spends the afternoon at Nkemanang's residence and travels in the night for Nwangong. *Saturday 19 July 2014*: Burial and Funeral. The Fon, Chief Fosanoh, and Caro [Fossungu], please do well to acquaint Nkemanang's family with this information even though I will be calling them when I get back to station (Windsor). Since I cannot get to everyone through this medium, do well to also inform any other interested persons. Thanks. PAF (Momany Fossungu, personal communication, 23 June 2014).

Figure #9: Mafor Fotale'eh, aka Mrs. Ndem: née Esther Asongnkeng Fossungu
Source: Fon Nicasius Nguazong Fossungu

It has to be stressed that Momany's only half-sister (Esther in Figure #9) was one of the resident principal organisers who needed to be acquainted with the information in the email above. On the same day, Chief Formbuehndia Bernard Mbancho of South Africa noted that the communication had been received and promising to react accordingly.

That action of his came in on the same day (23 June 2014) with counsel that the Yaoundé community be informed through Mr. Paul Agafina. The next day Momany agreed with Bernard's suggestion, saying he was sending an email right away to Paul Agafina. Mr. Agafina and other Yaoundé acquaintances were thus at the 2014 event in Nwangong. But that is not what is so important here; the thing of significance being that Fon Nicasius Nguazong Fossungu (in Figure #10) also wrote back in "Re: Funeral Update" and indicated that:

Figure #10: HRM Fon Nicasius Nguazong Fossungu
Source: Fon Nicasius Nguazong Fossungu

Message received and instructions to be executed. I was at Nkemanang's and we designed this programme for your appreciation. You have to respond in confirmation or rejection of a death celebration or a burial and 'cry die'. Here attached are: the biography and the initial programme, if you confirm the death celebration [that is funeral], then we will modify the programme. If not, you can correct mum's biography or complete it. Hoping to hear from you... I hardly go on the net this time (Fon NN Fossungu, personal communication, 27 June 2014).

I will not be handling the issue of 'burial and cry-die' and the entire programme here but simply be inviting readers to peruse one of the attachments the Fon was talking about; which is the following biography inserted here.

Biography :
Name : Regina Akiefac Fossungu
Date of birth : 1931
Place of birth : Nwangong-Fontem
Daughter of HRH Chief Fonge Ngecha
Mama got married to Karlemon Taleeh Mbunnyi Fossungu in 1947
She left behind many children and 13 (6) grandchildren to mourn her
[The confusing figures here are explained in the text following]

Source: Fon Nicasius Nguazong Fossungu & the Nkemanangs

It is not known exactly why, for grandchildren, they put in 13, and then 6 in brackets. But it would appear that they were in a way saying 13 grandchildren all together (from Momany and his three *blood* siblings: Vincent Awandem Fossungu in Figure #11, Esther Asongnkeng Fossungu, and Dieudonné Asongu Fossungu in Figure #12) but 6 from Mamie Regina's biological children – Dieudonné (1) and Momany (5)? Whatever it may be they were thinking, Momany simply asked for the bracket-figure to quickly disappear. Meaning that he does not see any need for making a difference between the grandchildren of Karlemon Tale'eh Fossungu based on who their own biological grandmothers (who are both Tale'eh's wives) are. Truly, family unity and progress would not be promoted by such irrelevant characterisations. If you don't quite grasp this very important message at this point, then I am positive that the 'Estate Catastrophe' in the second part of this Chapter would not fail to wonderfully do the job for you. Is Momany not entitled to be so happy

15

that (like he himself) his children just love themselves without caring about which womb they came out of? That appears to be the clear message of Figure #13 which shows Momany's Canadian children (from two different mothers). But would that family love and unite to survive with the obvious intoxication from their *biological* mothers?

Figure #11: Vincent Awandem Fossungu (aka Nkwetta Fotale'eh) in 2002
Source: Photo taken by Momany Fossungu

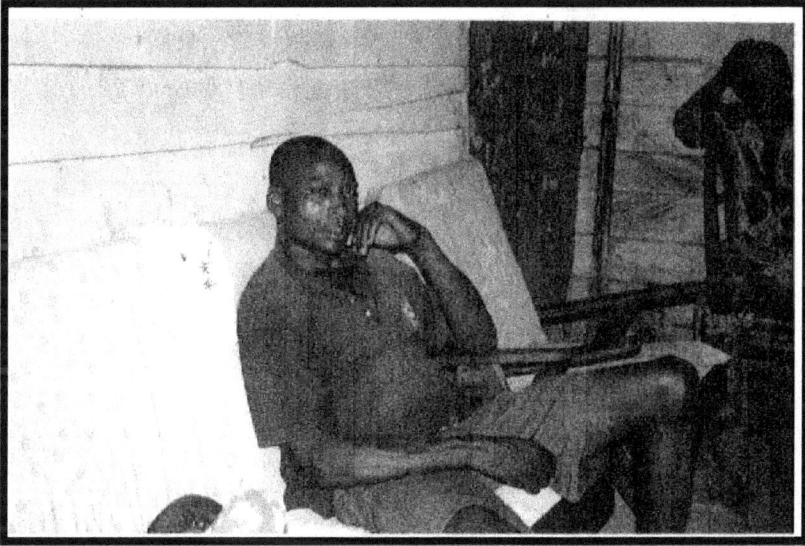

Figure #12: Asa'ah Fotale'eh, aka Dieudonné Asongu Fossungu in 2004
Source: Photo taken by Momany Fossungu

Figure #13: The Canadian Fossungus in 2010 (L-R): Ngunyi, Junior, & Nguajong
Source: Photo taken by Momany Fossungu

Issues of Family Distrust and Disunity Affecting Burial-Funeral Event and Combined Death Celebration

Talking of family unity and collaboration, the Chief Formbuehndia burial and funeral programme of October 2002 was not only altered without the knowledge of Momany who was coming from abroad; but it is also strange that even the Friday activities of the changed programme were not respected and everything was jammed into the Saturday plan. As Momany made known in an interview with the video person who covered the occasion:

The programme which had been given to me while I was still in Canada was changed while I was on my way without me being kept informed of the alteration. So, when I arrived here, everything was just so out of place from the initial schedule I had. But I have done my best to fit in and still do what I have been able to do so as to make papa's farewell ceremony one that would be remembered for a long, long time (Momany Fossungu, private communication, 19 October 2002).

I am not going into all the gymnastics of the alteration right now but merely to further note that the unbecoming programme alteration greatly contradicts the demands of family unity and trust, with the combined death celebration communications providing ample evidence. Crisebacologists truly think that if no one is bold enough (and no one that is a lover of the truth would afford not to be) to define Marie-Claire (and the likes of her) as hypocritical onesidetakists, then it is surely not this writer. She is a fat clumsy hypocrite; a *deceptionist* especially if one also reads her own homework-doing instructions to Scholastica, as well as on the issue of talking about what she is ignorant on.[1] Marie-Claire is also a

---

[1] Here is the entire email of Marie-Claire, for those who want a better handle on the whole sad story of a Royal House that is being led rather than leading:

Hello Miss Scholastica Asahchop,

This is in reference to the contents of your Email dated Friday 4/ 2/10. London, Canada. I was not only embarrassed, I was [also] disappointed with the way you ridiculed a young, talented, and respectable personality in the name of the Fon of Nwangong. He is not only a Fon to the people of Nwangong, he is also a father to some of us, and we know him better than you claimed you do. So please I do not know if this is Ignoran[ce] on your part, or you need help to put a certain message across.

You NEED TO FOLLOW THE PROPER PROCEDURE when you are about to broadcast any piece of information about him in the internet next time, OK? That

big bridge-burner. This bridge-burning attitude is especially perplexing when coming particularly from Chief Fofah Marie-Claire who would be minus zero today but for the invaluable non-discriminatory support she got from Momany both in and out of the Chief Formbuehndia Household. There are several other reasons for this assertion about Marie-Claire's bridge-burning mamiteelizalist comportment. Marie-Claire Efuelancha Afueh's instruction to Scholastica for the latter to do her own (love and devotion) homework well cannot be tenable. In short, it leads us directly to stiffly question if Marie-Claire herself does her own homework well enough to realise that one must not burn the bridge after crossing it so as not to prevent others behind from also crossing. Let me

---

means you need to discuss any information you intend to put in the internet with his representatives in USA and CANADA, a unanimous decision agreed upon, before it goes to the internet. The fact that he is poor does not in any circumstances allow you to reduce him to your level in the internet.

We have freedom of speech and expression in North America but not to use that in a negative way to degrade an excellent Leader and his Fondom. I would think that being in North America for these amounts of years would entail some wisdom in terms of the way we choose our words, but it does not seem like it. You might have had some good ideas behind your email but the manner in which it is portrayed is disgraceful and ridiculous. It's never too late to learn Miss. Leaders do not destroy. They protect, they repair, they guide, they caution and they communicate effectively.

Regarding matters of development in that village, you can write whatever color of email you wish and do development, it is your village. But, when it comes to his CHARACTER AND INTEGRITY, Please don't even Mess with it. For your information, his representatives in US and Canada are: Chief Forfah – USA; Dr. Nkemtaleh Fossungu – Canada. Give my kiss to the children and do your homework [this paragraph altered]

20

just use this brief instance of death and chieftaincy communications to bolster the theories concerned.

Bridge-Burning Death and Chieftaincy Communications and Acquisition

On Saturday, 26 November 2016, Chief Formbuehndia Bernard sent this message (captioned "Combined Death Celebration") to both Chief Fofah (Marie-Claire) and Chief Fotale'eh (Momany):

Dear Chiefs,

By this mail, I wish to inform both of you that the combined death celebration of late Formbuehndia E.N. Fosungu, Mama Thecla A. Fosungu, Br Joe Njumo Fosungu, Asaba Theresia Fosungu, Beatrice Fosungu, Gladys Fosungu [Annastasia Fosungu,] and Mrs Elizabeth Ngong Mbancho Fosungu has been programmed during the last two weeks of December 2017.

Chief Formbuehndia Bernard omitted Annastasia Fosungu. But that is not so much the essential point; which is rather that the following day (Sunday, 27 November 2016) Marie-Claire swiftly responded (in "Re: Combined Death Celebration") with the following:

Dear Chief Formbuehndia and Fortale'eh,

I saw the email. The timing is not good for me. It is too close for me to take any time off now. I will support you for whatever it takes for us to put a closure to the horrible past in the history of the entire family. Just looking at the list of lost family members was very hard for me. Not to mention those we lost in the Palace and those we lost on my mother's side of the family. It was a horrible period, and we pray NEVER TO EXPERIENCE THAT AGAIN. Extend my heartfelt and warm Greetings to the entire family. Forfah Marie Claire Afueh

Momany saw the two emails on Monday, 28 November 2016 and his brief response (in "Re: Combined Death Celebration") on that Monday was:

Well, it's in a year's time; quite some time for getting set. I am just wondering if Chief Fofah read 2016 instead of 2017. Also, in view of what the family as a whole has been through with these deaths, perhaps it would be better to have more time and proper coordination and sensitisation in order to have a wider celebration once and for all. In this scenario, two or three (max) years could do. Just my humble opinion. Chief Fotale'eh

For close to a month there was no further clarification or response from any of the two other Chiefs. But Chief Formbuehndia Mbancho later wrote on Tuesday, 6 December 2016 as follows:

Dear Fofah and Fotale`eh,

Firstly, my apologies for the belated acknowledgement of receipt of your respective responses to my mail and I would also like to thank you very heartily for that.

Secondly, from your mails, the conclusion I have gathered is that you are not ready for next year 2017 because we need enough time for proper coordination and sensitisation.

Thirdly, I would like to inform you that it was an uphill battle for me to convince most of the family members back home to postpone the celebration from this December to December 2017.

In this regard, I wish to plead with you that regardless of your very hectic schedule let us all try not to programme this celebration beyond December 2017. There has been a general outcry back home whereby many family members have attributed their numerous misfortunes to the fact that this death celebration has not been organised till date and they were hell-bent on organising it this December in order, according to them, "to perform the cleansing rites". Uniforms had already been bought to this effect but it was postponed only thanks to my persuasion that we abroad needed enough time to prepare.

Furthermore, I wish to inform you that I have forwarded your mails to the Fon in order that they serve as supporting documents for our proposal that we need enough time to prepare. Once I get his response, especially on whether the people back home are willing to wait beyond December 2017, or they would decide to proceed with the celebration whether we are ready to be physically present or not, I will keep you posted.

Thanks so much for your cooperation, and may the good Lord continue to bless and protect us all. Formbuehndia.

On Thursday, 8 December 2016 Momany read Chief Formbuehndia's email and wrote back in "Re: Combined Death Celebration" as follows (duly copying Chief Fofah):

Dear Chief Formbuehndia:

Thanks a lot for the additional information provided. It makes things a little clearer as well as explaining away some things that my earlier response was concerned about. Now that I know you weren`t alone in taking the decision for December 2017 (but done with approval of most of the people back home who even wanted it this December), I am comfortable with the December 2017 date (which wasn't really a problem with me personally, if you read again my previous response): except that I was particularly considering many others back there who (like the Fon and other village dignitaries) are to be heavily involved too.

Frankly, on some of these matters, waiting for ALL of us to be properly prepared can only mean NEVER having the thing done. You (as the head of this central family in the Royal House) must, in conjunction with the Fon, LEAD and the rest of us must simply have to find a way to fall into place. Thanks for informing us at least a year ahead. Chief Fotale'eh

Chief Fofah would appear to have completely dropped out of the dialogue as nothing is heard anymore from her end, and this cannot fail to remind me of her astonishing demeanour in October 2002 when Chief Formbuehndia Nguajong died (see Fossungu, 2016: 95-99). Absolute silence is now the rule on Chief Fofah's part: just as it has been with regard to the Chiefs of Nwangong since the chieftaincy that Marie-Claire got during the enthronement ceremony of Fon NN Fossungu in December 2007. It is thus not far-fetched to suspect that grabbing the chieftaincy title might even have been the sole reason for her presence at that 2007 ceremony in the Emollah Palace. Otherwise, how does one properly explain her conspicuous and unexplained absence at Chief Formbuehndia's funeral in 2002 and her present comportment towards the combined death celebration?

On 29 December 2016 Chief Formbuehndia wrote and made known to "Dear Fofah and Fotale`eh" (copying Fon NN Fossungu) that:

After a broad-base consultation both at home and in the Diaspora, it has been unanimously agreed that the Combined Death Celebration will be held during the SECOND HALF of December 2017.

The exact date will be communicated to you once the practical modalities have been finalised.

You will also be briefed on these practical modalities in due course. Wishing you and your families a very happy and prosperous New Year 2017.

Kindest regards, Formbuehndia.

Only then did Chief Fofah write back on 30 December 2016 (also copying Fon NN Fossungu) as follows:

Good morning Formbuehndia and Fotale`eh. I saw your email regarding the death celebrations. December 2017 is a good period of time to plan or make arrangements to travel. That said, I probably didn't take note of the year 2017 when I replied to your first email regarding this same issue. Not a guarantee but I will see what I can do. I am still struggling to put food on the table here but I will keep trying. I wish you and your family a happy and prosperous New Year 2017.

You can get a better orientation of the disunity problems also from Momany's further response to the interviewer's question seeking to know what message he had for "those here present and those not present?" The October 2002 interviews were conducted all through in French (and Pidgin) because Benjamin who covered that occasion is French-speaking. But, now speaking directly in English, Momany said:

My final word here would be some few words of gratitude to those who have made this possible. When papa died I was not on the spot. Of course, it is not just about money. I would have stayed in Canada, sent money here [such as just the flight ticket cost] and people would drink and eat. But the fact that I am not there makes all the difference; and I really feel it for my brothers and sisters who could not make it because, I can tell you, if I had just sent money, I would never have gone through what I have gone through. A lot of friends were there to help us out.

24

One problem, though, was that I arrived a bit late because the programme I had been given while I was still in Canada was changed without me knowing. But I have done my best to fit in and make Papa's farewell ceremony something we will live to remember. Thank you (Momany Fossungu, private communication, 19 October 2002).

The estate and other family disasters will now also be used to reinforce the unity and progress theories.

Troubling the Metrics of Mamiteelization with the Estate Catastrophe and Other Family Disasters

Whatever response anyone else would also give to the prejudice directed at certain children, if the case of Josephine (whose mother was Chief Formbuehndia's legal wife, with the child being obviously adopted by the man just like Peter was) would still raise biological classification questions in the circles of family bio-lawyers, no such problems could be presented by the inclusion of Therese (whose mother had long been sent off or divorced), who is even the *Asoba* (some Bangwa versions have it as *Asaba):* the controversial tradition-breaking post that must be explained as we study the estate catastrophe that raises as well the *asobarism* issues in so far as Therese Nkengafac Fosungu in Figure #14 is concerned.

The Estate Calamity Resulting from the Myth of Education and Gender Roles?

The response advanced to the central question here would largely depend on whether or not one opposes this modernity or certificate-education thing which would again and again be seen to be overly predominant in trampling on the people's culture or philosophy, which is undeniably the root of their existence and authentic evolution. The Royal Succession to the Nwangong Throne best illustrates the point. It is not to be delved into in this book but the headlong plunging into *Asobarism* in its respect could show easily that this 'meaningful meaninglessness' (as Fon DF Fossungu has intelligently defined *asobarism*) is apparently not different at all from an overturned Africa. An *Asoba* in Royal Cabinet parlance indicates that the normal successor (first or eldest child) has been circumvented.

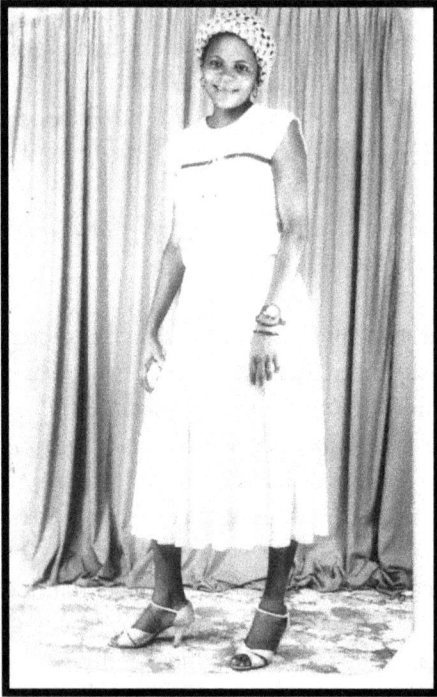

Figure #14: Therese Nkengafac Fosungu in the mid-80s in Kumba
Source: Therese Nkengafac Fosungu

Talking of the culturally offensive consequences of *Asobarism*, no one, of course, would be saying that Bernard Mbancho Fosungu doesn't merit his position as Chief Formbuehndia's successor. The point being also made now is that the new Chief Formbuehndia Mbancho concurred in his interview on the day of his coronation with what Commandant Michael Njumo also said while paying homage to the newly crowned Chief. One of the questions posed to Chief Formbuehndia Bernard Mbancho in his interview with Benjamin was: "What do you think about your papa's decision to see to it that you are now occupying his place?"

Answering the query on 19 October 2002, Chief Formbuehndia Mbancho of South Africa said that "I think it is a great honour for me that my father accorded me that confidence and I promise him that I would never fail him." Bernard (as the only other *biological* son) thus merited his place; the more so *en plus* after the Josephizationing-Letters renunciation (see Fossungu, 2015: 87). Bernard thus merited his place, if we have to go by the logic of *The Royal Palace* (the Nigerian movie) or African Royal Succession generally that usually looks at only male children, because it would have been crazy to expect Joseph being named by his father as the next of kin – except the deceased dad had to be emulating his own father, 'the King Solomon of Nwangong' (as Fon Sunday Tendongmo Fossungu is also called).

In the course of the educative Fossungu Family reunion of October 2010 Therese is shown not to be satisfied with her useless *masoba* position: "Another problem came from Maurine Fossungu that Masoba Formbuehndia (Nkengafac Therese) had sold all the houses that she could have stayed in and she is bringing a lot of disorder" (Fossungu Family Meeting Minutes, 28 October 2010). According to Paragraph 3 of the Will, "Nkengafac Therese [Fosungu] should own the house at Yoke near the Yoke water. She should use the farms but she has nothing to do with other properties." The perceptive role and influence of Constance Tumekong Fossungu (in Figure #15) could also be well noted during said family meeting. She is Momany's celebrated aunty and babysitter (see Fossungu, 2014: 22-23); also being Therese's age mate who quickly left Chief Formbuehndia's Household in total opposition to 'The Therese Pepper Incident' in Yoke (see Fossungu, 2013: 39-42) – one disreputable family episode that has legitimately provoked the question: "Was papa really someone who treated his children without bias?" (Fossungu, 2013: 40) Like several other critics of the tradition, Marceline Awa, for example, has also argued against that male-only tradition when "I encourage Cameroonian girls to engage in judo. They should abandon the old belief that women who practice judo can't bear children. That is just a myth. It is a false conception" (Sa'ah, 1997: 11). Pointing to her seven-month-old son, according to Sa'ah's (1997: 11) report, Marceline

27

Awa said: "This is the proof of what I am saying." It is thus greatly wondered if the role-sexing thesis is at the root of the brain-bursting succession formula from the Nwangong Royal House.

Figure #15: Constance Tumekong Fossungu (Momany's famous aunt & baby-sitter) in July 2014
Source: Derick Abomego

Role-Sexing Theory Engendering the Trilogized Succession Formula?

Could Chief Formbuehndia's woes with his own traditional successor (Joseph) be tied in any way to Chief Formbuehndia's own disrespect of Fon Sunday Tendongmo Fossungu's Will? Should Chief Formbuehndia also have emulated his own father (who Joseph Njumo Fosungu himself describes as "a very, very good man, a man of great personality" (Fossungu, 2015: 78)) by still making Joseph his next of kin despite Joseph's renunciation? Much more importantly, did Chief Formbuehndia think of Marceline Awa's *Role-Sexing Theory* above when he made his male child (Bernard) the successor but also excluded him from administrating his estate, in preference of the female child (Anastasia)? The concerned portion of the Will (Paragraph 1) entirely ordains as follows:

The whole administrator is Fosungu Anastasia. She is assisted by Fosungu Justine and Fosungu Maureen. The successor (next of kin) is Bernard Mbancho Fosungu. The Nkwetta is Njumo Joseph. The Asaba is Nkengafac Therese Fosungu. The Mafor is Fosungu Justine. The caretaker for all the farms is Nguazong Nicasius.

What value is in 'the next of kin' when the administration of the estate is out of your reach? A Unique Succession Formula too from Nwangong Fondom? I am not here going to venture into the stories floating around how Anastasia's moneyintriguist husband 'conned' Anastasia (who was then the preferred 'eyes' of the blind living father: see Fossungu, 2016: 119-20) into transferring all the wealth to themselves (himself, no doubt) and then subsequently eliminated the wife after the deal was done: in order to have a very free hand in "enjoying his life" with other ladies. After all, was he not already very rich to have one woman tie him down? That is the chitchat which, again, I would avoid tackling since I cannot (and am not at all in any position to) verify. One of the said assistant Will administrators (Maureen) is seen in her youthful days in Figure #16.

Figure #16: Maurine Nkengafac Fosungu in the 80s
Source: Photo taken by Momany Fossungu

It is hard to plunge into verifying some of these issues floating out there because even Anastasia's own and other mysterious deaths in the family Momany only heard from strangers and not from family members. You can get the proof from his white friends in Edmonton (Canada) who in September 2004 were "just wondering how things are working out with Scholastica and the kids. Are you in the same place in Montreal or do you have a new address?" (Nancy Whistance-Smith, private communication, September 2004). Momany then responded in the 2nd paragraph of his "Re: Thinking of You", stating that:

I lost a sister back home. She was thirty-one, married, with children. Two days ago I learnt her death was not usual, that a certain cousin of ours is responsible and that all of my late father's children, including me, have been booked for the same faith. The next in line is another sister who is a gendarme in Yaoundé, followed by me, etc. This is all coming from a soothsayer that they consulted last month after the burial. I just don't know what to believe anymore. And I hear they were in the village to perform some rites regarding this story. Surprisingly, I have only heard all this stuff from a stranger (a nurse in the heath post in the village), and not from any member of the family. I am so confused and don't know what to do. Extend my greetings (Momany Fossungu, private communication, 18 September 2004).

You can also hear Scholastica herself too declaring in one of her 'Numerous Communications on Children' (see Fossungu, 2014: 67-68) and more specifically her 1998 'children-insisting' letter (which is studied below in the third part) to Momany (while she was still in Cameroon) that 'Most rumours in Cameroon are always true'. Also remember though how it is said that 'there is no smoke without fire.' Did that fire actually consume Chief Formbuehndia's enormous wealth (and thus leaving his progeny deprived) because of his singularly distinctive 'Succession Formula'? And what could actually be behind it?

What is the Invisible Hand behind the Formbuehndialized Succesion Trilogy?

Of course, there is another ignored girl (Beatrice) between Therese and Anastasia but it is good to stick here with just *Asobarism*. So, if there must be a female administrator apart from the male successor, why was Therese (the first daughter and first child) also side-lined here? I cannot pretend to have the answers right away. But what is quite obvious is that Therese could not have ignited the *Asobarism* issues. You have nevertheless seen her still somewhat challenging her relegation to the 'uselessly useful' *Masoba* (female version) 'nonsense' by selling property even against the prohibition in the Will:
Fosungu Beatrice should be given two rooms in the compound at Yoke (near the market). This should be on a semi-permanent basis. Nobody should claim any property for his or her own self-interest. None of the

property should be sold out. The compound at Yoke should be jointly developed by the entire family (Paragraph 5).

Does postcolonial education also lie behind the succession trilogy or what is it that actually influenced it? To add to the allure of the questionable 'postcolonial-education-based'

Nwangong Royal Succession in the Fondom itself in 2007, is the fact also that the victorious young Fon NN Fossungu in that majestic 'life-and-death' fight is not only the namesake of late Chief Formbuehndia (Nguazong) but also began his title-holding journey as Chief Formbuehndia's *Asa'ah* (4th Royal Cabinet position), as heavily testified by Figure #17. The Will of Chief Formbuehndia Nguajong, in the first paragraph (as fully outlined above) also makes him the caretaker of all the farms, being only too clear for any altering.

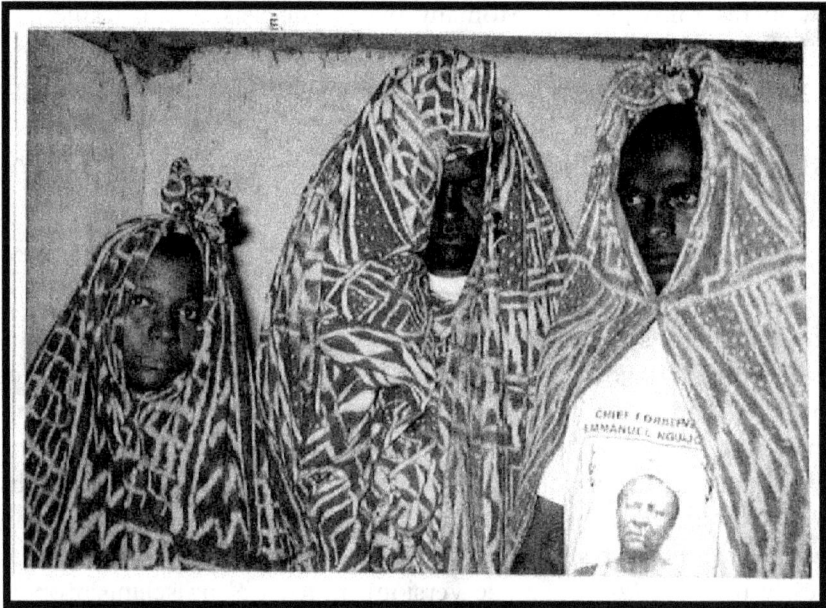

Figure #17: Three of the Members of the Chief Formbuehndia Cabinet: Mafor Formbuehndia Justine, Chief Formbuehndia Bernard, & Asa'ah Formbuehndia Nicasius
Source: Benji Photo-Video, Dschang

You can then see that it might not just be by accident that Nicasius Nguazong (as he then was) would not only be in Chief Formbuehndia's cabinet but also assuming a position that is not the lowest (like Peter's). Do the *succelogists* or 'succession-biologists' have something valid to say here? That is, are they going to audaciously declared that Asa'ah Formbuehndia is actually Chief Formbuehndia's biological child or what? Furthermore, by the man's Will, Nicasius Nguazong is also the caretaker of all the farms (Paragraph 1); and it does not just end there. By the same Will, Nicasius Nguazong's mother (Prudencia Memala Fosungu in Figure #18) is also caretaker of the only house in the village:

The caretakers for the compound at Letia in Nwangong village are Chief Foletia V.A.S. and Memala Prudencia Fosungu. Fosungu Beatrice has no right to control the cocoa farm at Munyenge or to put a worker in the farm. The administrator, Fosungu Anastasia, should always give 25.000 francs after every cocoa season to Madam Josephine and 25.000 francs to Madam Beatrice (Paragraph 6).

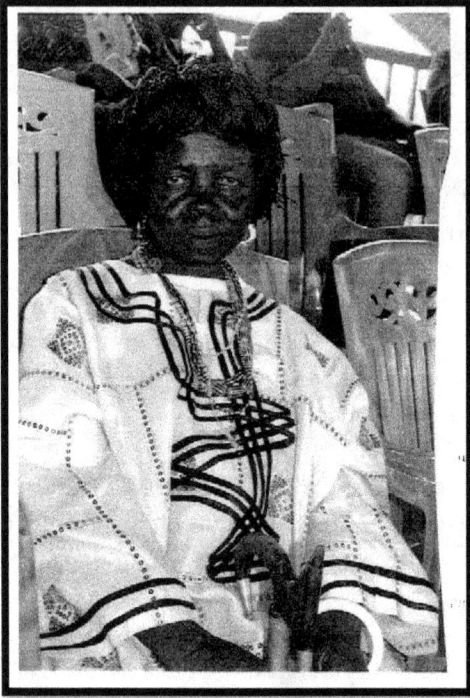

Figure #18: Prudencia Memala Fossungu
Source: Fon Nicasius Nguazong Fossungu

Yeah, the *Formbuehndialized Succession Trilogy*: successor not *the administrator* of estate; successor not *the caretaker* of estate; successor just *successor in name*! How could this man's mammoth estate ever have withstood the moneyintriguing tempest? Two of the most prominent factors that have been advanced as being behind the overturning of Africa are the identical twins of moneyintriguism and onesidetakism. What was/is behind the trilogized succession formula: frustration with his (male) children's skills or what? What does biology really have to do with it? Fon David Foncha Fossungu (who is seen again in Figure #19 during the said event) would appear to have the essential piece of the Trilogized Puzzle in his 'Thank You Speech' on the occasion of the Nwangong Generator Gift of 22

June 2004 from Momany (see Fossungu, 2013: 107-111). In the course of the vocalisations at said event, Fon DF Fossungu mentioned that Momany's heart is just like Chief Formbuehndia's. If someone could make a child that is not his biological child his successor, then he [Momany] is the one who would be Chief Formbuehndia's successor today. Chief Formbuehndia even brought up the idea to me and I flatly rejected it; because I just do not know where my own head would be today if I had let Chief Formbuehndia go ahead with this idea. I am talking about the interminable war that would have ensued from it and engulfed all of us (Fon DF Fossungu, private communication, 22 June 2004).

Figure #19: Fon David Foncha Fossungu (the "illiterate" Possessor of an intriguing amount of Four-Eyesism) is seen here flanked by some of his wives during the very significant and eye-opening June 2004 Palace Generator ceremony
Source: Photo taken by Momany Fossungu

The Chief Formbuehndia Estate Catastrophe would then seem to be a standard in family tragedy resulting from family disunity that is initiated and promoted by unhelpful Mamiteelizalist categorisations. The experts do not think I need to go on again pinpointing. But if that is still essential, then just imagine (from the narratives of Chapter 4, for instance) what Momany has been doing to uplift this particular family from (self-imposed, I must say?) poverty with the meagre financial means he could personally come up with. And then put that alongside what he would already have done with the deceased's gargantuan estate under his harmonious control and direction. But then the questions persist. Would Momany have been able to successfully do the job while being stiffly confronted with what Fon DF Fossungu has very prophetically described as "the interminable war"? And this 'four-eyes' Nwangong Fon is not far from the point, viewing that the traditional biological heir made it very clear in his highly circulated Josephizationing Letters that "I am a blood man. I wouldn't mind risking my life in prison for what I stand for and believe in" (cited in Fossungu, 2015: 77). Add to all that the fact that Momany was never told anything about anything during or after the burial-funeral; not even being aware of the existence of the Will or its contents until 2008 when:

Already in the course of realizing this particular Canada College project [in regard of Mafor Formbuehndia Justine], at one point (as in the just noted case of asking for photos) he asked for certain documentation from Justine so as not to rely solely on what he had in his head as her essential information. Precisely, Momany wanted her birth and academic certificates to be sent to him. Justine sent the requested documents while also including a copy of Chief Formbuehndia's Will, a paragraph of which touches directly on what Momany was even then doing without knowing. Could Justine just have included that Will simply because it mandated what the man was doing? I am talking about the 7th paragraph of the Will which ordains that "Madam Justine Fosungu should take her studies very seriously and be careful the way she uses her money (finances). Peter Ateafac Fosungu, Marie-Claire Afueh, Mbancho Bernard [Fosungu] and Njumo Joseph [Fosungu] should take proper care for Justine M. Fosungu for her education problems" (Fossungu, 2016: 103-104).

Would it also be by divine intervention then (using the moneyintriguist and dragdownist Asahchopination (see Fossungu, 2016: chapters 1 & 4)) that Momany was never able to answer to Chief Formbuehndia's earnest request for Momany to come over and see him (Chief Formbuehndia) "for some important discussions"? In his 'Centrality' interview during the Chiefs funeral, Momany had also made it clear in a paragraph that:

Before his death, I tried all what I could to come and see him as requested, and the idea was to get here by December this year or ending of November. Unfortunately though, in October I learnt he had left us. It wasn't easy at all but I have done all what was possible to be here. As you must have noted, everything appears to be going well. That's all I can say for now because I'm unaware of whatever instructions or other information that papa left. Events have just been following, one behind the other, and I haven't had the opportunity to be briefed on anything. I am hoping the others who were on the spot would give me some briefing afterwards (Momany Fossungu, private communication, 19 October 2002).

Whether or not Momany got that briefing, etc, makes no difference to what was happening that day in Nwangong, a Fondom whose family law and politics would evoke a lot of unanswered questions. For instance, was Chief Formbuehndia actually intending to ignore Fon DF Fossungu's advice on the matter and still make "his able son" (as he himself describes Momany (see Fossungu, 2016: 119)) the *gérant* of his estate: just as Fon ST Fossungu (despite then Emmanuel Nguajong Fosungu's refusal) had still handed the Nwangong Throne to him "to do whatever he wanted with it, hoping perhaps that my father would in the end see the need to be the central pillar of the family" (Fossungu, 2013: 155)? Would there even have been the possibility of the "interminable war" in the matter but for Mamiteelization? Is there any doubt then that Mamiteelization has upside-downed the Nwangong Royal Family in the same way as postcolonial education has indubitably done to Africa?

In somewhat responding to the question as well as cautioning the biological mothers who have been found in the next part of the Chapter to use children as "mere commodities for acquiring wealth" (Fossungu, 2014: 82), it has been firmly advised that:

No child should have to go through all what I went through simply because of some particular individual's selective definition of family or child; a designation, moreover, that would be exclusively geared toward making readily available resources for educating children unavailable to some children. A child must not be considered a child by the parents only insofar as the child's services are concerned but regarded not as a child when it comes to the education and other needs of that child (Fossungu, 2013: vii).

Biological Mothers and Children in the Money-Getting Business School of Canadian Institutions: Africa Defines Family Conceptions

This third part is an expibasketical or experience-based assessment of Canadian children welfare perspectives which would appear to largely disappoint the visiting Marsian explorer. It digs into the issue by handling children's general upbringing using the Canadian institutional case involving some African women in the unthinking/calculated ruining of children's future, with the active support and collaboration of the same Canadian institutions that are supposedly there to protect and promote children welfare. This portion of the discussion can only be a short addition to what readers can already find in *Canadian Institutions and Children's Best Interests* ((Fossungu, 2015d), a book that is "Dedicated To The Millions Of Children Undeservedly Suffering Solely Because Of The Scheming Of So-Called Parents, Fortified By The Complicity Of Canadian Institutions" (Fossungu, 2015d: iii). Said book is a significant volume in the domain since, according to Professor Mawere of the Faculty of Culture and Heritage Studies of Great Zimbabwe University, it is one of the most interesting and critical but nuanced texts I have reviewed in the past few years. It's more of an anthropological text on Canadian institutions based on rigorous ethnographic findings. The text is important in that it reverses the common trend, particularly in disciplines such as social anthropology, cultural studies, and ethnology that have a tendency of studying African societies without committing their resources and energies in understanding European and American societies (Fossungu, 2015d: back cover).

Readers are thus invited to reflect well on some definitions of family conceptions from African customary lawyers, such as Ndi Nkemanang Calestus Fossungu's important definition of motherhood. I will appositely and reiteratively instruct strangers to African family law and politics to further visit the same Lebialem (as Bangwaland is administratively called in Cameroon) for some clarifications of some family conceptions especially concerning children. The Bangwa provide amplification of certain family conceptions, not necessarily attaching biology to the definition of children or parents; this being most probably because there a child is not just that of the parents that combined in the 'doing of bad thing' to bring him/her into the world. It is the child of the community. Therefore, any elder who finds a child misbehaving takes it as his/her responsibility to correct (or discipline) the child without the biological parents making a fuss of the situation (Fossungu, 2015: 137).

Picture #20: Ndi Nkemanang Calestus Fossungu
Source: Fon Nicasius Nguazong Fossungu

Let us therefore listen attentively to what one Bangwa notable has to contribute here to (African) family law and politics. Ndi Nkemanang Calestus Fossungu (who is seen in Figure #20, in alluding to the irrelevant discrimination between children in a household particularly and community generally) did theorize on 18 July 2014, during the burial of Mamie Regina, that "someone's mother is not just the woman that carried him or her in the womb for nine months. It could be anyone that you even meet on the streets and who is caring enough to treat you as her child in the real humane sense of the word." The grand family-unity advocate called Momany appears to completely concur when he too postulated long ago that:

I think Mami Thecla could be summed up as the one woman that has greatly impacted on my life by not understanding and appreciating me for who I really am (e.g., as a child who never saw her in any other terms than a mother); this misunderstanding having had across-the-board

40

consequences on most of my junior brothers and sisters of the household whom I raised and babysat (Fossungu, 2013: 5).

Crisebacologists wouldn't need to go very far then to say that Nkemanang could be quite correct. The correctness is especially strengthened (among others) by these facts: (1) Nkemanang himself is splendidly bringing up children in his household who are not his biological children; (2) Mamie Regina was being cared for by Nkemanang and wife and not by her own biological child called Dieudonné Asongu Fossungu who was right there in Cameroon; and (3) one can comfortably relate his thesis to the plot-selling headaches in Chief Fonenge Vincent's household that is studied in Chapter 3, a tragedy which is not any much different from the estate disaster in Chief Formbuehndia Nguajong's household (as seen above) that is a typical example, and being the direct result of said discrimination of a household's children based on mere biology. Quite a disappointing biological motherhood awaits you in the rest of this Chapter! Readers really have to digest that African motherhood definition well before handing over the stage to the money-getting equation of short-sighted, children-abusing *biological* mothers, with Bangwaland's 'Village-City Multidimensional Man' (Fossungu, 2014: xv-xvii) called Momany who you see in Figure #21 still squarely being the pivot! He is just rightly all over the place, including particularly Canada, a country that surprises a lot in the domain, especially in discriminating against caring fathers in favour of scheming mothers, most of whom ruthlessly use children simply as money-making instruments.

Figure #21: Momany & Henriette Flavie Bayiha in 2009 in Montreal
Source: MJR Production, Montréal

Let's hear it all uncensored from a knowledgeable Canadian family lawyer! "Imagine for a moment" with Karen Selick (1996b: 46) "that you've just come from Mars and you're trying to understand Canada's laws on child support and custody." Maitre Karen Selick sees only frustration for you because, as "Children" have become "The New Excuse for Everything" (Selick, 1996a: 46), she is very certain that "you [would] climb back into your spaceship and return to Mars, disappointed that you have once again failed to find any intelligent life-forms elsewhere in the universe" (Selick, 1996b: 46). Here is just a little bit of exactly why the experienced family law advocate does certify so:

Most women fight like enraged grizzly bears to keep their kids out of dad's hands. Once they're through with a man, they think he's an irresponsible moron, even though he was good enough to marry, good enough to live with for several years and good enough to procreate with – not just once, but in many cases two or three times. Then these women frequently go out and get married to some other woman's cast-off irresponsible moron. But let the kids live with dad? Never (Selick, 1996b: 46)!

Flavimyring the 'Threatening' Letter to the Family Irresponsibility Office

The Canadian family lawyer here is not just talking in the air because "I have personal knowledge of at least 12 such cases, in which I've been involved as counsel – and I am just one lawyer in one small town, there must be thousands" (Selick, 1996a: 46). Not only the numerous conscientious and humane family lawyers vouch for it, but also a lot of these women's 'irresponsible morons', including a famous one called Momany. For instance, in view of his futile attempts to set eyes on or talk to his children, Momany wrote the following letter to the Quebec Child Support Bureau (call it properly the Family Irresponsibility Office, FIO, according to Fossungu (2015d)), hoping they would intervene and stop their mother from continuing her torturing of the innocent children. Written on Tuesday, 6 September 2016, the 'moron' or "the elastic and unbreakable bridge called Momany" (Fossungu, 2014: 82) theorized in it as follows:

Dear Sir/Madam:

Rights And Obligations Under Superior Court Decision Nº 500-04-060196-137

Take notice that until your Office can *fully* enforce the rights and obligations in the court decision above, I would rather also *fully* violate them than continue to *only* partially do so (as I have been pushed into doing since May 2015). Put in simple terms, I mean to say that I will stop paying *pensions alimentaires* until I can be made to:

Have some form of access to the children for whom I pay *pensions alimentaires*; and

Know to what institution (with complete contact information) I have "to continue paying les frais de garderie daycare costs in amount of 158.16$ for Peter Jr. directly to the garderie".

That is in the court order that your Office is charged with, and to fully enforce, I must assume?

Here are the facts behind this decision of mine to violate the court order in toto (and not just in part) unless your Office intervenes to stop the other party (the so-called CREDITOR) from choosing to enjoy only rights while jettisoning her obligations (or others' rights) in the court decision [most of these facts following are already outlined in Fossungu, 2016: 5-6]:

On Friday 29 May 2015 I called Filomena Pina Gonzalez's day-care (on 4251 Badgley in Montreal, H4P 1N9; telephone # 514-XXX-XXXX) only to be schooled in regard of many incomprehensible acts of Henriette Flavie Bayiha, including her serving the day-care provider with a letter that attempted to prohibit Filomena from allowing me to come to the day-care to see the children, or talk to them on the phone while they are there: without Flavie's express authorization. As Filomena also narrated to me, the children ceased attending her day-care on Tuesday, May 26, 2015. I was totally unaware of this move and have since not have information regarding their new day-care (if they do attend one at all).

To my email observation (of Tuesday March 8, 2016 at 8.09 AM) to Filomena that "I just do not know where and whether the boys are going to day-care/school", she responded on Wednesday, March 9, 2016 at 6.06 PM as follows: "Hello Peter: I have no idea where the kids are, last time she [Flavie] spoke with me she sa[id] that, she w[ould] bring Peter to school near where she lives, and Peteraf to day care there at the same school there in Cote St-Luc. Thanks. Filomena." Since May 2015, I have been calling just to talk to the children but Flavie's cellular phone (438-XXX-XXXX) would never be answered even as it always rang. On Thursday, 6 May 2016, I drove to Montreal to be able to see the children over the weekend. While in Montreal, on Friday, May 7, I called only to be told that the number was no longer in service. That number had been available a day or so before and I had left a message concerning my weekend trip. I then went to her apartment (#109-5023 Emerald, Cote-Saint-Luc, QC H4W 2S6) that evening at about 7 PM and rang the door bell but there was no response till about 8.30 PM when I left. It was the

44

same story on Saturday. Had they also moved? I returned to Dolbeau-Mistassini on Sunday morning without being able to set eyes on the kids. So, tell me what is actually going on?

How on earth do I know that the children for whom I pay *pensions alimentaires* are still alive? Do these children also not have the right to access to their father? Does 'sole custody' mean that the sole custodian has the open-ended right to just trample in any way she likes on the rights of the children and of the non-custodial parent? Does your Office's job entail enforcing *all* payments and other obligations under this *most unusual* court decision, or only those relating to *pensions alimentaires*?

Thanks for your comprehension and cooperation.

Sincerely yours.

You would normally expect that Momany would receive some explanations from the addressee of the above letter. Not at all with the Family Irresponsibles of Canada! They do just the one thing that their entire moneyintriguist heads know best: Dig the money out for the woman at all costs! Readers should deepen their understanding of the matter of the Money-Getting Business School that is frantically housed in the Revenue Quebec Campus by knowing that the above letter was sent together with the September month cheque for *pension alimentaire* which these Family Irresponsibles duly cashed on Thursday, 8 September 2016, at the same time as Momany's pay slip of same date would show deduction by his employer under the rubric of 'PENSION SAISIE'! No one is writing fiction here (fiction is not and would never be my style); see it all in Document A on which an 'X' has been marked to help with easy identification of the money seizure. That 'money seizure' continued despite that the man was still paying the full *pensions* amount every month. It is such a long ugly tale of the Hypocracy being called Canada. "Canada is not only a Hypocracy; it is also a *Copyocracy*. Call it Copyocratic Hypocracy or Hypocratic Copyocracy, the choice is yours. Be fearless in doing so" (Fossungu, 2015b: 133, original emphasis).

```
                                                      36473

*************************** MILLE CENT QUATRE-VINGT-TREIZE 02/100

                                    08/09/16     ****1 193.02


TER ATEH-AFAC FOSSUNGU
IB, AV. LOUIS-HEMON, APP. 15
LBEAU-MISTASSINI (QUÉBEC)
L 5X3




16  AU  03/09/16
    08/09/16    PER.:   36
EGULIER        2 112.00          CUM:    13 602.20
OFRAIRE            0.00          CUM:         0.00
PAYEES             0.00          CUM:         0.00
YES                0.00          CUM:        31.85
L                  0.00          CUM:         0.00
UR SALAIRE         0.00          CUM:         0.00
======================================================================
MENT D'EPI        64.48          CUM:       544.09
MENT KM            0.00          CUM:         0.00
======================================================================
SSENCE            91.00          CUM:       488.80
IECES DED.        41.00          CUM:       265.00
IECES N-D          0.00          CUM:        20.00
GIE                0.00          CUM:         0.00
'EPI               0.00          CUM:         0.00
ENSION            52.00          CUM:       335.00
EBERGEMENT        50.00          CUM:       325.00
RANSPORT           0.00          CUM:         0.00
IVERSE             0.00          CUM:       472.50
'AVANCE            0.00          CUM:         0.00
MENT PRET          0.00          CUM:         0.00
----------------------------------------------------------------------
VINCIAL          264.95          CUM:     1 728.78
ERAL             200.34          CUM:     1 332.18
                 104.66          CUM:       679.56
                  11.50          CUM:        74.71
 EMPLOI           31.92          CUM:       207.28
----------------------------------------------------------------------
NSION,SAISIE     156.08          CUM:       156.08         X
======================================================================
S TOTALES      1 003.46          CUM:     6 104.91
----------------------------------------------------------------------

ET            1 193.02          CUM:     8 073.23

ACCUMULES         84.40          CUM:       545.36
N POUR
                   0.00          CUM:         0.00
```

46

Source: Aménagement MYR Inc.

As you can see, Momany's 'threat' was just to push these Family Irresponsibles to talk some sense into the woman's head, if they are actually there to look after the children's interests at all as well. As you can also clearly see then, that is "clearly none of their 'SCREW THE MAN UP' business" (Fossungu, 2015d: 64) which makes them "actually true partners-in-crime to the Child-Support Business Scholars" (Fossungu, 2015d: 89). It just does not matter then to these Canadian institutions that Peter and Peteraf actually go to school/day-care (to leave out proper feeding and other emotional trauma). These children are in Canada, not in Africa, it must be overly stressed. Only what the woman wants and must get is their entire raison d'être. Yet, as Maitre Karen Selick (1996a: 46) has sagaciously pointed out, "examine almost any hot issue today and you'll find someone trying to curtail freedom in the name of protecting children. The anti-tobacco lobby [for instance], having virtually abolished smoking in so-called public places, like airplanes, that are virtually private property, now seeks to invade the privacy of smokers' own homes. They insist that sidestream smoke is killing kids." Children whose education and welfare they would not really bother about! Hypocrites! Frantalkism and Crisebacology must land in northern North America, if only for the sake of the education and welfare of children! But these two Giants must not be limited to North America because Africa's Kelie Tsopzem Fossungu's overpoweringly complex case also justifies their landing in *The Dark Continent* as well. Kelie is seen in Figure #22 wondering and not comprehending in the least why Africa should be left out of the Landing Show!

The Famous 'Children-Insisting' Letter and the Celebrated 'Child-Complication' Letter: Breaking and Exposing the Child-Affixing Scheme

Kelie could be quite correct because "[t]o say therefore that children have now become mere commodities for acquiring wealth would not be to stretch the point, an argument that is reinforced by Schola's own share in

47

the Pregnancy Story" (Fossungu, 2014: 82). To further expibasketically aid comprehension of Maitre Selick's incisive point on the use of children as new excuses for everything, just also listen to Scholastica in Figure #23 who in her numerous letters will be using and harping on children (while she is still in Cameroon) as the imperative reason why she must have to quickly join her husband in Canada (see Fossungu, 2014: 67-68, 2016: chapter 2).

Picture #22: Kelie Tsopzem Fossungu in December 2015
Source: Photo taken by Momany Fossungu

Figure #23: Momany & Scholastica Achankeng Asahchop in Douala in 1994
Source: Momany Fossungu

But what happens to these children once Scholastica is in Canada? Children are not only no longer in her definition of family (not to even talk of the husband she depended on completely). But also (among other things) these children must be wantonly killed – the modern 'corner-kicking' name for it being abortion – if they even remotely threaten the furtherance of her own selfish interests and those of those persons in her new definition of family – siblings and parents (see Fossungu, 2014: chapter 3). Let us have here, for instance, her very lengthy and famous children-insisting letter of 24 December 1998 that also brings to the foreground a lot of other pertinent topical development and family law and politics issues such as moneyintriguism and onesidetakism (which opposes the 'give-and-take' concept that is undeniably tied to African communalism). In 1998 Scholastica wrote to Momany as follows:

My dear Power! In five days time we shall be clocking five years in marriage. It keeps disturbing me that we are not together especially when

I think of how we have spent more years apart [than those spent together].

I don't as yet know how Christmas will look like. I am tired of staying alone and don't even know when and how the problem can ever be solved. It seems as if one can succeed in having a visa only to a different country and how do I get to Canada if we should do that? I hear that while in a different country, you can apply to visit a friend (preferably a white friend) in Canada.

Thanks very much for the things you sent. As I told you yesterday, the shoes are not of my size and are all old-fashioned shoes. I think it is better to inform you so that next time you know what to do exactly. My size is big size 39 or small size 40. Please, take note and next time I would prefer one pair of shoes and the rest of the money used for dresses. The shoes were too many but if they were dresses one could increase dresses especially now that most of my dresses are worn out. The rings and the cards were quite good.

Stephen said when I call you I should greet you and also thank you for the card you sent to them.

My graduation was very nice and many people came from Douala as you will see from the cards. I am afraid the cards will not be nice. I had a disappointment on the camera I was to use and just hired one around the campus. I don't know how viable he is. Pa Michael Tatuh who was to bring a video camera from Douala also failed me. I wanted to send the cassette to you. Anyway, it was not his fault, these Douala people left him behind and he did not have money to come on his own. I was very angry and disappointed. Dear, I did my best to satisfy people, though at my own expense because now I don't have money again but do not bother. Such things are necessary once in a while. I don't just know how I will manage to go to the village and how I will live in that place for long without money. While in the village I shall try to go to the hospital and also try to take traditional medicine. I am not going to go there alone. I will go with my aunt and maybe your mother. My aunt has been troubling me ever since to visit a traditional doctor who is very good but I always refused. Now is the time because I have a bit of time. I intend to stay in the village for one month. After that I don't just know where to go and what to do. It is very difficult to be living in people's houses for so long. A problem can likely occur when you stay for so long with people. You best know how your people are and one succeeds with them because I minimize many things and only pray that God should try and join us. I keep praying that we should come together even if it means having nothing to eat.

I really miss you and long to see you. I could have loved to come back from the village and do computer alongside with business if there was money. There is no money for me to do that and I don't just know what I am going to do. Dear, idleness and loneliness will kill your wife in Cameroon. Having a job is not also good morning here. I could have applied for one if it were easy. My head is working seriously now and I keep thinking of what to do or I can do. I shall go to the village immediately when I fill that form. What will delay my going immediately may be lack of finance.

Dear, please, do not leave any stone unturned as concerns my joining you over there. I know that you are doing that but I must still mention it. Imagine the money that we spend because of this separation. The money we spent at the embassy, telephone bills, etc. If we were together, we could have been using that money for something else. It may be investment or whatever. When I also think of our ages and the fact that we have no kids as yet, I really feel bad. I keep thinking of when we shall have our own kids and bring them up.

Dear, do you know something? If we should meet each other and waste no time in having a baby, I would be very glad. In that case one will know that God made the best decision for us. Imagine that if I had a baby, the baby could have been suffering because I am not really stable anywhere. I am only waiting to see when one will come, to conclude that God made the best decision for us. That is the more reason why each time I go to the hospital and consult I always indicate that I had a problem in taking in when I was with my husband. Dear, I pray that God should consider us now and join us in a grand way. Do you understand what I mean? That is, He should join us while giving us a baby and a

51

good job. I don't know why tears are flowing from my eyes as I am writing this letter. I am not really sad as such. They are tears of imagination.

I told you yesterday that I saw Dr Fonyam and he was asking if I have talked to you. He said you can apply from Canada directly to the Vice Chancellor because I said you can come and they would start frustrating you again. I prefer that we should stay out of Cameroon for sometime because it would be very difficult to refund the Whistance-Smith family's money from Cameroon.[2] I also hear there is going to be

---

[2] Talking of said money repayment, Nancy Whistance-Smith's email of 25 September 2001 is captioned 'Your Letter' and makes not only the divine intervention case but as well provides a model case of the bridge-builder's Hercules and solidifying as well the Theory of Onesidetakism and that of burning the bridge after crossing it that Scholastica is also well known for. In it Nancy theorised to Hi Peter as follows (beginning from the 2nd paragraph):

As I'm sure I have shared before, when Andrew and I left Kenya some seven years ago, we vowed we would never lend money to an African. I still chuckle at God's sense of humour bringing you and your Ph.D. into our little world. But you are different, Peter, you have a passion for your country and, as far as I can tell, a realistic view of the greater world as well. Unfortunately, Schola is not so blessed. Obviously she does not think we "miss" the money we lent you, or she would feel more obliged to help you pay it back. Not only that, does she not feel some obligation to send money in support of your ailing families? Also, what about your status here in Canada? Has anything been determined yet, or do you have to still leave the country by a given date? If so, what are Schola's plans? To stay in Canada with Ngunyi rather than support you? How my heart aches for your situation! However, we must continue to pray and trust that God can see far beyond these current troubles you find yourself in. Now that you are aware of the games that Schola is playing, it may be time to redivide up who is paying for what. If you pay for the very basics, food, shelter and diapers, it may be harder to

a second devaluation in January. I keep imagining how things will look like with that second devaluation. Many people are preparing for it now and I doubt if it is true. Most rumours are always true.

Bridget [Asahchop] came for my graduation; her own graduation will take place in January. The date has not yet been announced. Brother Emmanuel also came from Mamfe. You will see all those who came in the cards.

Dear, I presume I have exhausted most of the things for now. Accept greetings from Sister Odette. She was very happy with the card you sent. She said she could have preferred 1000 francs but asked me not to tell you because sending the card meant that you thought of her. I gave one of the cards to Mr. Tasong Dominic and he was actually very happy. Dorothy also had one. She is not happy with you at all. She keeps saying that she never knew you could least think of her like that.

Have a nice time and let's keep praying to God to just join us.

Your darling, Schola (Scholastica A. Asahchop, personal communication, 24 December 1998).

---

blackmail you. Ngunyi does not need brand new clothing (all my children wear used clothing from friends and neighbours) and I can certainly send you clothing for her that Emily has outgrown. I have not sent any so far because my sense is that it is an insult to Schola. Yet, we were able to send you money each month precisely because we spent less on ourselves and our children. I know, I am preaching to the converted.... you who lived on next to nothing for years as you worked on your Ph.D.

I can only assume that this latest series of trials will continue to prepare you for the difficult road that lies ahead of you. As I said before, I can offer no advice, just love, support and my prayers. "Trust in the Lord with all your heart, And do lean on your own understanding. In all your ways acknowledge Him, and He will make your paths straight." Proverbs 3:5, 6.

Please keep in touch – via email is fine. Love, Nancy (omission is original) (Nancy Whistance-Smith, private communication, 25 September 2001).

Readers should then juxtapose the contents of Scholastica's letter with her disheartening attitude towards children when she is already in Canada. These children are then only good for money-making or they are as good as dead. She commits abortion as if it is no big deal! But the hypocrisy doesn't just end there because there is also the other calamitous issue of Scholastica appearing to be an ideal person and spouse, a role model to others that she even counsels but actually not living as such in her own marital home. She nevertheless takes cover for her surprising behaviour behind the existence of another innocent victimized child; a narrative which you can also quickly grasp here from paragraphs 3 and 4 of Momany's famed 'child-complication' Letter of 4 November 2001 to Andrew and Nancy Whistance-Smith of Edmonton (Canada) who you see in Figure #24. The child in question here is Kelie, the daughter of Mafor Odette Ateafac who is seen in Figure #25. Said letter lengthily theorised:

Figure #24: The Whistance-Smiths in December 2013 (L-R): Emily, Andrew, Nancy, Greg, & Tim
Source: Nancy Whistance-Smith

In discussing with my wife, I made her to understand that, much as I trusted the success of our marriage, I was aware of the fact that we both have the choice of deciding who our partner should be. But a child like the one in question hasn't this choice. And that, given that Kelly is my daughter (and I'm sure she is, considering that the matter could not come forward like that unless she [Kelie's mother] is absolutely certain about the child's paternity), then I must have to assume my responsibilities in her regard. Scholastica had to make up her mind as to whether to walk out of the union or stay, knowing the facts and the complication. She apparently chose to stay and complicate the life of another innocent child before getting out. If people like you are only now hearing of this episode of my life, it is simply because I never, since December 1998 [i.e. when he was told the news], wanted to have her embarrassed on learning that I'd discussed it at all with anyone else. But I was wrong because, now that she seems not to be getting what she must have thought staying on will bring, she has gone wild with announcing it to everyone she calls these days. Who is she trying to embarrass?

Not me at all. The only person I would have been embarrassed telling this story to, is Scholastica. But I discussed this with her level-headedly. On the contrary, she is now demeaning herself in front of everyone by trying to do same to me. If she thinks she's had enough and wants to quit, it is that simple: do so quietly, if not for herself, at least, for Ngunyi's sake. The false impression she gives to people, including myself when we discussed it, is that she only got the news from me. But from her discussion on the phone with one of her friends in Buea [Edith Rose Khumbah, that is], I gathered she knew about it before getting here. Another false impression she gives to those she talks to is that all this child thing happened when we were already married, and that I knew everything "from A to Z" as she puts it. I must simply be a real monster! What else can I say? (Momany Fossungu, private communication, 4 November 2001)

From the abovementioned two paragraphs of Momany's letter, it is undeniable that he views children's education and welfare through an unbreakable and purified lens that some mothers appear to contaminate and break easily with their moneyintriguism. Nancy Whistance-Smith of Edmonton could not have put it any better in her aforementioned email of 22 September 2001 to Momany, titled "Your Letter", when she stated in the first paragraph that "I received your letter yesterday – what a difficult situation you are in! How I wish we could provide easy answers. Children bring such a different dimension to marriage and, as you are now seeing, provide the perfect form of blackmail" (Nancy Whistance-Smith, private communication, 22 September 2001). For a woman to knowingly pin another man's biological child on an innocent trusting man is quite reprehensible. Mafor Odette Ateafac's case goes well beyond reprehensible. Some women get involved in such inexcusable deeds with the child's education and welfare supposedly in mind – that is, if you also believe the Child Support Business Scholars.

Figure #25: Mafor Ateafac Odette in December 2015
Source: Photo taken by Momany Fossungu

Odette's case is said to have gone beyond that because, were it in line with the supposition just mentioned, she would not have: (1) been telling Momany, the supposed father, only in 1998 and also asking him to keep his paternity of the child a secret that remains just between the two of them, and (2) refused, despite the supposed dad's insistence, to give him the child's vital information as he earnestly requested. Odette was, therefore, just after the money (like the child-support business scholars) irrespective of how ruinous her gratuitous deception was to the child's education and welfare (to leave out the supposed dad's agonizing situation). But just see how 'the Criminal Love Thesis' (Fossungu, 2015a: 83-84) works to expose moneyintriguist dragdowners. Odette's factor #2 which, to her, was a nice means of eating her cake and still having it, has eventually uncovered the entire child-affixing plot: since the supposed father adamantly rejected lying to cover up her cover-up scheme in factor #1. What is being said in plain terms is that the need for using DNA testing in the child's Canadian sponsorship application would never have arisen but for Odette's stubborn refusal (especially between 1998 & 2001) to let Momany (the supposed father) have the child's essential information to include in his own Canadian permanent residence application that was made in 2001 (see Fossungu, 2015d: chapter 3). So, was Odette in the least thinking about the child's wellbeing and future or solely after the money directed to her for the child's sake? Like the children in Canada for whom child support is paid, Momany's child in Cameroon, in addition to being provided with her school and other needs, also receives a basic monthly allowance of at least forty thousand CFA francs. Table 1 captures and evidences some of the *recent* financial support issues.

Table 1: Some Recent Money Transfers For the Benefit of Kelie Tsopzem Fossungu (KTF) to Mother Odette Ateafac (MOA) and Brother Eclador Tsackeng (BET)				
Money	Amount	Amount	Receiver	Transaction

Transfer Number	(FCFA)	($CAD)		Date
5763503290	50,000.00	133.25	BET	April 7, 2014
1034464406	200,000.00	507.00	BET	March 15, 2014
2463751725	100,000.00	232.03	BET	May 7, 2011
6193010298	200,000.00	447.03	MOA	November 27, 2010
3841305197	50,000.00	149.88	MOA	January 12, 2004
9363916660	100,001.00	251.66	KTF	February 18, 2014
3141559957	40,000.00	103.00	KTF	April 14, 2014
1784216154	50,000.00	126.50	KTF*	December 23, 2014
73187999	40,002.23	99.57	KTF	2015/02/08
86389971	40,003.97	94.97	KFT*	April 12, 2015
49541941	50,279.55	120.98	KTF	May 15, 2015
88493025	80,005.00	188.78	KTF	June 22, 2015
76972538	100,000.67	248.03	KTF	August 9, 2015
99647769	40,001.58	105.76	KTF	28 August 2015
22079442	49,990.00	134.41	KTF	February 16, 2016
41997080	41296.04	105.00	KTF	April 13, 2016
44471783	45559.16	117.00	KTF	May 3, 2016
46616459	50001.38	128.58	KTF	May 19,

				2016
67302717	40,000.20	102.71	KTF	June 3, 2016
97944707	60001.98	149.23	KTF	June 30, 2016
29390357	60001.55	149.40	KTF	July 3, 2016
29468726	41114.60	105.00	KTF	July 26, 2016
40988702	251952.12	604.00	KTF	September 1, 2016
61126837	42506.76	110.00	KTF	October 5, 2016
81259899	40545.53	105.00	KTF	October 7, 2016
23018669	40309.25	105.00	KTF	November 7, 2016
37873261	101278.96	247.00	KTF	November 14, 2016
96513212	50,006.90	124.70	KTF	December 3, 2016
97387856	202,997.47	477.00	KTF	December 8, 2016
59791688	50000.52	122.87	KTF	January 5, 2017
89320840	40001.05	99.17	KTF	February 2, 2017
31167281	40001.17	99.41	KTF	March 2, 2017
22918571	40007.19	100.34	KTF	April 3, 2017
65324201	70001.95	173.36	KTF	April 20, 2017
99417296	50001.16	131.99	KTF	May 17, 2017
35224973	40001.15	106.10	KTF	June 5, 2017

90945832	200002.81	496.57 ˙	KTF	December 7, 2017
Total	3,307,791	6697.85		

Source: Momany Fossungu's Financial Documents
Received by a 3rd party (Odina Idryss Teneteu Ndeffo & Nkengafack Akefac Henadel) because of the expiry of her national identity card

If moneyintriguism and nonoselfism are not the driving forces here, how does one then explain the fact that this same woman called Odette had refused Momany's marriage proposal on the basis that she was too old for him but got herself impregnated by someone her age and then came around to pin the child on Momany, and doing so only when he is already in Canada? Could another brand of "African Overseas Culture" be detected here also? Most probably! After "The Third World War and the DNA *Roundaboutism*" (Fossungu, 2015d: 126-131) was eventually won and the requested DNA Test exposed the paternity scheme, it is known that the real biological father is now covering up his own role in the devilish plan by saying he does not want anything to do with the child since the mother knew quite well (as he himself) that he was the biological father of the child but decided to pin the child on someone else "simply because I am not overseas like him." I do not personally know who Kelie's biological father is (except that he is even a married man) but it is quite clear to me that no genuine man would just lay low like that in this circumstance. From Odette's perplexing comportment (that Momany says cannot be accurately documented here) until the DNA results in late 2016, it is suspected that the biological father is merely trying now to whitewash his own role in the moneyintriguist child-affixing scheme.

For instance, with the endless complication on the child's sponsorship applications (consequent on the fact that she was never included in Momany's own permanent residence application), Momany thought the singular way out was for him to marry her mother and bring both of them to Canada. He discussed this option with Odette who accepted the proposal during their phone conversation but later was very uncooperative with Momany's agents in Cameroon. In May 2014 Momany was in Cameroon and asked Odette in person about her attitude and her response was that when she consulted her children on the matter they objected. Momany's only question in response was: "Did Kelie also refused the marriage plan and is she actually part of your children consulted?" Who actually must have made the decision for Odette to have Kelie stuck in Cameroon: her other children or her boyfriend (Kelie's biological father)? Could having the child held back in Cameroon not be their joint plan to continue using the child as their calculated means of uninterruptedly sucking money out of 'the ignorant and stupid supposed father'? Whatever it actually is, the essential query from Kelie's biological father's own Overseas Thesis remains: Was Momany's initial 1993 marriage proposal to Odette turned down then solely because, at the time, he was a mere taxi-driver in Douala (not then being better off financially as Kelie's married biological dad)?

The Terrible Marriage Proposal Narrative Exposing Blood-Sucking Onesidetakism.

Talking of marriage proposals brings us full circle to the Asahchopination, part of which Odette too is: making the full circle talk a non sequitur in the manner of lawyers, I should guess? Whatever those people of the law *black-letterly* think about it does not affect the hell endured with some of these "sisters" of ours who Chief Formbuehndia Bernard Mbancho has described as Terrible Ladies in *The Terrible Marriage Proposal Narrative*. Talking of 'these terrible sisters of ours' (and brothers too, of course) who would not want to work hand-in-hand for the progress of the lot, Chief Formbuehndia Mbancho, for instance, in his popular "Terrible Ladies" message sent to Momany on Sunday, 16 August 2015, stated in the 3rd paragraph that: "Even Scholastica, your first wife, is showing no remorse to the fact that at least both of you are from the same village, and moreover neighbours." He then went on in paragraph 4 to strongly argue that:

I am always disagreeing with Mr. Paul Agafina on the issue of insisting on marrying a lady from Lebialem. It is not a guarantee of love and commitment. Last month when I called to greet him, he started talking to me about a lady from Esoh-Atah, whom he is proposing to me as a wife. I remember that he had also proposed this your very Scholastica to me long before you even first came into contact with her.

The South Africa-based Bangwa Chief is obviously bringing out Scholastica's smokescreen; with the best exposition of her camouflaged "model role" coming from no other than Violet Maylatey Fonenge in her 'Maylatelizationism' (see Fossungu, 2016: 12-15). Could this camouflage of Scholastica's be responsible for some noted cases of people having 'positively' proposed her for marriage to others? Guess who (apart from Agafina and company in Yaoundé) also proposed Scholastica to Momany: Asa'ah Forsah whose mother is not only a Fossungu princess but also the Mafor of Fon ST Fossungu (see Fossungu, 2016: chapter 4)! In his paragraphs 7 to 8 Chief Formbuehndia Mbancho then stated that:

Congrats on your new book. Are copies already available in bookstores? Well Chief, despite the challenges in our lives, let's keep on praying for one another. My 4-year-6-month-old son is always crying and asking me about the whereabouts of his [dead] mother. How could he really understand what has happened to her? He keeps on telling me, 'I want my mama, take me to my mama' and so on. This is one of the challenges I have to surmount.

On his part, Momany responded in "Re: Terrible Ladies" on 22 August 2015, indicating in the first paragraph that "sorry, I have been out of network area for a while, which is why I am reading your email only today." He then moved on to the next paragraph to advise the Bangwa Chief based in South Africa that:

On the question of wife, you should know better than to bow to other people's choices. The more so as you have children that any incoming woman MUST HAVE TO synchronise with. You have just used the right expression: Love and Commitment. I have used Love and

Understanding in my 2014 book titled *Africa's Anthropological Dictionary on Love and Understanding: Marriage and the Tensions of Belonging in Cameroon*. Oh! How painful it must be for your son! How challenging also to explain why he cannot be taken to his mother! How do you actually cope without her too?

How some affected persons cope with some of these things, especially those put into place by doublesidism, is difficult to explain to some people who have never tasted it. It is just good that Momany has the natural capacity to surmount some of these challenges; explaining his rare reaction to one of Chief Formbuehndia Mbancho's questions in the same Terrible Ladies email about Elias Akendung's deeds at the Douala Airport (as to more of which, see Fossungu, 2015: 125-28) which he outlined in the fourth paragraph of his response to the Chief, indicating that:

As for Inspector Elias Akendung, I just don't know what to make of all his actions. The good thing is that I don't stock my mind with bad things, and that is what aids me in advancing in spite of the multiple roadblocks. You could find more on the topic in my *Family Politics and Deception in Northern North America and West-Central Africa* (2015). All my books are in bookstores worldwide, especially in online bookshops. Just Google my name and decide on which/where to order.

Momany then advised in the concluding 5th paragraph for Chief Formbuehndia Mbancho to have "Courage, brother [because] God is in control." God has actually been in control despite the endless moneyintriguism and the notorious desire of some family members like Elias Akendung in Figure #26 and Chief Fofah (Marie-Claire Afueh) to be 'the only one' forging on. The two of them are the architects of *Efuelanchakendungism* which "Means a Family against Itself Must Fall" (Fossungu, 2016: 95-99). You could cement that seemingly innocuous theory with this small-Big taxi story. Elias Akendung has many taxis on the road in Douala, one of which belongs to his elder half-brother (Commandant Mbo Denis Nwedjong) who does not reside in Douala, but in Bafoussam. But every time that one of Elias' cars needs repairs, whatever part that needs fixing is taken off his brother's lone car and put in his own and the brother's vehicle becomes the one that has been repaired! The costs of garage are therefore unjustly passed on to the absent trusting brother. Family unity and progress indeed! This is even worse than open *onesidetakism*, true or false? Onesidetakism opposes *giveandtakism* (theory of give-and-take) which promotes collective progress, not the *"I, the only one"* mentality of onesidetakists and takebackists.

Picture #26: Inspector Elias Akendung
Source: Photo taken by Momany Fossungu

In the place of 'the only one' advancing, Scholastica would speedily put 'the only family' (which excludes husband and children). She too does not only burn the bridge after crossing but also focuses her energies almost entirely on parents and blood siblings; brothers and sisters who are unlike those that the Globavillagist (as Momany is also called) would be attempting to work together with so as to uplift the entire family and Nwangong Fondom from poverty and misery but only be getting the moneyintriguing and bridge-burning things in response. More of that moneyintriguist bridge-burning is found in Chapter 4 particularly which Scholasticalizes and evaluates the Family Illiteracy and Poverty Eradication Projects, with Scholasticalization being ably godmothered by Scholastica Asahchop whose dubious *children-loving* letter brings us full circle (correctly, this time) back to the yearly Support-Indexation letter of the Family Irresponsibles of Canada, Quebec to be more precise. On Friday, 9 December 2016 Momany received the Quebec Bureau's letter of 7 December 2016 with subject being "New Payment Order Further to Indexation of Support". It narrated the usual *bla-bla* until, "Consequently, as of January 1, 2017, you must remit to the Minister of Revenue the sum of \$348.21 monthly" (3rd paragraph). Interestingly, its 7th paragraph makes known that: "We wish to remind you that you must notify us immediately of any change affecting your file, such as change of address, a new support order, *or any other situation that you believe we should be informed of*" (emphasis supplied). Was what Momany's September letter to them is all about not captured by the emphasized 'situation'? Yet, they have written their nonsense of a letter now without in the least talking about or even acknowledging receipt of that letter! Just the Hypocracy called Canada, eh?

Concluding Remarks

Whatever response anyone else would give here, I wonder if anyone would here also dispute with Ndi Nkemanang Calestus Fossungu's sane definition of someone's mother above by saying that women like Flavie, Scholastica and Odette directly occasioning this discussion of the Family Irresponsibles of Canada here would actually be the 'mothers' of said children just because they 'excreted' them for purposes of the infamous Child-Support Business School. Amazing best interests of children in Canada! Make it northern North America, please, because some experts

65

have equally condemned the 'prurient interests of American children'. Thus, as Maureen Dowd explains, the expected '60 Minute'-type Bill and Hillary brawl wasn't Melania Trump's style, "and that idea got dropped. Melania did issue a statement calling her husband's comments 'offensive' but saying that he had her support and suggesting that everyone 'focus on the important issues facing our nation and the world'" (Dowd, 2016). Maureen Dowd wouldn't fail though to ponder about "Who knew that the important issue would be a pussy bow?"

A French intellectual has answered the question somewhat, explaining it with "the moral McCarthyism that prevails in American society when it comes to the issue of love, and which has been denounced by the more clear-sighted Americans for a long time" (Bruckner, 2011). He then goes on to appositely query:

What was the real point of the Dominique Strauss-Kahn and Clinton cases? They were a perfect vehicle to condemn eroticism in order to be able to talk more about sex. For weeks, even months, American people licked their lips over every intimate detail: about felatio, sperm, genital organs -- always with a false indignation. The fact that the alleged victim's lawyer Kenneth Thompson talked about the 'assaulted' vagina of his client Nafissatou Diallo with obscene jubilation is a tell-tale sign of this phenomenon (Bruckner, 2011).

I truly wonder if in their presidential elections, Americans are out to elect a Commander-in-Chief or a 'Commander-in-Scandalous-Sex-Attacks'. The Trump presidency has obviously greatly extended the *'Commander-in'* title to include those like 'Commander-in-Cheat', 'Commander-in-Lie', 'Commander-in-Fraud', Commander-in-Send-Her-Back-Home' 'Commander-in-Bully', Commander-in-Open-the-Economy' 'Commander-in-Tweets', 'Commander-in-White-Supremacy', 'Commander-in-Collusion' (just keep on going...). Whatever the case, it is amazing that some of these African women like Scholastica and Flavie would also be in the Cameroon Goodwill Association of Montreal (CGAM), for instance, loudly singing children welfare and the like. Those are African parents in Canada whose sing-song is 'my so much love of the children' even to the point of their gratuitous preferring of these same children growing up without the balance-giving presence of the other parent! Love of the child-support money indeed! Or is it simply an essential difficultizing part of African Overseas Culture? Once more, does being a biological mother in cases like theirs really make any sense in contradicting Ndi Nkemanang's definition of the real mother of a child?

CHAPTER 2

GETTING AFRICA INTO AFRICA AND MAKING OBAMA'S MOTHER LAUGH: AFRICA'S CHILDREN NAMING PHILOSOPHIES EXPURGATING HYPOCRISY AND ENGENDERING THE FATHER-GRANDFATHER WAR IN CANADA?

I must stress over and over that this book is non-fictional and frantalkist, meaning that it fearlessly calls a spade a spade as indicated earlier. It is believed, moreover, that sensible readers would "quickly agree with me that doing otherwise would also be unnecessarily depriving most of those concerned of the proper recognition for their enormous contribution to a better or enhanced understanding of" the issues concerned (Fossungu, 2016: 3). This Chapter explores children wellbeing politics as well as the philosophies behind the names given to them. According to some experts, "[t]he significance of children and women to the development of any society cannot be over emphasized. While children are the future of any nation…, the women folk are also imperative to the development of the society" (Yinusa et al, 2018: 279). The lengthy discussion of the importance parents generally but particularly North American parents (including those in the CGAM who are originally from Africa – hence also justifying the talk of 'importing' and 'African Overseas Culture'?) attach to their children's wellbeing and development can be shortened here with the help of Roger Ekuh-Ngwese (the 2015-2018 CGAM President) who sent out the following instructive message to CGAMers:

Dear Members of Goodwill Montreal, The end of year is around the corner and as usual Goodwill members are again looking forward to stunning and impacting the community with great steam of the End-of-Year party. I know this time will not be different, and we are all looking forward to that. Hey! Don't get me wrong! I am not a member of the EOY party committee. You want to know who I am? CHAIRMAN OF THE CHILDREN CHRISTMAS PARTY!!! Yes that's me. Fellow

Goodwillers, while we look forward to hitting the jamboree for ourselves, let's not forget those whose presence gives even more meaning to our existence: "OUR CHILDREN!" As in our tradition, we shall be organising a fun Christmas party for our kids. To this effect, I am inviting the following committee members for an exploratory meeting on Monday, 13th November 2011, at 6:00 PM. This date/time is subject to change depending on members' availability. The Venue: 410 Avenue Lafleur, Suite 61, LaSalle QC H8R 3H6. [The concerned members are:] Mrs Berri Nsame (Co-chair), Roger Ekuh-Ngwese (Co-chair), Mr. Tene Emmanuel (Member), Mr. Mohnkong Yacubu (Member), Mrs. Priscilla Folefac (Member), Mrs. Agbonyor Tanyi (Member), Mrs. Marie Diegoue (Member), [and] Pastor Epizitone Anabi (Member). I am assuming that we all receive mails through this forum. However, I will personally hook-up with members of this ad hoc committee on phone. We shall also be contacting our resource persons to get some advice: Dr Magnus Ajong and Dr Mrs Ibeagha. I am also calling on all parents of this Association to forward the names, ages and gender of their kids. To do this, simply reply to this mail. Enjoy the week as it unfolds. Best Regards. On behalf of the Children Christmas Party, Roger Ekuh-Ngwese (CGAM Forum, 8 November 2011, paragraphing altered).

Picture #27: Roger Ekuh-Ngwese (the 2015-2018 CGAM President)
Source: Photo taken by Momany Fossungu

The Intriguing Naming-Love in Cameroon Real-Naming Africa?

Emmanuel Fokoua Tene was vigilant enough to point out to **Roger** that said Monday was the 14th of November 2011 and not the 13th. Figure #27 shows Roger Ekuh-Ngwese (middle: who is godfather of Peter, Jr.) flanked by Farrel Ayah and Ginette Ndonkeu during the 'after-baptism' reception at home on 28 January 2012 in Montréal. The baptism in question was a double-baptism involving the two sons of Flavie and Momany. That said, how then do Africans go about naming and educating their children to ensure their significance in societal development? There is no better way of kick-starting the response to this central query than with the intriguing naming-love in Ibalikumato, Cameroon. That is, if we go by Dr. Wanaku's 'naming argument' in the

70

Southern Cameroons National Council (SCNC) Forum in January 2001 that:

In Ibalikumato, when a child is born, every relative 'qualified' to give a name does so. They do so out of love and the more names you have would show how much love you are getting.

At a regional level, we might be having the same problem. Our region is so loved that everyone wants to give it a name – in whole or in part – from Southern Cameroons, West Cameroon, Federal Republic of Southern Cameroons to Victoria-Limbe, Mamfe-Manyu, Bamenda-Tisong, Kumba-K-town etc ... This probably is proving that there is a need for protocols to be written to establish naming conventions [including street naming – so the postman can know where you are] that future generations can work with. If we do not do it, someone will in the future. But please do not bring back names like NA [Native Authority] (cited in Fossungu, 2013a: 44, original square brackets and omission marks).

That was the naming-love in Cameroon which has focused here more on the calling of some portions of the country; but the child-naming question persists in the education and welfare business. An exquisite response to this and the aforementioned imperative question (in the Introduction) must also swiftly take us back to Africa, the celebrated home of *parentology*, defined as the act of parents wanting and forcing children to live parents' dreams and not the children's own. Discussing the 'Fundamental Human Rights of the African Child' (Yinusa et al, 2018: 280-82) and the 'Predicaments of the African Child and implications on the Development of the African Society' (Yinusa et al, 2018: 282-87), Professor Yinusa and colleagues who explored the issues found out that some of the fundamental rights of the child include right to life, right to education, right to good healthcare, right to food and water, right to freedom, right to identity and right to be protected from all forms of economic exploitation, torture or inhuman treatment (Yinusa et al, 2018: 291). All these rights appropriately go into the basket called *welfare* or wellbeing. But education is most often singled out of it for special focus, notwithstanding that most of these rights and predicaments

71

of children and their impact on societal development are still exposed in this frantalkist contribution.

The philosophical tale on their naming and education is quite long for exhaustion but I would try to shorten it in this Chapter of the book that also exceptionally provides authentic hardly available education on African culture and philosophy, especially the philosophical version called Bangwalangwalism; the term defining a unique branch of African philosophy coming from the 99-sensical Bangwa in Debundschazone of Cameroon. It is here that white Mama Obama would be choking with laughter at rootless Africans. The 7th Fon of Nwangong and a few other parents (to be seen below) apart, these days a lot of Africans just name their children without significance, or without even finding out at all what the names they wrap their children up in do *mean*. Of course, meaning can also be meaningless when it means exactly what it means. If you are finding this piece of Bangwalangwalism very difficult, then let me break it down with this meaning-crazy or Pandalogistical couple that decided to name their children with the part of their dwelling where the children were conceived in. Their children are thus called Backyard, Bathroom, Bedroom, Garage, Kitchen, Living-room, just keep going until every 'doing bad thing' corner of the home has been named; not forgetting that some of them would also bear Abroad, Hotel, and Motel. You may also want to check out this other pair of 'bad thing doers' who named the innocent child 'Condom-Burst' because that is what actually happened to give the unwanted 'thing' passage into the world!

That certainly could hardly be the 'sensefully' senseless meaning being talked about here. What crisebacologists just mean to say is that most of the concerned Africans just give the name simply because some American or European bears that name. You will even easily find some African parents in Canada who would be making moves to change children's nosexonomical African names so as to "give them English names"; and I just do not want you to journey right now to Cameroon's Douala, for instance, to be amazed by the huge number of Francophone children going by the Clinton name (from Hillary's Bill, of course)! Some authentic African parents exhibit their four-eyesism (or far-sightedness) in the domain. For example, Dr Fongot Kini-Yen Kinni's parents "had the sense to give me a name that would determine my life research forever" (Kinni, 2015: vii), not forgetting that they also "matched these words [of encouragement in education] with deeds" such as "sending me money while I was in Europe, even though I was on scholarship, and encouraged me to travel to other parts of Europe and discover things for myself" (Kinni, 2015: xiii). There are thus two intertwined arms – (1) children-naming philosophies and (2) the education and welfare predicaments of African children. As noted already and needing reiteration, the Kinni parents' name-giving ingenuity is also seen in the exceptional prescience of Nwangong's HRM Fon David Foncha Fossungu (1) in naming his upright daughter and (2) in avoiding the future breaking open of his son's head by the *takebackists* in order to reclaim their postcolonial education (Chapter 3 handles this second arm). The first arm and the equally fascinating name-saking theory known as *Elizachoppism* constitute the two parts of this Chapter of this untraditional book audaciously meant for the traditional academy.

The Wonders of Four-Eyesism: Immaculately Correcting Juju Error, Hypocritical Fowl-Killers and Opportunistic African Administrations

The 7th Fon of Nwangong is Fon David Foncha Fossungu who you have already seen in both Figures #1 and #19. He actually named his daughter, Immaculate Fossungu in Figure #28, who resolutely rejected profiting from the *Etoughs'* mistake to become the *Mafor* or female second-in-command to the Fon or Chief. That happened on 8 December 2007 at the enthronement of the current Fon Nicasius Nguazong Fossungu when the *Etoughs* (jujus) 'caught' someone else than the person whose name had been called out for the prestigious female position of Mafor. It was only the desperate and impassioned plea of the 'caught daughter' (as she was being carted away in the manner of the CGAM *doggy-baggist*[3]) that helped the *Etoughs* to quickly rethink the situation before Immaculate Fossungu had been completely taken off the *attehttah*. They then speedily released her and promptly went for the right person – Violet Mbunchop Fossungu.

A lot of people have regarded the truthful daughter, Immaculate Fossungu, as stupid for having done what she did; preferring that she should have stayed quiet and become the Mafor since it was not her fault that she was wrongly caught. Wow!! That is precisely demonstrating to readers how a lot of these *modern* Africans (especially those in positions of authority) have now come to see dishonesty as the rule rather than the exception. Africa can never get into Africa with such deceitfulness. This is comportment (to stay within family circles with it for now) that you can also see in both the acts of the Asahchops (1) Praising an in-law Internally but Condemning him Externally and (2) Being an Externally Ideal spouse while being the Worst spouse Internally. The fowl-killing narrative is employed immediately to expibasketise the first arm especially, while the second branch is handled in other Chapters by the dependency syndrome created and fostered by the postcolonial African governments and other administrations of Black groups around the globe.

---

[3] I am adopting here from Paul Takha Ayah who, on Christmas Day 2012, perfectly nailed the issues of innovation and critical thinking in place with the doggy-bag thesis when (in contributing to the food shortage controversy in the CGAM) he stated:

Merry Christmas to all Goodwillers!

I would like to congratulate the chair of the food committee for a job well done and for being daring enough to try new things. To prepare food for a Goodwill party for $700 is unheard of. This is an example to emulate as far as efficiency is concerned. Even more, to return almost $200 to Goodwill coffers from the food budget is also unheard of. Gone are the days when the success of a party was measured by how much food is left over and carted away in doggy   bags.

(CGAM Forum, 25 December 2012).

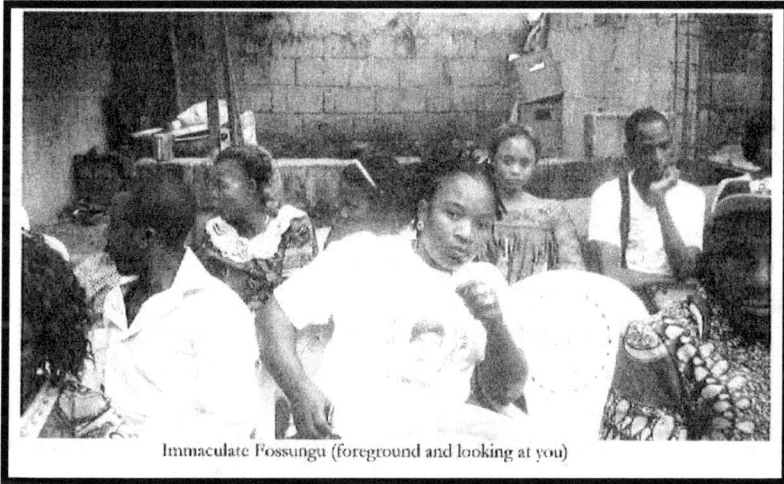
Immaculate Fossungu (foreground and looking at you)

Figure #28: Immaculate Fossungu (foreground and looking at you)
Source: Derick Abomego

The Fowl-Pig Killing Narratives on Family, Marriage and Commitment: Killing the Bowie Family Interest Theory

I am here discussing the act of the Asahchopination rejoicing in private while publicly killing the man's reputation regarding the same thing they are rejoicing over with by the taking of an innocent fowl's life. To begin giving concrete demonstrations of the two-facedness of the fowl-killers, readers are asked to listen attentively to how the Asahchop family (Asahchopination) goes around the entire planet painting their in-law called Momany as somebody 'who doesn't give a shit about our family,' whereas privately and within/among themselves they know very well that they are grossly lying to the whole world. Africa cannot get into Africa with this kind of untruthfulness; it can only do so through fossungupalogy "that is [defined as] the science of straightforwardness, necessitating the fearless looking at truth in the eye" (Fossungu, 2015a: xi). For the painting thesis, Momany has again advanced a portion of his

75

famous and very interesting 'child-complication' Letter of the previous Chapter that he addressed to his renowned friends in Edmonton, Alberta, Canada. "Dear Andrew and Nancy," the first paragraph of the said 5-page handwritten letter went on to lengthily theorize on family, marriage and commitment as follows:

I write this letter with mixed emotions. The positive side is however predominant. I have been technically without work here for a month, come tomorrow. My work permit, as you know, expired on October 5, 2001. At moment of writing I'm still to obtain a new one. It has not been easy at all especially as I'm the sole and only breadwinner for this family of three. Through these thirty days of uncertainty and worries, I've learnt a lot that I didn't know but thought I knew. My so-called wife has been really unconcerned about the whole situation, only adding more stress upon my already stressed up mind and head. Only her schooling is important. And because this time no dime was able to be released through her usual tactics of using Ngunyi (and this time the money wasn't just there), she has really brought her real self out. She's been calling every person imaginable in Canada, United States, Cameroon (and who knows where else?) and telling them how since she got to this country it has only been suffering and suffering and suffering for her. That I am a worthless irresponsible person not fit to be a husband and father. That she does everything and I only know how to sit and wait until food is ready and I open my big mouth and eat without shame. She says to everyone she calls, sometimes even when I am sitting right there, that I don't give a damn about her family (dad, mum, brothers and sisters). Can I even catalogue all the nonsense I've been hearing of late from her? (Momany Fossungu, private communication, 4 November 2001)

As to the internal rejoicing theory, you can hear them, for example, privately praising the fact that the 'accused' in-law named his very first child (with their own daughter) after the head of the Asahchopination. It is all coming from the 3rd paragraph of Elizabeth Elizachop's secret letter to her daughter, Scholastica. The full Elizachoppism letter is outlined in the second part of this Chapter. This 3rd paragraph of hers constitutes the backbone of the children naming theory known as *Elizachoppism*. To Elizabeth Asahchop's secret letter must now be added the following confirming paragraph from Belinda Chopazem Asahchop who also secretly wrote to "My dearest sister" (Scholastica, that is) as follows:

How are you and the child and father over there? Hope fine! For us, we are fine and very soon we are going to close [from school] and I'm sure that I am going to pass because I wrote [my exams] very well. We heard the news of the baby and were very happy especially on the day that the pictures came. Papa said because the child [Ngunyi] is named after him, he will kill a big fowl and he did so and [Mamie] cooked it with rice and everybody ate very well and was happy (Belinda C. Asahchop, private communication, 6 June 2000).

That was just the first paragraph of Belinda's secret letter. Readers must obviously be wondering how their copious 'secret letters' have come to be public dot-connecting materials and also in the hands of this writer. It is quite simple because Fossungu (2016: 165) has explained that "Peter Ngunyi Asahchop's very good 'secret-keeping' daughter was chasing so much money and 'property-sweeping' to London, Ontario, that she forgot their 'secret letters' that you are now having the privilege of publicly reading and to connect the dots." This intriguing Scholamany (Scholastica-Momany) marriage just seems to have caused a lot of unnecessary trouble to fowls and pigs, not to over labour the point mentioning children education and welfare here. Pigs too because you must be told that Fon NN Fossungu has also lengthily discussed the kind of huge pig that his predecessor (Fon DF Fossungu) slaughtered on the day that the Scholamany marriage took place. I am now *Crediting the Pig-Killing Story* which also distinguishes its University of Dschang Lecturer from the Bowie Family Interest Theorist called Marie-Claire Afueh (née Fossungu). Unlike Marie-Claire's onesidetakist definition of 'showing interest in family', HRM Fon NN Fossungu takes some considerable amount of credit for the manner he came into the issue of the Scholamany marital entanglement. It is obvious the Nwangong Fon must have read one of the many books on Deceptive Family Politics when he wrote his "Greetings from Ongola-Cameroon" email. Addressed to both parties of the Scholamanyist marriage, the 8th Fon of Nwangong theorised:

Hope you and the kids are doing great. I have read with tears the letter to Dr Fossungu. From the little I know, not an idea of the exact year or date that the whole Nwangong community gathered at Pa Asahchop's residence at Letia in Nwangong, a place known as "Store". The weather was bright and was just reflecting the 'heart' of the couple, Schola-Peter, and the entire happy population with the great people of that time; Pa Asahchop and family, Pa Emmanuel Nguazong and the Fon himself representing the family and the Fondom. All was bright and clear, your hearts were united and the rest was food and drinks for the masses, all in good footing because I remember my dad killed the biggest pig in the Palace only with the help of hunters because no human efforts could have killed such a giant pig without firearms. I know all was well and that I still believe it continued with God's guidance and blessings for the two kids you are blessed with.

I know your parents for the good things they do to us and the world. I know Doctor grew from the Palace through the Fosungu Emmanuel family. The two backgrounds are very assuring and promising for a better future that was expected from you people. My doubts are that, why has the devil exploited your differences to make things get to this level? I am of the opinion that the kids could never have known the details of your differences. We are learning from you as our elders and we are expecting good examples and models especially given that you can blend African and Western cultures to produce a somewhat hybrid model. Really, you can bear with me that none of you is at peace and I can think the separation is regretful. Can you not reconcile your differences for once and for the sake of the kids? Everybody is liable to making mistakes and forgiveness is a divine recommendation.

Please, I will recommend that you propose to me the very best possibilities that we can mitigate this situation. You and I know that no one knows the root causes of these problems other than you. I still believe that no one else will seek a solution that can be most appropriate than the one that you both can provide. Do this for the sake of the kids and the better days you once experienced.

It will be my greatest delight if this "cold war" finds an end and if both of you have peace of mind in a more sustainable way that will affect your siblings as well. Accept my greetings (Fon NN Fossungu, private communication, 9 September 2013).

Figure #29: A few photos of the infamous Nwangong 1993 marriage that the Fon is talking about
Source: Photo Dave, Yaoundé

The few scenes in Figure #29 are designed to help readers in assimilating what the Fon is trying to pass on in regard of the celebration of said marriage. The young Nwangong Fon's lectures on the incomprehensibility of that failed marriage that had "raised a lot of hope in regard of the many good things to come to the lives of many" (Fossungu, 2013: 153), is also straightforwardly frank and, as well, stands very far from the hypocritical fowl-killing narrative of the

Asahchopination's praising in hiding but 'finishing' the man's reputation in public. Marie-Claire Afueh too certainly does not like Momany for surely knowing that "family" is not the synonym of "slavery" and for also clearly not being Asahchopinationist in these matters. That is, to simply jump into a family's trying issues just from the narration from one side to be condemning the other side: because it is his sister, or daughter or brother, etc. making the complaint. Fon NN Fossungu's 2008 email to Momany indicated that:

Sister Marie-Claire told me that she is not in good terms with you because when she had those problems with the husband you showed little or no concern. Please know that you are a man besides being a senior brother to them and so you have to always keep that possibility of keeping us together both at home and abroad. Brother, your influence should be felt at all times in our lives (cited in Fossungu, 2016: 102).

That is the Bowie Family Interest Theory and I would want to think that Fon NN Fossungu's pig-killing approach here is very far away from what Marie-Claire was expecting from Momany in order to pass her funny test of "showing concern". I think crisebacologists would certainly have too much quarrelling with the supposition that "showing concern" entails Momany going to another man's household to give orders regarding how they should conduct their affairs there, simply because his so-called sister has complained about the husband to him. Like the Fon of Nwangong has ably demonstrated in his lectures, this is also what Momany often told Marie-Claire when she complained. That there is no household (marriage, if you like) without its own problems; with those that we regard as such ideal homes being simply those within which the husband and wife solve their issues without letting the outside world meddle in them. That, although extended family members may sometimes come in, it would be nice and productive only when both parties invite them to do so; and these family members, on their part, would only indicate where the solution could lie after hearing from both sides, not just from one party. Now, if anyone objectively regards that counsel as not showing interest, then I think any deserving crisebacologist must personally congratulate Momany for not being educated and experienced enough on/in the matter to show such interest. On the other hand, the same crisebacologist (in my view) would also say 'sorry!' to those who are not mature enough to handle the truth and rather prefer those who would appear from nowhere to *verser* more kerosene on the small fire in their home. Africa must get into Africa, saying a big 'sorry!' to the backstabbers and other dragdowners.

Readers could even get the gist of all what Momany had advised Marie-Claire on the issues she raised, from Momany's reaction to this message that was sent out by her own 'blood' brother, Ignatius Akendung Fossungu, on 12 May 2010: "Here are more pictures of the graduation. Go sister, you are the best. This is our moment, this is our time." In his "Re: Graduation" of 12 May 2010 (addressed to Ignatius Fossungu, Cedoline Fossungu, Marie-Claire, and the other original recipients too of the first or initial message), Momany had stated:

Hi Everyone,

To Ignatius, I direct my thank you for sharing this wonderful event in pictures with us. I was not there when it happened but I think I can now say I have abundantly lived the event live!

To Chief Fofah [Marie-Claire], I say thank you abundantly for making us all very proud. Not just because you made it to graduation with honours; but most importantly because you did so not without your family, your husband especially. I have never doubted your ability to correctly sort out things for yourself.

To James [the husband in Figure #30 with her], I say we are all sharing in this honour but the honour is, first and foremost, yours. Savour it, brother.

Bye now. Dr. Nkemtale'eh [this paragraph altered].

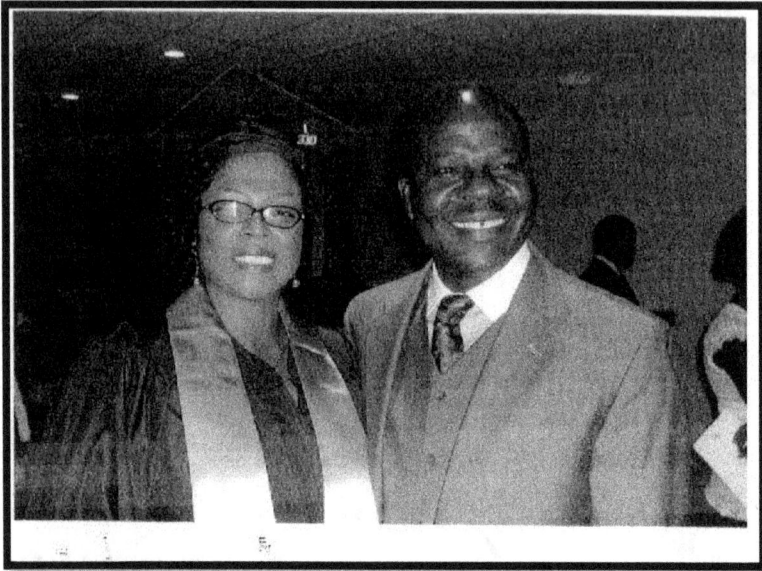

Figure #30: Marie-Claire Efuelancha Afueh (née Fossungu) & James Afueh during her graduation
Source: Ignatius Akendung Fossungu

Africa can only get into Africa through frantalkism. Frantalkism is thus the backbone of the Immaculate Freedom, Unity and Development Theory and is also seen in and fortified by the reaction of Momany to the bad news from the USA sent out by the Afuehs. Titled "A Fallen Hero" and coming directly from James and Marie-Claire Afueh, their forwarded message sent to Momany on Sunday, 16 June 2007 had declared the news and the extensive follow-up programme to the North American Cameroon community:

Fellow Cameroonians, Brothers and Sisters,

Another Cameroonian Hero has fallen again.

On behalf of my wife and family, it is with deepest sorrow and regret that we announce the passing away of her Brother/my Brother-In-Law, Mr. Joseph Fosungu – a great Lebialem Son.

God called Joe (as we often called him) at the young age of 43 years on June 6, 2007, in Parkland Memorial Hospital, Dallas, Texas. As painful as it is, we ask for your prayers and support.

My Brother-In-Law Joe was a Heart Patient with a Pace Maker. He was recently admitted into hospital for serious pneumonia, where he died two days later. We loved him, but GOD LOVED HIM MORE.

We are hereby asking each and everyone to do whatever they can to help so that his corpse can be transported to Cameroon.

We will be gathering in our home in Maryland on Friday, June 15, 2007 at 7:30 P.M. at 16403 Everwood Court, Bowie, MD 20716.

WAKE, VIEWING & CHURCH SERVICES are as follows:

WAKE KEEPING

Date:	Friday, June 22, 2007
Time:	8:00 P.M.
Place:	Celebration Plaza
	2921 Galleria Drive, Arlington, TEXAS 76011

VIEWING AND CHURCH SERVICES

Date: Saturday   June   23, 2007

VIEWING:

Time: 3:30pm - 4:30pm

CHURCH SERVICES
4:30pm – 5:30 P.M.

Place: THE MAJOR
FUNERAL HOME AND CHAPEL
2811 Galleria Drive, Arlington, TEXAS 76011

RECEPTION: 6:00 P.M. – 7: P.M.
CELEBRATION PLAZA
2921 Galleria Drive, Arlington, TEXAS 76011

Contact Information:

MARYLAND:	James Afueh	240-XXX-XXXX
	Marie-Claire Afueh	240-XXX-XXXX
	Frederick Temenu Fossungu	301-XXX-XXXX
CANADA:	Peter Fossungu	514-XXX-XXXX

TEXAS:	Pastor Folecfack Francis	817-XXX-XXXX
	Joseph Mahop	817-XXX-XXXX
	Maurice Asonganyi	214-XXX-XXXX
	Boniface Forzi	469-XXX-XXXX
ATLANTA	John Nguafac	770-XXX-XXXX
NEW YORK:	Fabien Fotabong	646-XXX-XXXX
ARIZONA:	Stephen Formenchia	520-XXX-XXXX
OHIO:	Christina Fortaw	614-XXX-XXXX

Thank you very much for all your help and support.

That was the bad news from the USA. So sad indeed! Reacting to the devastating news, on Tuesday, 12 June 2007 Momany told Marie-Claire Afueh that:

I do appreciate what you have done a lot even if I haven't really found the right way to say so. I have been so overwhelmed by situations here that the news of Joe's death completely flattened and paralysed me. In the face of it all (and despite the obvious difficulties) you stayed extremely strong and moved some mountains! I am very sure that dad (from wherever he is now) is extremely proud of you. I am too.

Thank you also for the advice you vented out during our phone conversation while you were still in Dallas. You had every reason to be upset. I understood then, but do understand even better now. As you rightly put it, money alone is not everything. I got really revamped after we talked and thereafter was able to formally communicate the sad news to members of Goodwill Montreal as per the attached forwarded message.

It's not yet over, but I am confident we shall overcome. Continue to stay strong, therefore, my dear sister; for you are now the source of my own strength and, together, we cannot and must not let daddy down here. God bless us. PAF

That is precisely what immaculate family unity and progress should properly entail. Frantalkism is at the base of this Immaculate Family Unity and Development Theory from Africa. It remains to be seen though whether that holds reciprocally and generally in the said Royal Family especially and Africa generally. The mentioned 'attached

84

forwarded message' is also graphical to the points and would need to be set out for readers' perusing as well. That setting out is graphical to an appropriate comprehension of "*Frantalkism* (or the science of love frank talk) [which] had come into existence on Sunday, October 2, 2005 at 1:50 PM with Momany's 'What on Earth Happened?' email to 'Hello Odilia'" (Fossungu, 2016: 181, original emphasis). I am thus referring to this email message titled "My Brother's Corpse in Dallas, Texas" that Momany had sent to the CGAM on 10 June 2007. "Dear Goodwillers," it announced,

As most of you already know, on June 6, 2007 I lost my junior brother – Joseph Njumo Fossungu – who, at time of death, was based in Dallas, Texas, USA. His corpse was released from the hospital last Friday to our sister, Mrs. Afueh (née Marie-Claire Efuelancha Fossungu) of Maryland, who had very ably rushed down to Texas to sort out things on our behalf. Joe's remains will have to stay in a funeral home down there in Texas for about two weeks while we grapple with the necessary arrangement to have the corpse sent back home (Cameroon) where it has to be buried.

This is a very trying moment indeed for both of us. Since the death of our father in October 2002, we have had to bury two other sisters (Beatrice Ngwika Fossungu in 2003 & Annastasia Chamo Fossungu in 2004) and a host of uncles, aunts, etc. But all of those, combined, would seem like child's play now in view of what we currently have at hand. The entire Fossungu Royal Family back home is in great need of your prayers and comforting but Marie-Claire and I who are out here with the deceased would cherish these the most. Indeed, Marie-Claire is so stretched out that I am imploring any Goodwiller who can do so, to give her a brief call at (240) XXX-XXXX and help me to encourage her to stay strong and level-headed. I truly don't know what I would have done by   now   without   her. Thank you very much. PAF (CGAM Forum, 10 June 2007).

Yes, indeed! That is how Africa can get into Africa because deaths and other such crippling events must not provide any reason for us to lose our sense of objectivity, an African leadership trait that Alamu (2015: 224-25) would also better school readers on. That is the vital message

85

that Momany also taught and dished out to CGAMers just a month after this Texas death (see Fossungu, 2015a: chapter 4). Readers would better grasp what Momany means by 'I truly don't know what I would have done by now without her' with knowledge that Momany could not travel out of Canada then because of the stumbling blocks of "African overseas culture", courtesy of Scholastica! It is apparent therefore that accusing Momany of not showing concern is just as hypocritical as the other accusation from the Asahchops. This hypocritical attitude that Immaculate Fossungu valiantly stood against in the coronation exercise is especially so glaring in the 'modern' African political sphere. This is precisely the reason anyone who (like Fon DF Fossungu and his upright daughter) does not take 'advantage' of the lucrative crookedness is ridiculed. How glorious Africa has been reduced to this! Get Africa back into Africa!

While 'non-four-eyes' Africans are still figuring it out, I will continue busying myself here with the hypocrisy issues that laboriously stand in the way of Africa getting into Africa. It is unnecessary therefore to detain readers any further with the questionable deeds of the so-called elites and other African administrators because I have a few queries for the crooked ones riling the blameless. Do those persons chastising upright Immaculate Fossungu even have an idea about what that woman's name means and why her parents might have chosen the name for her? If they are unaware of it, *Immaculate* signifies the following: spotless; clean and tidy; perfect; neat as a new pin; spick and span; faultless; and flawless. Yes, His Royal Majesty Fon DF Fossungu, you got that right. The Nwangong Fon's ingenuity in child-naming thus excluded the jujus' error from soiling the coronation process just as Africans' failure to remain authentic would provoke lots of ridiculing from North American children-loving white mothers.

The Contest of Cultural Theories: Africa Exports Nosexonomy and Bangwalangwalism to North America

This second part of the Chapter anchors on another version of children naming philosophies, viewing that the name given to a child can greatly determine his or her future. The theory particularly focused on here is one that necessarily falls out from the steadfast authenticity of some other African parents who avoid the useless foreign-naming trend by instead making namesakes in the family. I am particularly talking about Elizachoppism, a theory springing from the headache-germinating Scholamany marriage. Interestingly, Elizachoppism is godmothered by Elizabeth Njuafiack Asahchop in Figure #31. As already made known above, Scholastica's first child with Momany is called Ngunyi, being exceptionally named after Scholastica's father, Peter Ngunyi Asahchop. I say exceptionally because most African men would not do so but instead name their first child from their own side. Hear then Elizabeth Asahchop's Namesaking Theory on that rare honour Momany gave to the Asahchopination (a thesis which also collaborates 'The Asahndeming Lecture on African Tradition': Fossungu, 2016: 156-59). Elizachoppism, the namesake theory proper, is embedded in the 3rd paragraph of Elizabeth Asahchop's secret letter to her own daughter which was *confidentially* telling "Dear Scholastica" the following:

How are you my child? I hope you are really in good health with your baby and your husband.

We heard about your baby and we were very happy. I got the news on the 8th of March which was the International Women's Day. We got a letter from Eugene who was in Douala when you phoned Romanus. So he took that advantage and quickly sent us the information and we celebrated the day as if the child was being seen by us. Everybody who knows you in Fontem said when I am writing I should greet you. My reason for not writing so soon after I had got the news was that I wanted to receive a letter from you first and it was so, and I have written.

I was very happy with the name of the child. Because you are now not only my daughter but the mother of my husband and your husband is not only my son-in-law but the father of my husband. So many thanks to the two of you for that honour. In fact, this [delivery] was what everybody in the family was having [serious] thought [about] and a bit of mind problems. But the almighty God has solved the problem. So everybody in the family is happy with the happening. There is this saying that God's time is the best; so you have seen it with your own eyes that being patient is not a sin or a problem

When I went to the village and saw your mother-in-law and personally told her about the great happening, she was very happy to the extent of even crying. This was not because of crying but just due to the fact that happiness brings sorrow. She even went up to the extent of saying she had seen her own grandchild before the door will be opened for her by God. She is still in Nweh-Ncheng but it is not that she is sick but just that she wants a companion to stay with because when she was at the Palace she had nobody to stay with.

I am very sorry to tell you that my cousin Regina who was staying in Dschang died on the 12th of March but that is not a problem. It is almost becoming over. So just take it as it has happened. Greet Quinta and her children for me. Permit me to end here. Thanks, your mother, Elizabeth Asahchop [this paragraph altered] (Elizabeth N. Asahchop, private communication, 24 May 2000).

Figure #31: Elizabeth Njuafiack Asahchop
Source: Scholastica Achankeng Asahchop

Njuafiackism and Fobantengism: Circuitous and Confusing?

The Elizachopping 4th paragraph sub-thesis "that happiness brings sorrow" is here styled *Njuafiackism* and would appear to be off-beam until you are advised to grasp the fact that it is coming from Bangwaland, a place that is recognized for its hard-to-understand philosophies: just like the epistemology-ontology puzzle? I cannot really tell (regarding the equation) but Bates and Jenkins's disagreement with Collin Hay (their teacher) largely has to do with what Furlong and Marsh (2010: 186-88) do discuss as 'the relationship between ontology and epistemology.' Furlong and Marsh's discussion of ontology and epistemology is quite long and somewhat understandably repetitive in many parts. Understandably so because, among "other factors" peculiar to the subject matter (for more of which, see Stanley, 2012), we are told that repetition has its positive aspects, such as sometimes reinforcing our understanding of the points (Fossungu, 2014: 51). Here though is what I have essentially gained from their handling of this subject that is loaded with a lot of controversy (for more of the disagreement, see Mawere and van Stam, 2015). That each social scientist's orientation to his or her subject is shaped by his/her ontological and epistemological position; that even if these positions are unacknowledged, they shape the approach to theory and the methods which the social scientist uses; and that because these positions shape our approach, they are like a skin not a sweater; they, therefore, cannot be put on and taken off whenever the researcher sees fit. In the view of these authors, all students of political science should recognize their own ontological and epistemological positions and be able to defend them. This means that these students need to understand the alternative positions on these fundamental questions (Furlong and Marsh 2010: 184). Could that not quite explain why most Africans who do not even know their own culture are very easily brainwashed with 'African overseas culture'?

A tree-topper is someone who practises tree-topperism or midnight politics (see Fossungu, 2015a: chapter 1) and it is essential to add here that the foregoing theorization from Professors Furlong and Marsh makes a tree-topper always a tree-topper because tree-topping is not like a sweater that can be put on and off. It is only left for fossungupalogists or straight talkers or crisebacologists in the community to uncompromisingly destroy the trunks, if tree-topping has to be eliminated or curtailed "since my late father [from Nwangong Fondom called Chief Formbuehndia] would always fondly tell us that no tree-top can still exist with the trunk already cut to irredeemable pieces" (Fossungu, 2015a: 10). It is surely not for nothing that four-eyesism is being vigorously recommended for African schools (Fossungu, 2015a: xi & passim), since the perspective thus leaves little or no doubt about "the contribution of ontological and epistemological reflection to the process of instilling in students of politics a range of critical analytical skills" (Hay, 2007: 116) because 'context-independent research' cannot 'really be regarded as such' (Mawere and van Stam, 2015: 208). Thus, the sane argument is that "the inherited colonial education marginalises African indigenous knowledge systems and dismisses them as unscientific, pre-logical and primitive... Such a scenario entraps the African in a mentality of a foreign epistemic framework resulting in failure to think in alternative ways and come out of their poverty condition" (Gwaravanda, 2018: 256). Professor Atwell Nhemachena of Namibia carried the same thesis forward when he crisebacologically questioned:

If Afrikans become hybrids or chimeras, that is, half animal and half human, then how can Afrikans sustain the momentum towards Afrikanisation? If Afrikan genetic compositions are manipulated and reengineered, then how can Afrikans sustain the momentum towards Afrikanisation? If Afrikans become beastly queers, then how can Afrikans sustain the momentum towards Afrikanisation? Without Afrikan human essence, Afrikans vanish into the Fanonian zone of nonbeing, into the colonial and enslavement era nothingness. A form of nothingness that some versions of decolonisation would celebrate. Decolonisation should not be about the denial of Afrikan human essence. In other words, decolonisation should be in sync with Afrikanisation (Nhemachena, 2018).

The CGAM seems to have it all (like Sweet Mother Africa) but ends up not having it because of this persisting colonial education that excludes critical thinking and authentic African perspectives. I say so because a prominent CGAM President seems to have also made the above sweater-points with his 'our characters cannot hide' unity-message. In the traditional New Year message to CGAMers, Fidelis Folefac stated that "even though our characters cannot hide, it is important for us to establish a culture of healthy debate, leadership, dignity and integrity that will continue to make Goodwill and goodwillers proud in 2008 and beyond. Let our communications to goodwillers remain focused, mature and respect simple rules of public writing" (CGAM Forum, 1 January 2008). A useful symbiosis of most of these mentioned qualities (and more) of leadership in pre-colonial Africa, is offered by Alamu (2015: 219-27). Whether or not they actually live by their own instructions to others is something that is very commonly uncommon with 'modern' African 'leaders'. What should it actually be? *Children, Do As I Say Or Do As I Do?*

The instructors of the first alternative are clearly not qualified to be instructing children, a fact that would duly account for African children being the leaders of *a tomorrow* that is never coming, but instead remaining *yesterday* forever. All that being because it goes against the sane dictates of frantalkism which is the backbone of the Immaculate Freedom, Unity and Development Theory. Could the teacher like the one here talking to you be validly qualified to be preaching as such when he himself or herself acts otherwise? A YES would be conspicuously defining the hypocrisy Immaculate Fossungu preaches against; and Professor Hay (2007: 118) sufficiently agrees by recognizing that "as Bates and Jenkins's own intervention makes very clear, texts are rarely assimilated uncritically. The best way to guard against the dangers to which they rightly draw our attention is to instil in students from the outset precisely the same desire to 'pluck' at the 'laurels' of their teachers that most clearly animates their own contribution." The two former students did obviously charge their teacher with assuming the position of an 'intellectual gatekeeper' on questions of ontology and epistemology (Hay, 2007: 115). This is almost the same 'absolutism crime' that Collin Hay himself is well known to have charged the Faircloughs with (see Fossungu, 2018: 19-20). The students-teacher controversy here also illustrates 'the coming back at you' theory (see Fossungu, 2018: 17). Professor Hay does not see it that way though, indicating that his 'precedence'
argument, such as it is, is that no ontologically neutral epistemological claim can be made. In other words, to commit oneself to an epistemology is also to commit oneself to a position on a range of ontological issues. Moreover, *as I define these terms*, ontological claims logically precede epistemological claims. If, as I suggest, ontology 'relates to the nature of the social and political world' and epistemology 'to what

we can know about it', then ontology is logically prior in the sense that the 'it' in the second term (the definition of epistemology) is, and can only be, specified by the first (the definition of ontology). This, I contend, is a point of logic, not of meta-theory (Hay, 2007: 117, original emphasis).

I have been talking of hard-to-comprehend bangwalangwalism and you can get a bit of it from Chief Fobanteng Michael's answer to this simple question that was posed to him during his interview at Chief Fotale'eh's coronation in Nwangong Fondom: "What would you like to say to the sons and daughters of Nwangong listening to you?" He responded: "That it was a very great animation. That no one can take what is yours because only God can say what you would not be tomorrow. We have to bring up our children the right way; and he who is ahead or in front shouldn't think that the behind is ending. Life is only behind, not before. That's the only thing I can tell you." (Chief Fobanteng, private communication, 19 July 2014).

Chief Fobanteng's response as a whole is hard to easily grasp and his 'life theory' in it would seem very confusing until you are reminded to remember that it is a Bangwa Chief theorising on the unknown again (see Chapter 3)! Bangwalangwalism! Not to equate it with the seemingly circuitous *Nguafackism*, it is perhaps merely another proverbial way, for instance, of "echoeing Cameroonian musician John Minang that you should always be kind to those you meet on your way up because you may likely meet them on your way down" (Fossungu, 2016: 220).

Perhaps you would be able to comprehend his theory on God being the only one to prevent someone becoming what was destined, after perusing this book to the end. Would Elizabeth Asahchop not also have explained it off above with her 3rd paragraph thesis that 'God's time is the best'? Whatever the case though, people who are good at grasping Bangwalangwalism would not go all this distance to comprehend Elizabeth Asahchop's egg-riddle-like 'happiness-sorrow' postulation or Njuafiackism. After all, did Momany not *happily* marry their daughter only to end up *sorrowfully* soon after her 'miraculous' Atlantic Crossing? I guess I should better be counselling people to soon 'sadly' marry in order to be 'happy' after? What can Chiefoletialism also bring here to the discussion table, especially regarding the 'happy-to-sad' Mamie Regina's Canadian grandchildren in Figure #32?

Figure #32: Mamie Regina Akiefac Fossungu's Canadian grandchildren (clockwise from top left): Nguajong Forbehndia Fossungu; Peter Ateh-Afac Fossungu, Jr.; Ngunyi Ateh-Afac Fossungu; & Peteraf Karlemon-Ethan Tale'eh Fossungu
Source: Photo Aria, Montréal

The Logic of Nosexonomy: A Battler of or Partner in Denigrating African Culture?

The questions above would push us to find out if Collin Hay's logic could also aid matters at all with Elizachoppism (the namesake theory proper of her 3rd paragraph) which also pushes one to consider what could also be said about Nguajong who is named after Momany's own father? This question is raised because of an amicable 'boasting' between the two children (Ngunyi and Nguajong). They love themselves so much and you would hardly divine the senior-junior or boy-girl tendencies in their dealings. Furthermore, both of them are nosexonomically named. Nosexonomy defines the sagacity and authenticity of those Africans who still bear only their gender-neutral African names (see Fossungu, 2015b: 76). The two children are also both 'NGU' (short form) and so the alphabetical precedence thing too is logically beaten off (like Collin Hay's logical un-wearing of the 'gate-keeper' coat)? If affirmative, that could thus leave them with just being the fathers of their parents! Momany used to just love hearing them arguing it out even at their tender age as they were in Figure #33! *Ngunyi*: 'Be careful as you talk to your mother's father and your father's father-in-law!' *Nguajong*: 'Don't forget you're addressing your father's daddy and your granddad!'...

95

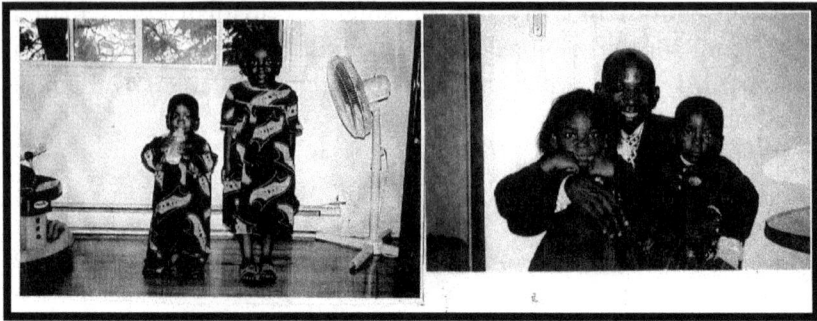

Figure #33: (Left) Nguajong & Ngunyi at home while they were still in Montreal with both parents & (right) Oh! How could they ever correctly understand why they can now no longer have all this?
Source: Momany Fossungu's album

Cube-Rooted Bangwalangwalism: The African Father-Grandfather Battle in Canada

Momany would truly be wondering now what the conversation would have become with the addition of both Peter and Peteraf. Would Peter just nicely shut all the others up for being 'just grandfathers' while he is *their* father? Would Ngunyi (whose middle name is from Momany) smoothly counter-attack with her also being *their* father? (You have already seen all four of them joyfully debating here in Figure #32). Talking of father, Chief Foletia Vincent who you saw in Figure #2 told Momany in a letter in 2004 that: "Over there [in Canada] you are the husband and father of Scholastica while she is your wife and mother" (cited in Fossungu, 2016: 114). Call it *Marriage-Chiefoletialism* to distinguish it from another version of Chiefoletialism on death known as *Royadeathism*. Could Elizachoppism be behind Chief Foletia's thesis that makes Momany 'the husband and father of Scholastica in Canada'? Don't think so because Momany's being the father of Elizabeth Asahchop's husband makes him the grandfather of Scholastica, and not father. Moreover, there is no way that (from Elizachoppism) Scholastica could also be 'Momany's wife [possible] and *mother* in Canada' [impossible] as the Chief-Foletia thesis also has it. Both of them being parents to

96

Elizabeth's husband, makes them husband and wife, for sure; but Scholastica can clearly not be Momany's mother in any way there from; not even his maternal grandmother: since none of their children is named after Momany's mother who is 'happily-to-sadly' sitting in Figure #34. Of course Scholastica can lay claim to his paternal grandmotherhood through Nguajong but the only woman who could have validly made the mother claim is Flavie, through Peter Jr., and the paternal grandmother one through Peteraf.

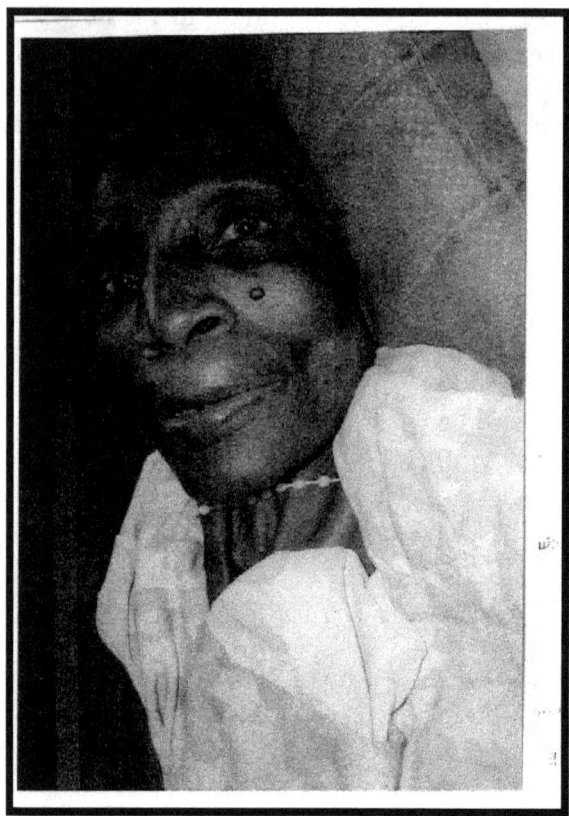

Figure #34: Mafor Regina Akiefac Fossungu in May 2014, barely a month to her death
Source: Photo taken by Momany Fossungu

Therefore, Chief Foletia's theory (Marriage-Chiefoletialism) could be inspired by other considerations, not taking any roots from Elizachoppism as such. What Marriage-Chiefoletialism (another interesting piece of Bangwalangwalism) would simply mean is that, because the couple is so far away from home and other family members (African communalism), they no longer have to just remain husband and wife to each other but must completely assume the roles of those unavailable (extended) family members in order to be able to weather and survive the isolation or their strange new home. This is positive 99-sensical Counsel that the couple in question never lived by since (because of predominating onesidetakism and moneyintriguism[4]) those 'absent

---

[4] Being two giants which are solely responsible for the excessive lateness in honouring the repayment of an invaluable life-saving loan. I am talking about the Whistance-Smiths' critically important loan whose repayment only began with Momany's letter of 26 July 2019. Dear Andrew and Nancy, it opened,

It has been more than twenty years since you wonderfully came to my rescue with your invaluable loan. Imagine that I had been paying just a thousand dollars yearly from when I completed my doctoral programme then the loan would already have been completely repaid! It was not then possible and I thank you once more for your understanding. Let me reiterate again that I can only be delayed, never stopped, from doing what I set out to do. Please, find enclosed here a cheque in the amount of six thousand dollars (6000$). I will see how much I can be able to pay back before October this year (time when my tree-cutting season ends). Whatever amount that will be remaining at that time is to be completed next season 2020.

Please, see this loan repayment solely as a necessary and logical revival of my Cameroon Project. I know you had written off the loan in 2003 (my gratitude once more for your rare comprehension). But if I can pay back a thousand-dollar *loan* from my so-called wife (when I was going to Cameroon to bury my dad), there is surely nothing

members' on one side were never really absent; being so, so negative-99-sensically present through 'Re-Conceptualizing the Meaning of Family 99-Sensically' (Fossungu, 2014: 75-82) to the extent of totally displacing and obliterating the other 'couple' or the "Canadian husband and father" (see Fossungu, 2016: 63-70).

Talking of 'Canadian father' must also lead us to another significant query. It relates to finding out who, between Nguajong and Tale'eh (Peteraf), would rightfully claim the title of 'father's father'? The issue is graphically important in view of Momany's 'Two Sets of Parents' (Fossungu, 2013: 2-19) – de facto and biological – in *Africans in Canada: Blending Canadian and African Lifestyles?* – a book that Dr Piet Konings of the African Studies Centre Leiden describes as "a captivating story" which "provides the reader with a number of useful insights in the complicated African family relations, which are otherwise difficult to acquire from standard scientific and more specifically anthropological literature" (Fossungu, 2013: back cover). Yes, 'standard scientific' and 'traditional' literature would not correctly educate you on some of these issues since they already assume things and have exclusionist frames. In her review of said book, Dr Rosita Coding of Examiner.com also did proudly "recommend that sociologists, anthropologists, historians, and educators (all) lend an ear to Fossungu's writing" because his "book provides the reader with a uniquely African philosophical perspective of cultural fusion" with the author "presenting a means for Westerners to see African cultures and communities beyond the veil of the exotic and

---

that can stop me (especially now that I have sorted out the numerous confusions that then prevented me) from repaying an interest-free loan that has helped me so much in attaining so much in life. I have never been as happy in the past two decades as I am now: just knowing that I am honouring my word to you. Please, go ahead and cash the cheque (as well as any other that will be coming later).

Extend my affection and greetings around. Sincerely yours, Signed. Peter Ateh-Afac Fossungu (this paragraph altered).

Orientalism" (Coding, 2013). You got that right, doctor, and it is about time for the waist-breaking laughter.

Obama's Mother Laughs at Pathetic Peripatetic Africans and the CGAM

More naming and education philosophies can be pursued in the other Chapters later. Right now you can thus multiply the African children-naming puzzles from here to here (if you do really like Professor Collin Hay's logic of un-wearing the uncomfortable suit). But what counts really is whether or not these children are even still immersed in their African roots now: especially as not long after their relocation to London (Ontario) in September 2004 their mother (Scholastica) began hotly talking of changing their names in order for them 'to have English names'! Question is: Are they of English or of African stock? As Dr Fossungu (2015b: 76) has pushed the advantages of African nosexonomy into the limelight and then pondered, "Am I looking forward to finding Europeans being called, for example, Mbinchang Okoro Mandengue?" Crisebacologists are sure that even Barack H. Obama's white mother never ventured around it (after their separation) to change the son's name in order to give him 'a white name' or 'a Christian name'. To cut a long tale of peripatetic Africans short, just imagine what force the Birther Movement in the USA would have had in 2008, if Obama's loving mum had been as unloving as to make the alteration and you would have grasped completely this talk about children's best interests in their welfare and education. So, would Barack Obama ever have become President of the USA if his mother had actually tampered with his identity information? Why can't we just educate our children to know and be at home with just who they are? How Momany must be enormously missing his lovely and intelligent children! How these children too must be missing his authentic upbringing and fatherly love and support in all their forms! Oh! How could they ever correctly understand why they can now no longer have all these things?

Mama Obama must really be dying laughing-to-crying here! And she would not be the only white North American mother doing so. As mentioned in the previous Chapter, the burning questions of family unity and development, both in and out of Africa, and the incomprehensibility of some of the mysterious happenings in villages particularly could be brought home here through one of Momany's aforementioned communications with his white friends in Edmonton (Canada) who in September 2004 were "just wondering how things are working out with Scholastica and the kids. Are you in the same place in Montreal or do you have a new address?" (Nancy Whistance-Smith, private communication, 18 September 2004). Momany then responded as follows (1st paragraph):

Hi Nancy, It has not been easy. They left on 2 September 2004. Only last weekend did I receive a note from Scholastica through a lady here (Paul's sister) that travelled with her to London, Ontario. I was supposed to drive them down there over the long Labour Day weekend but Scholastica changed her mind and decided on Tuesday that it was on Thursday (2 September) that we must go. I couldn't and she had someone else (who, I don't know) to drive them there. I only succeeded in moving over the long Labour Day weekend and I am now at this address: 7110-210 Chemin de la Cote-Des-Neiges, Montreal, Quebec, H3R 2L9. My phone remains (514) 884-9068 (Momany Fossungu, private communication, 18 September 2004).

In her "Re: Thinking of You" of 18 September 2004, Nancy Whistance-Smith wrote back, indicating that "you must miss the children terribly. Do you hear from them at all? Sad news about your sister. Is it common for cousins to rid themselves of relatives? Sounds quite horrific to me and is obviously very stressful for you. I will continue to keep you and your family in my prayers. Greetings from all of us in Edmonton, Nancy." Once more, why wouldn't African children, irrespective of where they are born, be brought up according to African culture, a custom that is heavily based on communalism? I strongly believed that we Africans are not forging ahead (as we normally should) fundamentally, if not exclusively, because we are cut off our authentic roots. Do Europeans, for example, ever Africanize while in Africa (Fossungu, 2015a:179-200)?

Just imagine again this other laughable case in the CGAM that seeks to impress on people that discipline and legality and the love of children's welfare and tranquillity (you name them), are the rule there. For instance, talking about the Children Christmas Party (CCP), we are made to understand this. That it was in order for the adults to enjoy the End of Year (EOY) party without the distraction of kids, and viewing also the damage from the loudness of the EOY party music to the tympanic membranes of these children, that it was decided during the October 2005 Assembly that a CCP (often shortened to Children X-Mas) should be inaugurated and to take place a week or so *before* the grand EOY party. Very thoughtful of these parents indeed! You can see some of these children in Figure #35 having lots of fun at their CCP.

Figure #35: Children having a lot of fun at their CCP
Source: Photo taken by Momany Fossungu

But this dictum is very far from being the case, as amply testified, first, by the Minutes of several January Goodwill General Assemblies (GGAs). The complaint against some members (parents) who always bring their children along has become so loud; and all that notwithstanding the sane provision of baby-sitting services for a negligible amount. For instance, on 28 December 2005 a famous '*Info Regarding Party*' communiqué from the Paul Ayah administration told Fellow Goodwillers that:

As the party draws near, here's some info meant to ensure that things progress smoothly. 1. *Babysitting*: Arrangements are underway to make provision of babysitting services on the night of the party in order to avoid having children at the party. For any concrete arrangement to be made, we need to know the number of people who would need babysitting services. Those interested in the service should contact Valy. A member has made his apartment available very close to the location of the party. The idea is to get one or two teenagers to babysit during the evening. Parents can drop off their children and pick them up after the party. A contribution of $2.50 per child will be required to help pay for the babysitters (CGAM Forum, 28 December 2005).

The complaint against the continuous bringing of babies along mounted so much that the January 2013 Assembly even threatened and suggested the putting of "NO CHILDREN TO BE ADMITTED IN THE PARTY HALL" on the tickets and enforcing same at the gate. *Well said than done* is all anyone who knows African and CGAM enforcement of rules would also say (see Magaisa, 2015: 259-64; Fossungu, 2015a: 55-64). The 'before-EOY-condition' too has not always been the case because you will find some CCPs taking place after the EOY party. For examples, you can get one from the 2009 CCP communiqué sent out by Eugene Lekeawung Asahchop on 15 December 2009 (which also informs you that a CCP committee usually re-forms itself into sub-committees – just like the End of Year Party Committee):

Fellow Goodwillers: After a successful end of year party it is now the turn of our kids. Let's make it successful for the kids just as it was for us last weekend. Below are sub committees to assist in various activities. The committee for Parcelling and Labelling of Gifts will meet on

Thursday 17th at Mr. Folefac's (Outgoing President's) residence at 6 PM for the labelling. Please if we all come on time it will take a maximum of 2 hours.

The leaders of the other committees will be responsible for arrangements either by phone or mail with their members.....

Thanks. Eugene (CGAM Forum, 15 December 2009, omission supplied).

If you are in the CGAM and just call all that irresponsibility or hypocrisy, you are then surprised to hear what quickly comes forth. This doublespeak surely confuses and brutalises children who are keenly looking up to these parents as role models. According to some experts on children studies, "the predicaments facing the African child that were also noted in the chapter include: child mortality, illiteracy, poor access to healthcare services, starvation, exploitation, sexual abuse, sale of children, child trafficking and abduction, violence, torture and displacement as well as harmful cultural practices" (Yinusa et al, 2018: 294). Do children all over the world face these problems or only children in Africa? I will let the detailed discussion of the CGAM children activities in the rest of the Chapter also insightfully speak to that.

The CGAM Children Diversity Programme and Children Christmas Party

One of the CGAM's three 'Special Organs' is devoted to children activities. These 'special organs' stand in contradistinction to the Special Events Committees (SECs), which are so many that outlining all might require two or more books in this one. For some examples (quite apart from the ad hoc committees on parties that are largely seen in this and other Chapters), one can cite the Scholarship Committee (Magnus Ajong as chair, Enongene Ekwe, Yacubu Mohnkong); the 2010 Loan Recovery Committee (Enongene Ekwe as chair, Sylvester Nchende, Hilary Fuh-Cham), 2013 Excursion Committee (Henadez Makia as chair, Fonderson Tataw Ashu, Roger Ekuh-Ngwese, Fidelis Folefac, Richmond Bassong, Julius Etaya Ashu), 2013 BBQ Committee (chaired by Evaristus Ngoe Ojah), Bylaws Revision Committees (BRCs), and Goodwill Projects

Committee (Fidelis Folefac as chair, Neba Georges, Prudence Ayuk, Wilson Anung).

According to Article 11 of the CGAM Constitution, the following special organs also contribute to the achievement of the objectives of the CGAM: 1. Goodwill Football Club (GWFC) is responsible for organizing soccer and other sporting activities for the wellness of members of Goodwill and any persons interested in participating in the activities of the club. 2. Goodwill Women Forum (GWWF) is responsible for the organization of special activities dedicated to the empowerment of Goodwill women. 3. Goodwill Children Diversity Programme (GCDP) is responsible for organizing events for Goodwill Children aimed at promoting cultural diversity and their integration into the Canadian society. That was the Constitution talking but it remains just words until put into action. Let's therefore talk a bit about the GWWF before taking the GCDP next, followed by the Children Christmas Party.

The Goodwill Women Forum (GWWF)

The CGAM's yearly celebration of International Women's Day takes place under the canopy of the GWWF which was founded in 2008. Some researchers have ably explored the African children and the African women and their fundamental rights in the society as well as the predicaments facing both groups in relation to the development of Africa (see Yinusa et al, 2018). Highlighted as the fundamental rights of the African woman are: equality and elimination of discrimination, elimination of violence against women, marriage, access to justice, education, inheritance, widow's right, economic and social welfare rights, health and reproductive rights (Yinusa et al, 2018: 294). Meanwhile the predicaments of the African women were found to include: gender inequality, gender oppression, violence, maternal mortality, stereotyping, discrimination, stigmatization and labelling and the problem of decision making in reproductive health. (Yinusa et al, 2018: 294-95). One of the conclusions of the report is that there is "the need for some African societies to take a cue from other developed societies by eliminating

106

these barbaric acts against the African child and African woman in order to make Africa a more civilised and developed society" (Yinusa et al, 2018: 295). So, how are these two 'vulnerable' groups really faring in said developed societies?

Previous Chapters and sections have provided some clues. The experts have highlighted some 'Fundamental Human Rights of the African Woman', as well as the 'Predicaments of the African Woman and Implications on the Development of the African Society' (Yinusa et al, 2018: 288-94). Some of the problems facing these African women specifically are, inter alia, Widow Inheritance, defined as "a cultural and social practice whereby a widow is required to marry a male relative of her husband, often his brother" (Yinusa et al, 2018: 293), Gender Inequality (Yinusa et al, 2018 289-90), Violence against Women (Yinusa et al, 2018: 291), Gender Oppression (Yinusa et al, 2018 290-91), Problem of decision making in Reproductive Health (Yinusa et al, 2018 293-94), Maternal Mortality (Yinusa et al, 2018: 291-92), and Stereotype, Discrimination and Labelling (Yinusa et al, 2018: 292).

The GWWF tries to ameliorate things in relation to some of these issues specific to women worldwide. As Florence Ngayap Nankam (6th CGAM president and 2013 GWWF chairperson) would circumscribe it for readers, the GWWF is a leading platform that brings women together to promote and foster their connections in the community. Its mission is to mentor, support and empower women in Montreal and Canada through their monthly networking and educational meetings, promotional opportunities and social events. The GWWF offers the opportunity to interact and socialize with other women who have similar interests and challenges. It also strives to create the opportunity to collectively develop how women can move forward on the issues that they care about; being a great platform where women deploy experience and expertise across all generations, offering as well practical discussions on how to overcome barriers and create new horizons not only for Goodwill women but for women world-wide.

Figure #36: Some scenes of CGAM celebration of International Women's Day
Source: Cameroon Goodwill Association of Montreal

Here, for example, is a list of the persons that were involved in organizing the 2013 celebration of the International Women's Day (from which the photos above come): Florence Ngayap Nankam (chair), Caren Osong Ayah, Catherine Yungong, Cecilia Ayuketah, Delphine Afor, Lorraine Fombe, Micheline Acheah, Pascaline Abongwa, Phyllis M. Ndonkeu, Precelia N. Folifac, Rosaline Tanyi Takang, and Tracy Leke. It has been done every year since 2008, the 2009 committee having been chaired by Berri Nsame.

The Goodwill Children Diversity Programme (GCDP)

The GCDP was actually initiated in 2008 through the Folefac administration's creation of a partnership with the LaSalle Police

Department (Unit 13) to support children activities as a way of educating and socializing them on the one hand and keeping them away from drugs and other street crimes on the other. Thus, Fidelis Folefac's determination to get the community some considerable amount of visibility and as a force to reckon with did not end with the creation of the Goodwill Football Club in 2005 (for more discussion of the club, see Fossungu, 2018: 127-31).

He then focused on creating activities for children and that's when the Goodwill Children Diversity Music Program was launched – a project whose objective is to group children together and give them a sense of responsibility, while making them aware of the multi-ethnic realities, through culture in general, and through dancing and singing in particular. Thanks to the partnership that he managed to establish with the sponsors and the Borough, he was also able to organize a Christmas party and an outdoor soccer team for children. In addition, he managed to build solid cooperation with LaSalle's police force, which provided him with soccer equipment for the children, thereby conveying a message to youngsters that the police aren't a force to fear, but rather people on whom they can count in case of need (LaSalle, 2010).

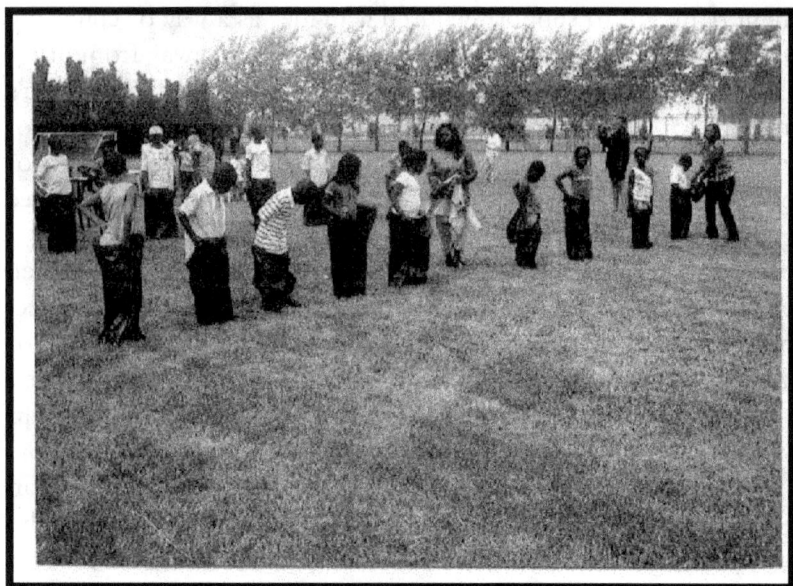

Figure #37: Sample Photo of Children Activities during CGAM's celebration of International Children's Day
Source: Photo taken by Momany Fossungu

The Picture above does represent some of the activities children are involved in during the celebration of International Children's Day by the CGAM. Many CGAMers have been active in seeing to it that the children programme is what it has been, is, and will be. For example, the 2008 committee for the celebration of the International Children's Day was chaired by Naya Ngala, 2009 by Florence Ngayap Nankam, and the 2013 one was made up of: Yucubu Mohnkong (chair), Agbornyor Tanyi, Delphine Afor Ndemaza, Lorraine Fombe, Richard Tegum, Richmond Bassong, Tracy Leke, and Yvette Fuh-Cham. But it would clearly be artificial to say even a word about the GCDP without mentioning one particular name (or the term *Evelibeagalization*) that is almost synonymous to it: Dr Eveline Awemu Ibeagha. That is the shortest way to describe her tireless dedication to the (Goodwill) children of the community, not only through the GCDP but also the yearly Goodwill Children Christmas

110

Party (CCP), dating back to the CCP's inception in 2005. Dr Eveline Awemu Ibeagha is seen in Figure #38

Figure #38: Dr Mrs. Eveline Awemu Ibeagha distributing gifts at Children Christmas Party
Source: Photo taken by Momany Fossungu

Funding the Goodwill Children Christmas Party (CCP)

Because of the visible importance that CGAMers attach to their children's all-round development, a circumscription of the CCP would be in order here before any other further examples of community participation involving children that may follow. A little sketch of its history and functioning would be important preparation for also grasping CGAM political, economic and social dynamics. The End-of-Year (EOY) Party Committee (EOYPC) is actually the oldest committee, being as old as the CGAM itself – which is not the same with the kids' end-of-year party (CCP). It has been important to situate readers well by re-baptizing them with the party spirit of CGAMers that also engendered the children one that readers will be hearing a lot about in CGAM circles and relating to the issues of this book, the disrespected philosophy behind its creation having been noted above already. The decision at the 2005 meeting was that each member should contribute ten dollars ($10.00) for the CCP. It has since evolved to the point where (1) its initial three-member committee now embodies the large number seen in Table 2; and (2) the Association now allocates funds toward this important occasion for children (and not only CGAMers' kids), with more and more sophisticated gifts (beginning notably during the Folefacist presidency) than when it initially began. That not only CGAMers' children attend this party can be seen, for example, in the CGAM President's message of 9 October 2009 titled *Children List*, in which Fidelis Folefac told members that:

To reduce the task for everybody, I have edited the 2008 list posted below. The ages will be updated by 1 year later.

Thus only parents who joined Goodwill in 2009 or have had new babies should provide the name, age and sex of their children/babies.

Also kindly alert if we have omitted any name. Once we know the number of gifts we have, we will ask for the names of [other] children you will want to invite to the event.

Parents: DO NOT WAIT UNTIL LAST MINUTE TO UPDATE THE LIST [which is omitted here].

Table 2 : CGAM Children Christmas Party Committees:2005-2013)	
Year	Committee Members
2005	Eveline Awemu Ibeagha (chair), Karen Najeme, Georgia Kometa
2006	Eveline Awemu Ibeagha (chair), Caren Osong Ayah
2007	Eveline Awemu Ibeagha (chair), Caren Osong Ayah, Rosaline Takang, Precilia Folefac
2009	Yvette Fuh-Cham (chair), Felicia Tatuh, Florence Etube, Eugene Asahchop. Resource person: Eveline Awemu Ibeagha

2011	Roger Ekuh-Ngwesse & Berri Nsame (c0-chair), Agbonyor Tanyi, Emmanuel Fokoua Tene, Epizitone Anabi, Marie Diegoue, Precilia Nkengasong Folefac, Yacubu Mohnkong
2012	Yvette Mbeh Fuh-Cham (chair), Caren Osong Ayah, Precilia Nkengasong Folefac
2013	Yvette Fuh-Cham & Delphine Afor (co-chair), Caren Ayah, Catherine Yungong, Lorraine Fombe, Micheline Achea, Phyllis Ndonkeu, Pascaline Abongwa, Tracy Leke

Source: Cameroon Goodwill Association of Montreal

Table 2 gives you more education on the committees and their members since inception until 2013 (with just two years missing – 2008 and 2010). The very first Children Christmas Party took place on Saturday, 17 December 2005 in the hall of St. Lawrence Anglican Church on 520, 75th Avenue, LaSalle. So too was the second in 2006 as can be deduced from the 'Children's Christmas Party' message from the CCP Committee chair (Eveline Awemu Ibeagha), a communication that also gives you a glimpse into the event's activities. Sent out on 15 December 2006, it announced to 'Dear Goodwillers' that:

This is to remind you all of the Children's Christmas Party scheduled for this Sunday, the 17th of December 2006. Venue: St. Lawrence Anglican Church, 520 75th Avenue, LaSalle, H8R 2P5. Time: 2 - 6 p.m. prompt.

Agenda: 1. Opening prayers: - General prayer by Nkem Folifac; - Prayer for Children by Ammah Adolf; - Prayer for parents by Atemkeng Folifac. 2. What is Christmas? Presented by Steve Komguep. 3. A song by the Foko kids. 4. The story of the birth of Christ, to be read out by Anna Mungwa, Berri Nsame, Caren Ayah, and Caren Najeme. Question and answer session to be handled by Caren Ayah. 5. Memory verse presentation by 8 children (Mamie Najeme, Folifac Jr, Solomon Ibeagha, Ngando Etube, Darlington Tebo, Michael Ammah, Tanisha Etube and Atemkeng Folifac). 6. A short drama presentation by 5 children (Bianca Najeme, Nsame Bawe, Solomon Ibeagha, Steve Komguep and Folifac Jr). 7. Singing of the joyous hymn of the day...Joy to the world; the Lord is come... 8. Dance competition by the kids and presentation of special numbers. 9. Entry of Father Christmas (to be assisted by Macalister Usongo) and presentation of gifts and prizes. And lots more........ 10. Food and dance. Come and support the children. Please, be punctual as we are allowed only 4 hours to use the hall. Eveline [paragraphing altered]

Figure #39: Sample Photo from pioneer Children Christmas Party in December 2005
Source: Photo taken by Momany Fossungu

The picture above cements the narration. As for the pioneer CCP, parents and children were reminded on the day before by Secretary-General Mubadang Emmanuel Ngwakongnwi to endeavour to be there by 2:30 PM so that the occasion could start promptly, stressing that "the leading organizers (Ibeagha Eveline and Najeme Karine) will also look to confirm the ages of all the children. You may want to give them a call." It was a ground-breaking and pace-setting beginning that has since brought Children Christmas parties to be the norm in all the other Cameroonian (and other African) associations in Montreal. A few of the numerous souvenir pictures of that pioneer children party (and others) have been given above. As usual, it is preferable to let the president better explain the whole dynamics to readers, as Paul Takha Ayah in Figure #40 thankyouologizes and congratulates the organizers and all CGAMers:

Figure #40: Caren Osong Ayah & husband, Paul Takha Ayah
Source: Photo taken by Momany Fossungu

On behalf of all Goodwillers, I will like to extend our thanks and congratulations to Evelyn Ibeagha and Caren Najeme for the great show they put on for our children on Sunday. This shows what can be achieved with great organization. Our thanks and congratulations also go to Aloys Ibeagha, our Santa; Patricia Atemba, Santa's favourite helper; Mubadang for assisting with the coordination; Jules Komguep for taking pictures and making them available on the Website; Irene and Edmond

Nankam for informing us about the cadets; all parents who braved the inclement weather to bring their children; and all goodwillers who showed up to cheer the children.

Remember that the important thing is not the size of the present that the children received but the excitement that filled their eyes as they sat with Santa and received their gifts and, of course, the pleasure of seeing all the children so happy.

For pictures of the event, please visit our Website http://goodwill.site.voila.fr/ [now http://www.goodwillmontreal.com] and click on Newsroom.

For those we called regarding our misplaced camera, please note that we found it in the church the next morning; it fell behind a couch.

It is now the turn of the end-of-year party committee to put on a great show! Info from a few members reveals that ticket sales are going on very well; the number of tickets reserved or sold now stands at about 70! Our target is 150, so keep up the good work. Remember to contact Patricia Atemba if you need more tickets (CGAM Forum, 20 December 2005).

"It is now [not] the turn of the end-of-year party committee", *Monsieur le Président*, because only the kids party merited being specially sketched here.

But participation is still going on though, with the adults (parents and teachers especially in Africa, unthinkingly, most of the time) trying to have total supremacy or Cameroon's *pleins pouvoirs* over children's education and (professional) orientation. Why do parents often exhibit this trait of wanting their children to do just what they (parents) want, and not what the children like doing as career? I mean to say: Is there actually a Dysfunctional Parent-Teacher Instruction War in Africa or simply the act of Living Parents' Dream, which this book defines as Parentology? The next Chapter attempts some responses.

CHAPTER 3

FOUR-EYESISM IS SEEING THE UNSEEN AND KNOWING THE UNKNOWN: THE AFRICAN-AMERICAN WAR THEORY 'TAKING-BACK' FAULTY EDUCATION THEORIES AND EXCESSIVE BIOLOGY IN FAMILY IN AFRICA

According to Fossungu (2015a: xi), "this book basically proffers the science of Four-Eyesism as a discipline that all African schools need to institute and make a compulsory subject: if the vandalized continent would have to be awakened to its realities." This Chapter employs the expibasketical science in accentuating the critical importance of Four-Eyesism or seething intellectualism. As already seen in previous Chapters, Fon DF Fossungu's seething intellectualism is not significant only in the children naming sphere; it is also overwhelming in the domain of some children education theories, including the *Thumb Education Thesis* that is fathered by Chief Fongangnet Romanus of Nwametaw (one of the nine Bangwa Fondoms) and which must eventually be "taken-back" together with the upside-down assistantship education theory whose scientific name is *Petasahchoppism*. This rare trait of the so-called "illiterate" Nwangong Fon has not failed to drag in the handling of issues relating to the philosophy of children education and welfare, including what is actually behind the names given to them; leading inevitably to the million dollar question: *Are Lessons in Four-Eyesism Really What Africa Really Needs for Its Liberation, Protection and Development?* That is, a necessity for properly *Getting Africa into Africa?*

Chief Fongangnet is well known for having told the Fossungu Royal House and Nwangong Fondom generally how "all your Fons will always be those who sign with their thumbs." That is to say people who cannot read and write the Whiteman's language; *whitemanly* illiterates to be clear. The Nwametaw Chief's *Thumb Education Thesis* was obviously referring to Fon DF Fossungu's heir apparent who is now Chief Fonkwetta Denis.

Empty Literacy! Vapid Literacy! Upside-down Literacy! Isn't it time to level-headedly 'take-back' both the upside-down assistantship-education theory and thumb education thesis and other frustrations (including the biological) facing sweet-voicing African children? This talk of sweet voice and 'star-like' traitors to their own community quickly brings to mind the Blacks singing in North America. BASS is the name of an American pop/hip-hop musical group of two guys. Their name, according to them, actually means *Black And Sounding Sweet*. They are quite right and it is hard to exhaust the list of these sweet-sounding Blacks but, since a few examples may be required, my dear readers can alphabetically have these: Alicia Keys, Aretha Franklin, Ariel, Beyoncé, Boyz II Men, Destiny's Child, Donna Summer, Freddie Jackson, George Benson, Janet Jackson, Jody Watley, Marvin Gaye, Marymary, Mase, Michael Jackson, Monica, R. Kelly, Sisters With Voices (SWV), Smokey Robinson, Teddy Pendergrass, The Deele, Tina Turner, Tracy Chapman, Usher, Whitney Houston, Will Smith.....

In fact, these American Blacks from Mother Africa do really sound sweet, if one even considers that Harry "Belafonte succeeded in charming his audiences with his husky but sweet and mellow voice luring them to adaptations of popular and West Indian folk songs including the inviting nostalgic Jamaica Farewell: 'Down The Way Where The Nights Are Gay' which won him a place in the hearts of his audiences and pushed him into the limelight of fame" (Kinni, 2015: 343).

If I may be permitted to ask readers to just listen to two other groups of four females and of four males, I would readily refer, respectively, to For Real's tracks on their album that is titled *Free* and Force M.D.'s on their *Step To Me*. Step to Me then, dear readers, if you are free and frantalkistically learn to understand community lielisticalism and hypocrisy and betrayal that have lamentably become Africa's signature. The foregoing names are just a few examples, since I cannot even be capable of enumerating all the Top Black American artists that have become household names worldwide and who, according to Tricia Rose of *The Guardian*, "have undeniably the greatest leverages, power, visibility and global influence of any period in Black History" (Kinni, 2015: 350).

118

But these Black stars have, sadly, for the most part (according to Harry Belafonte), not used "their celebrity to speak out against the injustices against Blacks, especially black youths who were disproportionately more in prisons and jobless than any other race sample in the United States of America" (Kinni, 2015: 350). But that is even not all the shame in it because, in addition, "today, I realize that the erroneous narrative of the sexually permissive black woman has found its way into contemporary African-American music videos and hip hop culture. Some rap artists make millions and win awards for writing misogynistic lyrics that label black girls and women as bitches and hoes. I worry that too many young African-American women think of themselves in those terms" (Rush, 2011). Substitute 'African' here with 'Black' and then ask to know if the Blacks at home (in Africa) are not entitled to expect deliverance from their own foreign-based 'celebrities' who are thought to be better off knowing the world's lielisticalism about/on Africa?

In other terms, would the castigated comportment of some of our veritable African intellectuals (using the *illiteracy* tag) not truly be another unique instance of seeing the unseen and announcing the unknown in Africa? It has largely been made known by Fossungu (2013: 155) that, "important as it may seem, formal education alone is just not enough for good and sapient leadership." Are all the dictators in power today in Africa and traumatizing Africans not formally educated? How do we correctly respond to the question posed at the close of the previous Chapter? In other words, how do parents help in the matter of creating or destroying community 'celebrities' in Africa? And how do the events in the other Chapters of this simple-looking discipline-defying book contribute to answering these African-development queries? To provide some far-reaching responses, the first part of the Chapter studies parentology and educational support and orientation while the second engages in the farsighted taking-back or deciphering of the camouflaged educational and other developmental dangers and impediments.

Lizaqueenism (or the Strange Love of the Strangely Unexplained) versus Parentology

The general argument is that "education curricula inherited from colonizers resulted in a society of job seekers rather than employment creators. The education curricula have in fact resulted in school leavers being subjected to oppression and exploitation thereby perpetuating poverty in Africa. This means that there is little innovation and creativity that is imparted by the inherited system of education" (Gwaravanda, 2018: 255). That is quite true but the answer to the earlier question whether there is a Teacher-Parent Dysfunctional Counselling War leans more toward parentology which has already been defined as the act of parents wanting children to live parents' dreams and not the children's. It finds particular significance in what Professor Gwaravanda has just been condemning, also being specifically linked to what is usually referred to as 'academic counselling or orientation'. The import of the query is lodged too in "The feeling of repugnance that current political trend in many African countries engenders and invokes, throw[ing] up the question of the relationship between culture, morality and politics. One wonders if these three variables which in pre-colonial African states were understood to be bed fellows continue to be understood as such in post-colonial African states" (Mawere, Mawere and Jovo, 2015: 270).

What role could (parental) poor orientation and inappropriate education and institutional support play in this awkward detrimental divorce that is obviously dragging down Africa?

For instance, you can easily find an African child who has no idea about (or liking for) the sciences being unsympathetically told by the parents – father in particular – to study and become a medical doctor. Most often the child's opinion on the matter is completely irrelevant or ignored. Just because a neighbour's child is a medical doctor! Most African leaders who are also parents thus unnecessarily screw up their children's life (and the community's somewhat, therefore) by assuming that everybody must idiotically dance to just their tunes: even when these parents cannot even measure up to the children's natural singing and other gifts in their magically sweet voice and towering IQs as Lizaqueenism can further demonstrate. I am thus taking Momany's parentally-inspired wasted voice magic to attempt a response to the questions posed above, particularly the one on the destruction of celebrities. I am talking about what *Lizaqueenism* (derived from both Liza and Queenta in Figure #41) can valuably teach us in the domain. Loving the voice so much! The case of Liza (Momany's one-time girlfriend during his stay in Manjo in Wourizone in the early eighties) is simply beyond exhaustion. Let me begin with Queenta (his fiancé then) who is well known too for seeking to just hear Momany's voice to be happy (see Fossungu, 2016: 31 & passim).

Figure #41: Queenta Ngum Afanwi in Nwangong in July 2004
Source: Photo taken by Momany Fossungu

"Un Coucou" is the title of Liza's email of 22 November 2006 to Momany, in which she states that "I thought you were going to call again

121

today so that I could listen to your sweet voice and familiar laughter that always mesmerize me" (my translation). Momany's voice and laughter would seem to charm a lot of women in general but the virgins in particular. Why? One of Liza's (and she is not alone) February 2007 emails to Momany is actually titled "I Want to Hear You Laugh." Even loveless Scholastica would not be comfortable when she wouldn't hear Momany laughing on the phone. Thus, she too wrote in October 1998: "Dear, I talked with you this morning and realized that you were not happy with me at all. Even to laugh was more than you" (Fossungu, 2016: 205). On 15 June 2015 Momany's French-speaking daughter, Kelie, too wrote an email stating that "....*Papa j'aimerais entendre ta voix et je suis vraiment impatiente de te voir encore*" (I am greatly missing your voice and I cannot wait to see you again) and the one of 18 April 2015 entirely went as follows: "*Juste pour te saluer et savoir comment tu vas. Je suis impatiente de te voir et de te serrer dans mes bras. Ta voix, ta respiration, tes paroles et ton regard me manquent. J'ai réservé un cadeau pour toi. Je t'aime énormement*" (In brief, she is saying that she is missing his voice again, among others).

In her "You Are the Only One" email of 29 November 2006, Liza (the famous Francophone 'anglophone' who was then already married to someone else) wrote: "My Love, How are you doing? I really love hearing your nice voice which I adore so much. I would have liked to be right there with you in Montreal, giving you a smooth bath, preparing your meals... how unfortunate that this distance stands between us! Are you sure I will be able to allow you go back to Montreal without me? I am feeling like I would have to come along with you, hidden in your luggage. I am still waiting impatiently for your call today as from 7 pm Cameroon time. I love you. Liza."[5] The love-lecturing thing is out of the scope of this book (instead generally see Fossungu, 2016 & 2014) but, to fortify

---

5 "*Mon Amour: Comment vas-tu? J'aime bien écouter ta belle voix que j'adore. J'aurais souhaité être là, auprès de toi pour te laver délicatement et te faire ton petit déjeuner mais hélas!!!! Es-tu sûr que je vais te laisser retourner à Montréal sans moi? Je risque me cacher dans tes valises lorsque tu seras ici. J'attends ton appel ce soir à partir de 19h, heure du Cameroun. Je t'embrasse partout. Liza.*"

the voice theory and the corner-kicking killing of celebrities under review, let's just also hear *former* lovers like Anna (and many more), for instance, exceptionally calling him long-distance from Cameroon, for that matter, only to tell Momany (who is already so scared that some bad news has arrived – since it is usually the only time most *Mbenguists* or *Allaighmeleughers* get a call like that from the majority of home-based Africans) that all they just wanted was "to hear your wonderful voice and laughter"! Pauline, his girlfriend in Canada who was then visiting in France, called him almost daily "to just hear your sweet and charming voice before I can go to sleep"! Wouldn't all that be more than enough to keep you seriously pondering on what it is that is in your voice (that you yourself cannot discover) that just keeps "killing" these women?

Jean-Pierre Panda, who is bent on marrying only his own virgin (see Fossungu, 2016: 193-95), must be so, so jealous to hear all of this. "I just wanted to hear your charming voice!" Is that taking us anywhere close to the mystery of Momany's virgiluckism? The term defines the luck of always having virgins falling in love with someone. In short, maybe Momany would have simply killed the *entire* world with his voice (even more than Belafonte) if he had seriously taken to the singing career? (What about the comedian role too, since most people are also always finding what he says funny?[6]) Momany truly loved singing and excelled at it, as even his Sasse College mates have quickly attested to. The question here only relates to his doing so against all the parental opposition at the time to students choosing that career path: as singer Prince Nico Mbarga has aptly epitomized it in his *Wayo In-law*. Prince Nico Mbarga is talking

---

[6] "For instance, one of them told me in the course of the Snake Lesson below that I was very funny and I responded with: 'Just wish that your African presidents were a little *funny* like Mandela[] – we wouldn't be here so stressed up and cutting Western trees, but instead contributing our own quarter to national and continental development in various ways, including cutting but African trees to shed more light in the dark forest!' Everyone almost died from laughter" (Fossungu, 2015c: 89; original emphasis, footnote in square brackets omitted).

about moneyintriguist in-laws. Moneyintriguism is a huge developmental problem for Africa just as the African-American War is to Black cohesion.

'African American' versus 'Black American': Long Memorizing Asianamericanism, Rosawhitism, and Arabotamelism

I am here deciphering and examining the lielisticalism and some of the other misnaming tools that are corner-kickingly employed to prevent Black consciousness or cohesion, being an important exposition of theories and concepts that would easily and greatly help readers to better grasp the misnaming that defines and maintains lielisticalism and/or upside-downism. The point of lielisticalism also relates to the critical issue of 'African American' versus 'Black American'. The appellation of 'African American' just ought to be dislodged for being anti-cohesional to Black people. I am here to further explain how and why there is this offensive Continental War. In discussing Sex and Racism in chapter 4 of their 1982 *Long Memory*, Mary Frances Berry and John W. Blassingame talk of 'White Women and Black Men' (1982: 119-20). It is important to stress that they correctly never said European American Women and African American Men. They are not alone in this oft-overlooked important issue.

The Government of Quebec too sees no point in using the continental adjective, preferring the racial. That is the correct version, as has been reiterated by James Brown's 'Say It Loud: I'm Black and Proud'. That the Quebec authorities are very much interested in realizing the full participation of Black [and not African] communities in Quebec society needs no over amplification. For instance, in his capacity as President of the CGAM, Paul Takha Ayah (who you saw in Figure #40) on 5 November 2005, in a communication titled *'The Full Participation of Black Communities in Quebec Society'*, stated to "Fellow goodwillers" that:

The Quebec minister of Immigration and Cultural Communities has set up a working group and a public consultation to look into ways of encouraging the full participation of black communities in Quebec

124

society. The working group is headed by Mrs. Yoland James, MP for Nelligan. I will be making a presentation before the group on Friday, November 11, 2005, and I encourage anyone who has suggestions that I can propose to the group to contact me. For more information on the working group: http://www.micc.gouv.qc.ca/52_2.asp?pid=912. To consult the report on the problems faced by black communities in Quebec: http://www.micc.gouv.qc.ca/publications/pdf/Consultation_communa utes_noires_anglais.pdf.

In addition to its emphasis on African freedom, unity and development which are currently 'without Africa' because of *la mauvaise éducation coloniale*, this book is also tendered with view to assisting the Quebec Ministry of Immigration and Cultural Communities particularly, and other Quebec and Canadian governmental departments generally in their presumptive goals.

Now, straight on to the main point at the epicentre of the Continental War, if other (North) Americans are described not by the continents they have their origin in but by their race, why must it be otherwise with Africa's: unless there is some 'hidden' or 'corner-kicking' agenda to it? Why can't we now see the unseen like Fon DF Fossungu and other Nwangongers? A very recent ground-breaking research on Pan-Africanism would rather prefer we use the 'continental' and not the 'racial' adjective when it very lengthily examines "The Racist American Dream and Renaissance of African-American Awareness" (Kinni, 2015: 1-177). It is not clear if one should see a paradox in Dr Kini-Yen Fongot Kinni's chapter 1 title here; but a lengthier 'four-eyes' discussion of the lielisticalism embedded in this Continental African-American War would push me to that direction. Let me tackle it straight on therefore, using (1) the *Asianamerican* theory, (2) the *Rosawhite* thesis, and (3) the *Arabo-Tamel* narrative.

Asianamericanism: Asians (mostly from the Indian sub-continent) that the trouble-making British brought to the African continent, for instance, would claim to be 'Africans' only in so far as that 'claim' gives them the advantage of continuously exploiting the local or native population that they wantonly call "kafar" or "kaffir".[7] Dr Akiti Glory Alamu, please, I am calling unto you to remain steadfast in teaching them too here.

---

[7] During his stay in South Africa, Gandhi routinely expressed "disdain for Africans," says S. Anand, founder of Navayana, the publisher of the book titled "The South African Gandhi: Stretcher-Bearer of Empire." The book which is "a serious challenge to the way we have been taught to think about Gandhi," advances the following sample of what Gandhi said about black South Africans:

* One of the first battles Gandhi fought after coming to South Africa was over the separate entrances for whites and blacks at the Durban post office. Gandhi objected that Indians were "classed with the natives of South Africa," who he called the kaffirs, and demanded a separate entrance for Indians. "We felt the indignity too much and … petitioned the authorities to do away with the invidious distinction, and they have now provided three separate entrances for natives, Asiatics and Europeans."

* In a petition letter in 1895, Gandhi also expressed concern that a lower legal standing for Indians would result in degenerating "so much so that from their civilised habits, they would be degraded to the habits of the aboriginal Natives, and a generation hence, between the progeny of the Indians and the Natives, there will be very little difference in habits, and customs and thought."

* At a speech in Mumbai in 1896, Gandhi said that the Europeans in Natal wished "to degrade us to the level of the raw kaffir whose occupation is hunting, and whose sole ambition is to collect a certain number of cattle to buy a wife with, and then, pass his life in indolence and nakedness."

* Protesting the decision of Johannesburg municipal authorities to allow Africans to live alongside Indians, Gandhi wrote in 1904 that the council "must withdraw the Kaffirs from the Location. About this mixing of the Kaffirs with the Indians, I must confess I feel most strongly. I think it is very unfair to the Indian population and it is an undue tax on even the proverbial patience of my countrymen."

* In response to the White League's agitation against Indian immigration and the proposed importation of Chinese labour,

"Although indigenous people are strikingly diverse in their culture, religion, social and economic organization, yet they are subjected to a stereotypal way of life by the world around them. Unwaveringly, this stereotypal way of the native is depicted by some people as the embodiment of spiritual values and political progress" (Alamu, 2015: 217). While that important teaching goes on with the enthusiastic approval of late Field-Marshall Idi Amin Dada, I will proceed straight on with the African-American War Theory.

How many of these Asians that find themselves in the USA would countenance being referred to as 'African Americans'? This same question applies so neatly too to *Rosawhitism* or the *Rosawhite* Thesis (from the Republic Of South Africa), as admirably exposed in the bewildering American colourless-colour classification in the Walter White Tale (*Wawhitetalism*, if you like). It is the story of a white woman from South Africa and her black husband (Walter White, an American) who went to India in 1949. As the woman (Poppy Cannon) has explained it,

We were guests of the Calcutta Association for the United Nations, a meeting hurriedly arranged. The president of the Association turned to me. "I have read in the journals," he said, "that you are white." He pointed to his snow-white cuff. "And your husband," pointing now to his coat sleeve, "is black."

Gandhi wrote in 1903: "We believe also that the white race in South Africa should be the predominating race."

* Gandhi wrote in 1908 about his prison experience: "We were marched off to a prison intended for Kaffirs. There, our garments were stamped with the letter "N", which meant that we were being classed with the Natives. We were all prepared for hardships, but not quite for this experience. We could understand not being classed with the whites, but to be placed on the same level with the Natives seemed too much to put up with."

* In 1939, Gandhi justified his counsel to the Indian community in South Africa against forming a non-European front: "I have no doubt about the soundness of my advice. However much one may sympathise with the Bantus, Indians cannot make common cause with them." (Asa'na, 2015).

127

Both of us looked across the table at Walter. "Obviously," I answered. And the whole table, up to the moment formal and solemn, broke into a roar of laughter. "These mad Americans"! (Berry and Blassingame, 1982: 127).

Rosawhitism (or the Rosawhite Thesis) and Arabotamelism: From the Republic of South Africa, *Rosawhitism* stresses the fact that (1) there is 'White South African' (see Goell, 1978; Marongwe and Mawere, 2015), not European South African; and (2) it is clear that White South Africans in the USA would also not be happy to be captured under 'African Americans'. A rather dark brunette white woman (as Berry and Blassingame, 1982: 127) describe her, Poppy Cannon was surprised to be regarded as black in India; the more reason also that she would not want to be captured by the lielistical 'African American' umbrella in the USA: notwithstanding that a South African (of whatever skin colour) is an African.

Or do crisebacologists correctly hear the Arabs of North Africa saying otherwise? *The Arabo-Tamel* Narrative (or *Arabotamelism*) appears to give an affirmative response since most of these North African Arabs claim not to be *Africans* but Arabs (see Fossungu, 2015b: 83-84). *Tamel* stands for Tunisia, Algeria, Morocco, Egypt and Libya. In addition to the exquisite exposition of the Arabs' role in trying to enslave and/or exterminate the Black race (see Kinni, 2015: chapter 1), crisebacologists would need to just add that these Arabs, too, would certainly not find it funny being called *African* Americans in the USA.

If, at the end of the day, *African American* is restricted to the Black person, why continue to use the confusing and anger-raising expression unless there is some ulterior motive behind such employment? Let us, therefore, be specific and clear about the fact that our black brothers and sisters (outside the continent) are NOT African Americans, African Britons, African Canadians, African Australians, etc., But BLACK Americans (Britons, Canadians, Australians, etc.). James Brown, Bob Marley, Peter Tosh (to name just a few singers) have been telling us the same thing for years but we have apparently not been grasping the unity message, the only one that can get Africa into Africa. I am here specifically talking about 'Black Consciousness' under which "[Steve Bantu] Biko called for an Africanness that was different from the colonially-inspired domination and othering, one that was philosophically grounded in Ubuntu that took pride in African traditions and heritage, African history, African unity against oppression and in the holistic liberation of Africans" (Marongwe and Mawere, 2015: 132).

That is then the correct version that has to be employed always for readers to better understand the lielisticalism and 'corner-kickism' involved, including those from unthinking parentological African parents.

Opposing certain careers by such parents would not just be the lone issue and Momany's affluent expibasketism continues to be very instructive. Momany's 'handwork-loving' father actually wanted him to proceed (from primary school) to a technical secondary school in Ombe in Debundschazone of Cameroon. Momany could do anything that he put his hands on. But he was not at all looking at the technical or "hand-work" field as the option. To be able to live *his* own academic dream, and not the father's, Momany (unlike many children) doggedly filled the college-going forms without his dad's knowledge. Some pro-parentologists would unthinkingly call that disobedience but some knowledgeable others (the expibasketicalists and crisebacologists) would correctly see it as doing the right thing! Following your dream! According to some crisebacologists, parents must have to be made to understand that:

To discipline a child is not synonymous to creating unnecessary fear in that child. At a certain age, a child becomes mature enough to know what he/she wants in life to be happy and successful. Most children know this but fail to stand up for the things that are required for attaining their goals, most probably because of the fear that is often wrongly equated with respect: *Janodilists* and *Annaspectists*. Respect goes both ways and encourages mutual and meaningful dialogue, the presence and availability of which would certainly have averted the calamities that befell the many children mentioned in this book (Fossungu, 2016: 218, original emphasis).

What we have today in Africa is a classic in African unity and development without Africa, as many of the other student cases catalogued herein also portray. Thinking for oneself even at Momany's young age is something to be highly encouraged in Africa rather than be chastised. But, as an expert in Nigeria tells us,

Unfortunately, the reality on the ground in many African countries is the fact that unsuitable educational and economic approaches are the principal causes of the continent wasting chances of development. Most African countries, particularly Nigeria pattern their educational institutions in line with colonial master's style instead of developing indigenous system. This attitude works against African rich pre-colonial education system. The pre-colonial African education system allows one to develop himself/herself and in turn contribute to the development of the society.

Functionalism in the light of common good of the greater number was the guiding principle of education in traditional African society (Nwosu, 2015: 297).

To the above criticisms must be added the 'Bottle-Necking and dual education approach' of the inherited colonial system (Gwaravanda, 2018: 260-62) which has even turned the deplorable colonial education to be a thing for only the rich. You thus see Government schools and colleges that are normally meant to take care of the children of the poor in society now being solely for the children of the rich who can buy admission into them (see Fossungu, 2019: chapter 2). Africa is not alone here though, as the recent 'Prestigious-Schools' admission scandals in the USA can sufficiently prove. Momany can validly obtain clean-and-clear or merit-based admission into any school in the world (see Fossungu, 2013: 53-54); but his father was very crossed on discovering that Government Technical College (GTC) Ombe was not the son's preferred choice. It was then too late to have altered the course of the boy's academic life. Or, could Momany's unnecessary academic battles (see Fossungu, 2013: chapters 2-4) be intimately tied to this anti-Ombe trick? Whatever the case, his dad's comportment could scarcely be equated to Mamiteelization (see Fossungu, 2013: chapter 3 particularly), being just a

130

father trying to make a child live the father's dream (parentology); reprehensible, no doubt, but still a very different thing from killing whatever dream that the child might have. Let us discover more of the anti-progress tendencies as we next examine positive support in education.

Positive (Emotional and Financial) Support in Education and the No-Education Cases

The parentological majority of parents really impose a dream on their children but also grossly fail in orientation and support/encouragement toward its realization. Leaving aside the defiant Elizabethanglocardistic husband-choosing cases (see Fossungu, 2014: 85-88), a parent would, for example, send the 'hair-dressing-loving' daughter to a very reputable aeronautics or aerospace school and think that is enough to create a pilot out of her. He just does not also care to find out from the instructors if she is okay with the courses that lead to the imposed chosen profession. Some parents who even find this out would gratuitously argue with a teacher that gives them his or her honest opinion, dismissing the teacher as unfair and the like. They thus push the poor girl to frustration whereas she could have excelled in the hair-dressing domain chosen by her, and thus contribute enormously to society in that domain. For instance, responding to the journalist's question regarding how long she has been doing it and why she took up the profession, Miss Anna Mokom (then President of the Bamenda Hairdressers' Union in Cameroon) stated that "I have been doing hairdressing for the past 13 years and I think what has kept me for so long in the job is my love for it" (Mbipgo, 1997: 10).

It is not to say, however, that parents should never try to choose a career path for their children. Guiding their children is their job, if not a duty. It is only that they should take the child's decision and preferences into account and give him/her all the necessary tools and environment that can aid towards realizing his/her dreams. As seen in the previous Chapter, this is what some parents like Dr Kinni's did when they not only had the sense to give him a name that would determine his life research forever but also matched their words of encouragement with deeds such as sending him money while he was in Europe, notwithstanding that he was even on scholarship, and also encouraged him to travel to other parts of Europe and discover things for himself. Chapter 1 has also shown such positive financial support in education being Kelielized in Table 1.

It was only in January 2016 that Momany really got to examine upfront what his daughter in Douala was doing in school. Kelie was then in high school and majoring in fashion design (*la couture*, it is called in French). On examining her books that she herself joyfully brought to him for the purpose, Momany realized just how much she loves and excels in *la couture*. Her main complaint was that of lack of the essential tools for more and more out-of-school practice and perfection. Momany was so impressed and touched. He immediately got a carpenter and an electrician to re-work her room and then went and bought her a 'do-all' sewing machine, telling her (like Dr Kinni's dad) to get to the source and summit of tailoring and be dressing, among others, the stars of Bollywood, Hollywood, and Nollywood. It is significant to note that Dr. Fongot Kini-Yen Kinni's parents (father particularly) told him simply "that I should not stop at anything till I am satisfied to have reached the source and summit of my endeavours and achievement" (Kinni, 2015: xiii). The significant issue here is that these fathers never determined what that 'anything' (the children should not stop at) must be, appropriately leaving that choice to the child, unlike the parentological parents. Kelie's mother is to be credited more with this free choice, of course, than Momany who only came in later – Mafor Odette Ateafac, of course, still to be saddled with responsibility for the lateness though: with moneyintriguism obviously lurking behind the scene, as seen in Chapter 1.

Of course, some of the academic or professional choices are somewhat 'forced' on the children sometimes by circumstances beyond their own control. This seemingly was the case of Anna Mokom who "visited my sister in Yaoundé and she took me to a salon. That was the first time I entered a salon. When I got into the place, I really fell in love

132

with hairdressing and because I was sent away from school for financial reasons, I decided to go into it" (Mbipgo, 1997: 10). That also appears to be the case with Momany who, for financial constraints that are rooted solely in biology, also switched from sciences to art (see Fossungu, 2013: chapter 2). Readers also have to necessarily meet Violet Maylatey Fonenge (below) who also abandoned her dream profession of journalism to something else called linguistics because of financial problems. The important thing though is that the abovementioned candidates' alternate professions/programmes were chosen by themselves as the most appropriate means of survival; not being directly selected by their parent(s).

A lot of these parents would not even 'force' any orientation or choice because, to them, schooling (especially for the female child) exists nowhere in their thinking. Having painstakingly surveyed illiteracy as one of the challenges faced by the African child (Yinusa et al, 2018: 282-83), some experts made known that research conducted by UNESCO in 2000 "has also found a disparity in access to education between the girl-child and the boy-child in Africa. For example, in some countries in West Africa, there is more enrolment of boys while the girls stay at home while there are also more of girls' enrolment than that of boys in some other areas where boys have to stay at home and tend to the family farm or engage in some form of trade" (Yinusa et al, 2018: 283). It is in this arena that Chief Fongangnet's Thumb Education Theory could hardly have been wrong in its speculation about the no-postcolonial-education which is so rife in Fon DF Fossungu's perspectives on school-going education. His ideas in the domain are totally in opposition to that of his predecessor, Fon ST Fossungu, who equally never went to the Whiteman's school but is fondly known as "the King Solomon of Nwangong" (Fossungu, 2013: 3). Quite apart from numerous complaints from Fon DF Fossungu's own biological children that I have personally listened to, it is no secret that Fon DF Fossungu would rather fill his Emollah Palace with more wives (most of whom could be his granddaughters) than send one (just because I cannot go anywhere below that to correctly talk of one-hundredth) child to college or secondary school. That is not news that I should be the one breaking. The cases of extremely bright palace children who have, since 1979 when he ascended the throne, been unable to see the four walls of a secondary school classroom cannot be exactly outlined. But does that necessarily make Fon DF Fossungu an uneducated person in the important African sense of being educated? Some answers are provided as we go, being led by Peter Ngunyi Asahchop who is sitting in Figure #42.

Figure #42: Peter Ngunyi Asahchop in October 2002
Source: Photo taken by Momany Fossungu

The Meetingpoint between Four-Eyesism, Takebackism, and the Upside-Down Assistantship Education Theory
Fon DF Fossungu and other so-called *unschooled* Nwangongers would now overwhelm you with their intriguing four-eyesism as they very beautifully 'take-back' generally unforeseen faulty education theories and other associated frustrations. It is true that some experts have recently done much lecturing on intellectualism in volumes such as *Democracy and Human Rights in Africa* (Fossungu, 2013b). At this point, I am more interested in taking readers back to about twenty years to two timeless

pieces that Dr Fossungu wrote on education and African villages which would also greatly help readers in grasping the controversies on inheritance and chieftaincy in Africa; a hullabaloo largely ushered in by the re-eminence of certificate-education, an unfortunate trend which is, itself, propagated by the brainwashed mind-set of city dwellers on the villages as witchcraft's true definition. As Fossungu (1998: 10, original emphasis) theorised more than eighteen years ago:

Cameroon, one could suspect, wouldn't be as peaceful as it seems to be if there was seething intellectualism available. In other words, freedom wouldn't be so easily crucified at the altar of dictatorship (*alias* Peace) in a society that is infested with intellectuals (except we must give this term a different connotation). The most conspicuous of such intellectuals, also known as lawyers, are considered everywhere to be the 'central figures' in society. Does Cameroon really have these central figures? Its own high rate of literacy (see Paul Biya, *Communal Liberalism*, 1986, p. 11; and Gilbert Tixier, *A Comparative Study of the Economic Policies of the Cameroons and Ivory Coast*, 1974, pp. 87 & 13) could certainly be okay as far as certificate intellectualism per se could be concerned. But intellectualism, I should suppose, must mean much more than just that. Academic certificates can clearly not be the synonym for intellectualism. What about the *certificateless* category?

The attitude of Cameroon's lawyers is a cause for concern because this group of professionals have woefully failed to live up to tasks expected of the profession, having become "watched dogs" instead of being watch dogs of society (see Fossungu, 2013b: 146-53; 2019: chapter 2). They have been variously shown to only talk human rights when their particular interests are at stake. To substantiate his points on the villages as places for acquiring necessary instruction, Fossungu went on to give an instance of what "could be a brand of the said 'ignorance and superstition'," stating that he has always said, "in regard of our Old New Deal or New Old Deal, Democracy (NODD), that whichever the reader/listener prefers is immaterial since OLD still persists" (Fossungu, 1998a: 10). That being because he cited Professor Mark W. Delancey who in 1989 (some six years after the old women in Nwangong – the young teacher's village) stated on page 70 of his illuminating 1989 book (*Cameroon: Dependence and Independence*), that "in many respects Biya did not alter the system he inherited; he merely tried to make it operate more effectively."

The education critic from Bangwaland then specifically asked readers to note well that "operating a dictatorship more effectively can only mean more dictatorship like never before" (Fossungu, 1998a: 10) and then went ahead to quote Delancey as carrying on that "the old laws and decrees remained in place and the ability of the president to concentrate all power and authority in himself remained. Just as he had ordered the police to relax, so too he could order them to tighten up" (Fossungu, 1998a: 10). With that citation from the American political scientist, Fossungu then proceeded to find out if the old Nwangong women who had seen it long before Delancey actually have ninety-nine senses: by having seen as far back as 1983 what others could not? (Fossungu, 1998a: 10). This is surely another unique instance of seeing the unseen and announcing the unknown in Africa again: yes or no? Was it not the same Four-Eyesism with Fon DF Fossungu rejecting Marie-Claire Afueh's offer of assistance with his son's postcolonial education?

You will be comfortably taken to that quickly detected *poisoned charity* from the Western world by passing through the run-way called the *Upside-down Assistantship-Education Theory* whose more methodical name is *Petasahchoppism* According to the 3rd paragraph of Peter Asahchop's very popular and instructive 1999 letter to Momany:

The mother of Nicasius Nguajong, the son of the Chief [Fon, that is], has brought to the Chief very big shame in his reign as a Chief. The young man completed [high] school last year and failed to go to the university and there are no prospects that he may go to school next academic year. The Chief wanted him to write *concours* in category D and C of the public service. I heard that Marie-Claire [Fossungu, now Afueh] had wanted to help but the Chief refused, [saying] that after it will be some sort of provocation. I wonder if you could write to him about it (Peter N. Asahchop, private communication, 3 June 1999).

136

This particular letter of his has not been described as *very popular* for nothing. Its entire contents are very important in different and varied expibasketising capacities. Two important issues from its outlined 3rd paragraph would need highlighting: (1) the assignment of the blame to the boy's mother (who you saw in Figure #18), which constitute the backbone of the upside-down education theory in question, and (2) the refusal of help from Marie-Claire (who you also saw in Figure #30) which exposes the Fon's overwhelming four-eyesism, being what I think Africa really needs for getting Africa into Africa, not postcolonial education.

The Shame Assignment and the Maylateyist Lectures on Education, Marriage and Family: Challenging Mamiteelizalist Biology in Children Education

It has to be noted that Peter Asahchop assigns the shame to the boy's mother (Prudencia Memala Fossungu) because it is believed in the culture that it is the responsibility of the Fon's (or Chief's, as the case may be) wives to predominantly take care of the education needs of their own children, with the Fon or Chief (in accordance with the Cameroonian government's upside-down manner of doing things in matters of education) instead being the *assistant*. As an authority on Four-Eyesism has argued the infamous theory out, Cameroon's 1998 Education Law:

[b]eing an apt example of the lack of self-control in this country, it is not very surprising then that one finds, for instance, that it is the central state (and not the regions) that will 'formulate and implement educational policy with the assistance of regional and local authorities, families as well as public and private institutions' (Education Law, section 11). I am inclined to think that in a situation of genuine biculturalism and decentralization the arrangement has to be the other way round. That is, the regional governments, including public and private institutions, should be those to formulate and implement their respective educational policies (within a national constitutional context) with the national or central government instead being the *assistant*. If it is otherwise, one

cleanly has to stop talking of decentralization and educational dualism (Fossungu, 2013a: 96, emphasis is original).

There is no need for me to go so far into the current schools shutdown in 'Anglophone' or West Cameroon (now known as Ambazonia) to expibasketise it since readers can also see the disreputable theory operating clearly in the instructive case of Violet Maylatey Fonenge who you see in Figure #43 below. To better grasp the Education-Mamiteelization Lecture, let us first get the instructive lectures of the victimized biological daughter called Violet Maylatey Fonenge (née Fossungu), a Nwangong princess whose middle name in Bangwa means "connecting" or "one following the other." Like Immaculate Fossungu in Chapter 2, Violet also lives up to her 'connecting' name to the extent that she is even cousin to both Momany and his ex-wife, Scholastica! Violet has thus helped us in expibasketising or 'connecting' the straying education-family-marriage dots in her lengthy and fascinating *Maylateyist Lectures* which she addressed to Scholastica:

Figure #43: Violet Maylatey Fonenge
Source: Scholastica Achankeng Asahchop

My only sister: It was a pleasure for me to read those sweet words of yours. My sister, the lord finally blessed my effort with a brilliant success. I had two papers, History and Literature, with four points. But due to circumstances beyond my control, my plans were all shattered. I could not go to Yaoundé or Buea, nor could I do the journalism that I have always loved. All this was due to financial problems. So I had no other alternative but to go in for linguistics since there is no department for journalism here [in the University of Dschang[8]].

---

[8] This Cameroonian university in Bamboutouszone is notorious in its own unique ways. You can also hear one of Frederick Temenu Fossungu's letters to Momany informing him

In fact, I have not been happy for all this time. I hate this Dschang and, as you know, it was never in my dreams. Well, after everything "Man proposes and God disapproves". Everything depends on the lord. I'm trying to see if while here I can communicate with Mr. Fomenky and register for ASMAC [Advanced School of Mass Communication] next year. But it seems as if all will not be possible because I did not have French. But I will write it next year. Your advice to me was very good. But, as I said, conditions could not allow me do what I want. Under linguistics, I'm reading English, French and German as my main languages and African literature is my minor course [what an African developmental inversion! Just like the Upside-down Assistantship Education Theory itself!].

Sister Schola, I'm doing my best to see into it that I do not tarnish my reputation. I always pray to the lord to prevent me from all the temptations that one comes across at this level. I want to be and always remain a responsible girl. Moreover, I was with Belinda [Chopazem Asahchop] during the holiday and did my best to advise her as you have always advised me. Just know that Belinda loves me as I love you and on the other hand, I love her as you love me. I did my best to advise her. She is a very good girl and I just pray that she continue with her behaviour.

My dearest sister, many people have come to me for marriage. I have realised that this is the right moment for me to make a choice. Among them all, the most serious and the one I like is the son of Chief Forteng in Nwametaw who is in the U.S. Sister Schola, as you said, I should be considerate before making a choice. In fact, I have seen that, despite all the struggles, my parents are facing a lot of difficulties every day. Mamie was seriously sick and admitted at Fontem just last month. She needs a special care. But who is there to care for her? If not of her, I might have

---

how "Here in Dschang… we are suffering in the hands of Francophones. All lectures, assignments, practicals, field studies are all carried out in the French language. Out of the 15 courses I am doing in level II, none is taught in English" (cited in Fossungu, 2016: 101).

stayed at home for this [school] year. But she sold her plot and all the money was used for my fees and other needs. My father wanted that I should stay at home for this year because of finance. And I could not blame him since I knew their situation. But it was thanks to Mamie. It has always been my wish to get married to someone who is responsible and caring, kind and faithful. One who will love my parents and be the one with whom to share life's challenges. In fact, I find some of these characteristics or qualities in Mr. Peter Nkengasong Forteng who is in New Jersey (USA). Though I have never met him, I have discussed with him over the phone and he seems to be the kind of person I like. He knows Mamie very well. And he once told me [that] "Kind people are always remote." He said Mamie was very kind. I have told him to look for you. I told him how dear you are to me. I gave him your phone number and address. He has sent many of his pictures to me. Well, my beloved sister, do not say that it is because I have heard of abroad that I'm excited. No. It is that I want a brighter future especially for the sake of my parents.

How do you spend your life there? I'm anxious to know. You said you will tell me something good. In fact, I'm anxious to know. I dreamt of you one day and it seems as if it was an indirect way for the lord to show me that He has blessed my sister. So it is only when you tell me that I will know if my dream was true. You can phone to me using this number: .... [number omitted]. When you call, ask for Mr. Azaomo Thomas Asaah's wife [and] tell her when you will call again and she will send for me.

How is Brother Peter? Extend my profound greetings to him. Those pictures were very nice. In fact, I was very glad to see them. Those friends [of mine that you know] are in Yaoundé. Accept special greetings from my friends here: Patience, Elizabeth and Nicoline. How are Sister Quinta and her kids? In fact, she is really wonderful [bizarre?]. I have never expected that she would be so less concerned as far as the family is concerned to the extent that she did not even care to ask about my results. And her own brother did not care to tell her. Well, after everything God is our protector and everything is in his hands.

My dearest sister, crave my indulgence to drop at this juncture while expecting to read from or discuss with you at any moment. Here is my picture [that is, Figure #43] for you. I took it on my graduation day. Extend my profound greetings to your new friends that way.

Thanks. With much care and concern, yours junior. Signed (Violet M. Fonenge, private communication, 25 October 1999).

Violet is obviously an outstanding lecturer on questions of education, marriage and family and her letter is just as important as Peter Asahchop's in exposing a lot of issues relating to Nwangong Royal Family politics on children's welfare and education especially. More grease to the elbows of beautiful and intelligent Violet! Even more than enough straightforward ink in her pens that wrote the confidential (but now public-dot-connecting) letters to cagey-scheming Scholastica.   In her remarkable lectures, the upside-down education theory is clearly seen in the fact that it was the girl's mother who struggled and sold her own plot in order to ensure that Violet get university education at the University of Dschang, an educational institution which was not even in the girl's wildest dreams. The option of multiple-wives Chief Fonenge Vincent Temenu (Violet's father who is seen in Figure #44) was that Violet should stay home till when? There is much to be decried here about the education inversion in Cameroon and the comportment of the 'many-wives-marrying' royals. But let's keep that for some other time and instead recall and emphasise the important fact on unity and progress not being helped by useless Mamiteelizalist (or biological-birth) categorisations or discrimination relating to children – the future of the nation.

Figure #44: Chief Fonenge Vincent, Chief Formbuehndia Emmanuel & Chief Foletia Vincent in 1993
Source: Photo Dave, Yaoundé

Mamiteelization and the Narrative of the Generous Unifyer

As seen in Chapter 1, Mamiteelization is godmothered by Mamie Thecla Anangfac Fosungu, second wife of Chief Formbuehndia Nguajong. The important thing right now though is the following. This talk of biological discrimination of children can certainly not pass by without involving the archetypal case of the exceptional Nwangong Royal Family *Unifyer*. This comes from the plot-selling tale of Mamie Julie Fonenge who is seen in Figure #45. Mamie Julie's narrative also cements the unfortunate ineffectiveness of the generous *unifyer* of the Nwangong Royal House called Richard Ngufor Fossungu in Figure #46. Relating it to Mamiteelization and the lack of vision or Four-Eyesism, it is to emphasize also that Mamie Julie would not even have been reluctantly selling her plot in the nineties (to be able to send her daughter to

143

university) but for her own short-sighted senseless discrimination against Richard in the sixties for not being her biological child.

Figure #45: Mamie Julie Fonenge & her father, Pa Tendongfac in 1993
Source: Photo Dave, Yaoundé

Figure #46: Nkemngu (Richard Ngufor Fossungu) in July 2004 in Douala

Source: Photo taken by Momany Fossungu

It is very certain that, had Richard been fairly treated in Chief Fonenge's Household and given the educational opportunities that were withheld from wonderfully intelligent Richard then on solely biological grounds, Richard would, a little thereafter, have very generously and enthusiastically taken splendid care of the other children and parents of that Household particularly.

This theory is firmly advanced especially because Richard Ngufor Fossungu appears to be the one precious Unity-Development-Generosity 'knot' that the Nwangong Royal Family never got the chance of effectively having: solely because of persistent Mamiteelization that discriminates children on biological-birth grounds. Because of that exclusionist categorisation, the best *Unifyer* and most generous member of the Fossungu Royal Family was not accorded the opportunity that he was supposed to be so easily given (in the Households of both Chief

145

Fonenge Vincent and Chief Formbuehndia Nguajong – his elder brothers) to have the sound economic base that is so imperative these days for a better delivery in the poverty elimination and advancement domains.

Even without that essential economic base handy, Figures #47 to #49 (among others) can tell readers plenty of what Richard would certainly have done having it, especially in the elevation of the Royal House as a whole. Unnecessary and indiscriminate discrimination just cannot get Africa into Africa. Thus, in Figure #47 Nkemanang and Mary Fossungu (Richard's 2nd wife) are seen at Momany's wife's graduation from the Buea University in 1998; while in Figure #48 Richard's 1st wife, Maria Fossungu, is also 'family-unitising' with Momany (who has Elias Akendung's 1st child, Beniece, with him) during the Douala Nwangong Family Meeting in the mid-80s; and, finally, in Figure #49 Richard himself (at far right) is at Momany's traditional marriage to Scholastica in November 1993 in Nwangong: on Momany's right is Mme Mary Foletia, wife of Chief Foletia Vincent – one of Momany's many uncles who "is well known to handle such matters with a lot of style that blends tradition and modernity in a way unique to Foletia" (Fossungu, 2013: 161).

Figure #47: Nkemanang Calestus Fossungu & Mary Fossungu
Source: Scholastica Achankeng Asahchop

Figure #48: Richard's 1st wife, Maria Fossungu, and Momany, Source: Momany Fossungu

Figure #49: Richard Ngufor Fossungu (far right) at Momany's marriage in 1993
Source: Photo Dave, Yaoundé

The said Households' Mamiteelizalist practices can be cemented, for example, with the charge of Joseph Njumo Fosungu (of Dallas, Texas, USA) in the Josephizationing Letters to his biological father (Chief Formbuehndia) that "Tell Richard in Douala that I say I don't like all of them. In short, I hate your Fosungu Family... Richard is a thief who wanted me to send him cars to put on the streets as taxi and failed to tell me you [Chief Formbuehndia] were trying to buy a bus and give to him" (cited in Fossungu, 2015: 106). The same biological theory thus even more forcefully applies to the Chief Formbuehndia Household not only in regard of Richard who was, again, heavily frustrated there; but also if one would properly imagine, for instance, that, after Momany's exceptional acquisition of the G.C.E. Advanced Levels in the lower sixth form (see Fossungu, 2013: chapter 2), Momany was enthusiastically sent to the Yaoundé University in 1981 – let alone to the USA, as Joseph, the biological son, was in 1985. All these enterprising and light-shining African children (representing the millions of others) were blocked just for not being the biological children of the Madams of the Households! As things have turned out, would one say that Mamie Thecla (who godmothers Mamiteelization) and Mamie Julie actually frustrated only their non-biological children and/or their biological children as well? Anyone farsighted and objective enough can easily see how this works also at the level of African unity and development and, therefore, in getting Africa into Africa. But biology does not seem to be the lone tool used by some *pretending* mothers to kill children's glowing future, if not the children themselves. Not only unthinking and short-sighted parents frustrate students with upside-downism and dragdownism in Africa. The brand of education and the academic institutions themselves contribute enormously in the matter.

Four-Eyesing Takebackism's Hidden Destruction and Frustration from "Paper" Academic Institutions

Frederick and Violet have been severally heard talking of the case of the Dschang University, regretting their not being able to attend the 'Anglo-Saxon' University of Buea. But you just have to also hear that 'Anglo-Saxon' Buea University's own disheartening story from Scholastica's best friend in Figure #50 who was also Momany's student at the University of Buea. In her letter to Momany, Edith Rosa Khumbah Nkokwo wrote to "My dear Power" as follows (beginning from the 3rd paragraph):

I tried getting into the Nigerian law school without success. The problem is that the University of Buea has not been officially accredited to the [Nigerian] Law School. Buea has not officially applied; and even if they do, they'll still have problems because the [Nigerian] Law School expectations are far more than what we have. They expect in a [Law]

150

Faculty at least 10 permanent lecturers, each with an office, a law library, etc which we don't have. So I have given up the idea of going to law school at least for now [this paragraph is already cited in Fossungu, 2019: 94].

As Schola did inform you already, I will like you to do me a favour. I am interested in doing a postgraduate programme in law. My field of interest is in the area of Environmental Law and Gas Law. I will be very grateful if you can help me apply to the universities around you that offer any of these courses. Gas law embodies everything that concerns oil or gas production. I will be very grateful if you can do this for me. If it were possible, I would like to start school between January and March. The order of my names is KHUMBAH EDITH ROSA NKOKWO. I don't know whether it will be possible for you to buy the forms and send to me or I send photocopies of my documents. I would prefer that you send the forms so that I discuss it with my mother and sisters.

Right now I am in the house doing nothing, just that I must be here till December, when my brothers and sisters will all come home [from the USA] for removal of my father's sad-cloth and laying of the tomb stone (Edith-Rosa K Khumbah, private communication, 18 June 1997).

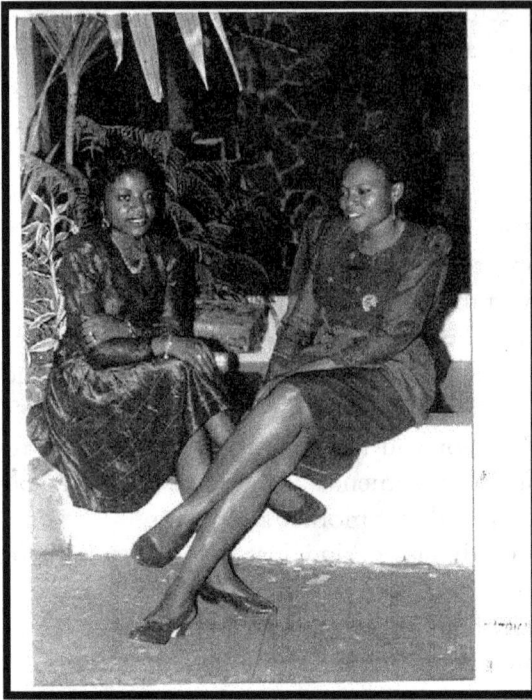

Figure #50: Edith-Rosa Khumbah & Scholastica
Source: Scholastica Asahchop

It must be added that there is even no Law Faculty in said Anglo-Saxon University of Buea, with the Department of Law there being just a department of the Faculty of Social and Management Sciences (Fossungu, 2019: 94). There is hardly any need for further comments on this preventable frustration of 'the leaders of tomorrow' except to reiterate with an educationist that "one cannot therefore speak of universities when one has not created appropriate infrastructures and other conditions necessary for the existence and smooth functioning of those universities" (Fossungu, 2013a: 192).

Why these academic institutions and parents fail in their tasks is directly tied to the unavailability of the 'Trilogy of Good Governance' (a non-existence which is also firmly tied to colonial education that excludes the imparting of critical thinking skills in students). The sad discovery at Cameroon's 'Higher Education' (alias Biggytitlemania) has sanely led to the thesis, which empty-certificateful heads of Cameroonians wouldn't even comprehend, that:

When we collectively allow the crooked-voice guy there in the Etoudi Palace to single-handedly appoint the V-Cs and *Recteurs* (to limit just to these here) and then turn around and expect such appointed officials to act as if they have a free hand, then I say we are all *nosifeans*. People with no schooling in four-eyesism, is what it means. *Hisofeans* [like HRM Fon DF Fossungu and Mafor Regina Akiefac Fossungu, for example] would not be pinning the problems on Nalova and Teresa Akenji (to stay west of the Mungo River). They would rather be fighting to have universities in this country run as autonomous bodies by the localities. And that cannot be limited to those academic institutions alone, since a university cannot be autonomously run by an entity that is not itself autonomous. That position would be no different from saying that the current governors of the regions (call them whatever you will) do in fact manage said entities. *Lie-lie*! Governors must be duly elected by the inhabitants of their various regions for that to effectively happen. How to make all that reality is already outlined in the TRILOGY OF GOVERNANCE [that] Momany has humbly brought forth and is here challenging us all to utilize to bring our people out of the *Quagmaticking* wilderness and into the Promised Land (Fossungu, 2016a, original emphasis).

That is the getting of Africa into Africa that I am talking about. Anyway, whether or not Africans really want to use the furnished Trilogy in the 'Africa and the Development Discourse' (Nwosu, 2015: 303-305) in order to make unity and development *African* (and not *without Africa*) and thus reach the Promised Land, the entire idea is that of imbuing students with the science of Four-Eyesism or farsightedness, the acquisition of which does not appear to be fastened to 'modern' colonial education but instead to pre-colonial African education. The kind of education that lets its holders' titles 'shine from under'; meaning that you should "just let the accomplishments that the titles are evidencing better

153

speak of the titles through your exemplary putting of the achievements to the service of humanity" (Fossungu, 2015a: 15). Yes, that properly defines Getting Africa into Africa. But how can all this be when the training of teachers and other cadres of state (including particularly lawyers and judges) is so notoriously wanting in instilling the very qualities demanded of these professions? What kind of education would students then receive from teachers who only became teachers through bribing their way into the profession? Can the same not also be said of using such questionable education to set aside the people's culture in royal succession? Are there still many Africans who can easily foresee all these things like the *unschooled* Fon DF Fossungu (for example) does?

The Birth of Takebackism and Marrying in America

That important question calls for a lengthy discussion of the help refusal that brings out Fon DF Fossungu's crushing Four-Eyesism. In rejecting the offer of helping with his son's postcolonial education from Marie-Claire Afueh, the Nwangong Fon was simply preventing what he far-sightedly saw as 'the breaking open of his son's head' later by Marie-Claire in order to 'take back' *her* education when the Fon would disagree with her on any point whatsoever: as per the Takebackism that Marie-Claire godmothers (see Fossungu, 2016: 99-102). Marie-Claire's takebackism or frederickeugeneckism got its naissance from communications like the following letters from both the 'blood' brother of Marie-Claire (Frederick Temenu Fossungu who is seen in Figure #51) and Peter Asahchop. The brother's letter would commence the show because it is very important in aiding us to solidify and explain Frederickeugeneckism (or Takebackism). Frederick Temenu Fossungu's letter to Eugene Lekeawung Asahchop stated:

Hello Mr. Eugene, How did you travel from Dschang to Buea, hope you travelled very well. We were so happy when we learned of Sister Schola's departure to U.S.A. and to Canada: she got to Canada very safely.

Sister Marie-Claire asked me to come to Buea and collect her things from you: they are her bed and mattress, her wardrobe, in short, she means that of Schola. She said she gave them to Peter and Peter gave them to Schola.

They are having some problems i.e. there is misunderstanding among themselves. I just wish to inform you so that you should be ready to release the things.

Eugene, I am only being sent, instructed, ordered, not that I am the one. Please, try to phone Peter maybe he will explain better.

I may come from May 26th upwards. She says there are many other things she has forgotten. Study fine. I am your friend. Signed.

N.B: If there is any doubt, write me using the above address or phone by this number XX:XX:XX. There you will have Tchali or Simplice, ask them to call me or arrange a fixed time (Frederick T. Fossungu, private communication, 26 April 1999).

Figure #51: Frederick Temenu Fossungu during his University of Dschang days

Source: Frederick Temenu Fossungu

Frederick is not alone in exposing its development though; of importance too is what Peter Asahchop, again, theorizes in his very important letter. In the 5th paragraph of his really famous (same *Petasahchoppism*) letter (note the date well) to Momany, he stated:

The last letter I wrote to you mentioned a small computer machine for the testing of blood sugar. I am always in the hospital. I kindly plead that you send me one to carry out tests in the house than going to the hospital weekly or monthly. I had an embarrassing letter from Frederick [Temenu Fossungu], the brother of Marie-Claire, saying that Frederick wants to collect things like wardrobe, mattress and bed from Eugene [Lekeawung Asahchop]. I want to know whether things Scholastica was using are the things of Marie-Claire. He mentioned the three items above and others which are not specified, and that you people have a problem with Marie-Claire and husband. I wonder whether the problem had existed before or it was when Scholastica came in. I beg you to quickly write for us to have clarification from you people (Peter N. Asahchop, private communication, 3 June 1999).

Yes, Momany has confirmed to me that his moneyintriguist-dragdownist father-in-law must be told right away that, to the Afuehs of Bowie (Maryland, USA), a problem has always been there because of the bitter truth that Momany flung into Marie-Claire Afueh's face in Nwangong in early 1993 which the two have since taken for a sin against them; thus leading to their comportment that solidifies "The Police-Family Thesis" (see Fossungu, 2015: chapter 4) or Onesidetakism. All that happening simply because Momany also stubbornly refused to lie to cover up Marie-Claire's own lie on the issue of 'no-one in the family then knowing' the person she was about to be married to. That is precisely what is actually behind the takebackist theory, not the Bowie Family Interest Theory that is merely being used as a hypocritical cover. Interestingly, Violet Maylatey Fonenge too is involved in it (for those who have not already studied the famous 'Marrying in America' lessons that gave Momany the bad name of 'the one who spoiled Violet's chances of marrying an America-based man' – see Fossungu, 2013: 142-45).

But Violet later thanked Momany for being true to himself always because that straight-talking stance actually led her to 'the real man' (Fossungu, 2013: 143). That is the real way to Getting Africa into Africa. The amazing part of the Violet narrative is that when Momany had bluntly told the America-based man to go and do his homework by himself, Momany did not then even know that Violet herself had never even met the man in question, as she herself was confidentially disclosing to Scholastica in her 1999 Maylateyist Lectures above. So, what is it really with the godmother of Takebackism in Bowie, Maryland? Could Chief Fonganet's 'illiteracy problem' with Fon DF Fossungu not then also be tied to the latter's possible farsighted rejection to "sell" chieftaincy to the former? Who then is the *wisemany* "illiterate" here? Of course, crisebacologists or balanced critical thinkers must say it is the *certificateful* empty heads that are blaming the sage. Which of these genres of intellectuals does Africa really need to make its unity and development authentically African and thereby easily get Africa into Africa? Are modern Africans really thinking correctly? How could they do so with *frozen* brains as those of the Black *prayerists*? The next section of the Chapter begins studying the candidate's determination and enthusiasm which the next Chapter further extensively harps on.

Windsorizing Frantalkism and the Student's Determination to Succeed: The Ghent University Dossier and the CGAM Do-As-I-Do Experience

It is essential to stress that support from others (including parents), as important as it is, could just not be sufficient for the student's success. As the narratives of other Chapters (the next one especially) can also attest, the candidate must first love what he or she has opted to do before support can have real meaning. In such self-determined cases success could still be achieved with or without parental aid, and with or without postcolonial education. Some crisebacological educationists have protractedly expressed this simple idea or philosophy in their "University Education, With Or Without Money" (Fossungu, 2013: chapter 2). It is only what an individual really loves doing (and not what s/he has been pushed to do) that can guarantee excellence and progress in the community. This truism is not only a defining characteristic of the African pre-colonial education system but can also be seen operating in Momany's loaded expibasketism. From it can be drawn for the reader's enjoyment and instruction the man's first-month experience with political scientists and their sweetheart of debates, especially on what Momany was then clearly a minus-novice. It is all about behavioural analysis that is lengthily discussed by Sanders (2010) and rational choice which is similarly handled by Hindmoor (2010). Students were required to post comments and questions on their class forum (or CLEW, as it is called in Canada's University of Windsor) before the actual face-to-face discussion in class. The course was actually beginning to be too abstract to legal-minded pragmatic Momany and really making him to feel like a fish out of water. Many others in his shoes would simply have given up and left the programme. The mere fact that a doctoral degree holder was there pursuing a Master's programme is enough to indicate resolve. Momany had stayed on not only because he was determined to complete the programme but also mostly because of what he learned at a very early age with Mandenguelovism (dealing with his one-sided love with his first primary school teacher – see Fossungu, 2014: 7-15). That experience duly taught him not to be ashamed of having a difficulty and to freely talk about it in order to get help. That is the walking ahead and looking behind but keeping on still walking and putting your troubles behind you, as Maitre Peterson Tesi has described it. Frantalkism it has been called; being the propeller to positive development.

That is precisely what Momany also did in the said CLEW discussions and earned a 50% (rather than a zero) with his September 2013 Observaquestion:

"Most of what I have to say may not be of much interest or significance to many of us with a political or social sciences background. But I think those of us without it would need to get clear on some of these things. For example, I have just observed that furnishing multiple sources in political science research methods it is *standard* to begin with the earliest and end with the most recent. Or, could it just be the preference of said authors?" That is just a little segment of the voluminous observaquestion, but the feedback from the others was amazing and did enormously aid Momany to quickly get a handle on the entire course. Come to imagine his pretending then to be alright with the subject/concepts when that was truly not the case: and you would have sufficiently grasped a lot of the debates in the

159

Postponementolodramacracy of the CGAM, as well as other arguments in this and other discourses – notably the Bowie Family Interest Theory in Chapter 2. Momany thus quickly learnt from just making his difficulty known to all. At the end of his lengthy observaquestion was the question wanting to know from the others if the discipline of law (his home-ground) is a part of the behavioural sciences or not.

Whatever is or is not behavioural, Celia S. Reeves gave Momany the handle he needed to suck in the matter. He had decided to consult Reaves' book (as suggested by one of his Windsor classmates) to see if she could help bring the subject closer to home. Reaves immediately kind of reminded Momany too well of what the Methods Course instructor (Dr. Jamie Essex) had said on the first day when Reaves notes in her Preface that "I hope to motivate students to see the research methods course as something more than an obstacle in their path. Instead, I want them to see it as a stepping stone they will need to reach their goals. This attitude will make it more likely that the things they learn will stay with them beyond the final exam" (Reaves, 1992: vii). Momany was thus beginning to like entering and discovering the supposed treasure Reaves might have in store. But, like in Christickinology (see Fossungu, 2014: 51-54), Momany became completely "imprisoned" in Reaves' work when in her 'Part I: Fundamentals' (and as if speaking directly to just Momany and his 'problem') Celia Reaves would open with: "Before studying research techniques and methodology, it is important to develop a general understanding of the scientific endeavor. Without such an understanding, you would be like an art student learning the chemistry of pigments and solvents without ever seeing a painting. You have to know what the techniques and methods are for – why they will be used – before they will make any sense" (Reaves, 1992: 5). Indeed, these techniques and methods thereafter began to make sense to Momany and would most likely do same to anyone without a background in the behavioural sciences like him. Get an appetising taste of the "behaving sciences" then, as they relate to children's education and welfare and the development of Africa, beginning with moneyintrighentism.

160

Moneyintrighentism signifies 'moneyintriguism hiding behind the Ghent University Dossier'. Moneyintrighentism began on Wednesday, 21 October 2009 when Momany wrote an email titled "Ghent University" to the current Fon of Nwangong. The issue of not always paying the required attention to, or making the necessary follow-up on, Momany's proposals for advancement is quite generalised in the Nwangong Royal Family and does not apply only to the 'After-Chief-Formbuehndia' funeral epoch as exposed in Chapter 4.

The scholasticalization stress in the next Chapter apart, some previous books have talked immensely about what people who are really interested in achieving a thing would go about doing to circumvent seemingly insurmountable obstacles on their way (see especially Fossungu 2013: chapters 3 & 2). Those people just being pushed by others or merely trying the moneyintriguist thing would never be able to see through the 'Hercules' in front of them. Otherwise, what would one say concerning what also actually held back the Fon of Nwangong's speedy follow-up that was required for the Ghent University dossier too?

It was not until Friday, 12 March 2010 that Fon NN Fossungu wrote back (in "Re: Ghent University") admitting fault of carelessness while forcefully stressing the necessity for his getting out of the country because of the grave danger to his life, a life which was more important to him than the throne. Well, that is encouraging, at least, when someone admits his or her fault. It has been posited times innumerable that it is very easy to teach a person who is aware of his/her ignorance but just more than an uphill task doing so to those who are ignorant of their ignorance (see Fossungu, 2015b). Hence, in his email of Monday, 12 April 2010 titled "Information Needed" Momany told the Fon that:

You will need to also send your Advanced Level Certificate. I also need to know the following:

1) Employment History (if any): name of employer, position of applicant, employer phone, employer e-mail, employment dates (from --- to----)

2) Whether you are currently admitted by a university institution and for what course

3) Research Areas: (a) a provisional title for your intended dissertation at the U of Malta and (b) a research proposal of at least 300 words. This item can be sent to arts@um.edu.mt not later than one week after submission of your online application

4) Head of School/Academic institution last attended: name, phone number, address, position held, e-mail.

5) A mailing postal address in Cameroon. (I have used my own address here provisionally but it would be better to use one over there. Can I use C/o MDL Maureen N. Fossungu?) I am trying to get you admitted in the University of Malta for an MA in Geography in the Faculty of Arts (1st choice), or for a Diploma in Management Studies in the Faculty of Economics, Management and Accountancy (2nd choice), beginning October 2010. The application deadline is 15 May. For Belgium, the deadline for application for next school year is already past (March 1). For the passport section, I have filled "In progress" but it is important you embark on this sooner. I will get back to you on this issue before this week ends but you can already start gathering the necessary information. I think I should simply leave out FOSSUNGU (as family name) from the application forms since all your other documents do not carry it, don't you think? I have indicated that you obtained the Maîtrise in 2008, is that correct? I will be submitting the online application as soon as I receive the missing information. So, do well to respond as quickly as you can. And also constantly check your e-mail.

Dr NPAF

As you have seen and will further see, Momany's helping hand has been extended to the Fossungus a lot but nothing fruitful has happened. Why is it so different with his family members? These questions really need to puzzle anyone. Especially, again, knowing that on Wednesday, 14 April 2010, the Fon of Nwangong wrote to "Dear Dr Nkemtale'eh" as follows:

I received the money yesterday and started the passport process immediately. I certified the required documents yesterday. Actually there is a problem I caused without reflecting on the future implications which is an obstacle to the progress of the passport issue. I made an ID card when I was enthroned in 2008 with the objective of including the family name and more importantly to compile my documents for chieftaincy classification. From investigations, it is clear that one of the IDs must be cancelled at the national ID centre SACEL in Nvan. I was there yesterday and today but could not find solution to the problem. The very last trial to this will be on Monday when the highest authority will be back from a journey. He is called Colonel FABRE. I much regret this inconvenience caused by myself and I will keep praying and trying.

Meanwhile I am attending some preparatory classes for ENAM and ENS. The preparatory classes will commence soon. I wish you should not be angry with me for this because I never knew the consequences could be so high. The colonel's secretary told me that the difficulty is due to the fact that the data bases for the identification do not provide any possibility for cancellation.

I still hope this problem will be solved by the colonel.

The money the Fon is talking about refers to the 100,000 FCFA sent to him on 12 April 2010 (Western Union # 805-873-9161). If you make a small trip back to what has been said above, then you would find that there is absolutely no problem or issue here except one the candidate himself is creating, perhaps, in view of having more money sent to 'solve' it. Moneyintriguism is an obvious giant standing on the way of Africa's progress. It even gets worse when the fact that it is not a problem is indicated and we still cling to our imaginary or created difficulty. After several other communications between them that portrayed some considerable amount of leg-dragging on the Fon's part, on Friday, 16 April 2010 Momany told the Fon (in "Re: Information Needed") that:

I will start with the Malta question. Nothing is odd in asking to know what one does not know. What is instead odd to me is not knowing and pretending to know. Malta is a European Island country lying between continental Europe and North Africa.

As soon as I have the documents/information still pending, I will complete the online application and submit it. I will then communicate the username and password to you so that you can check your file online whenever you like. Thereafter, all communication from them will be with you through email especially. Keep me posted.

If you want to make another birth certificate to tie in with your other documents, that is okay. But that would not alter the academic certificates, the documents that the school will largely be interested in. Just be prepared to tender the required explanation if they should ask. These are very authentic documents and I don't see any need for panicking. Have a wonderful weekend.

Dr NPAF

It has been essential to present this sequence of communications (like you will also get in the Canada College file in Chapter 4) since it is by following it through that one can easily grasp the point that comes in the nature of a conclusion drawn. The Fon wrote back to Momany on Monday, 16 April 2010, duly informing him that:

I have been trying things but there are some pertinent issues concerning me. I have investigated the ID issue and only 100,000 FCFA can solve the problem for now. So I will like that we do it later due to the fast approaching registration deadline. Another issue at stake is the fact that I have not been able to add our number (have a child), since 2008 when I was enthroned. No matter the difficulties I have faced and those I am still to face, there is a necessity to add this number so as to keep the legacy.

Though it is not easy but with God I think we will go through this. I think it is preferable that I intensify my effort in getting into the public sector here while trying to complete the master program here. If this is attained, we can then proceed with the Ph.D. programme through a study leave request.

For the concours, I have started with the preparatory classes for the ENAM, to continue with the other ones later. People are sending their support and I still feel encouraged and determined not to fail them. This is the way I propose we should take and I will like to hear from you as soon as you read this mail. Greet the family for me.

What an intriguing family of moneyintriguist doublesidists! What place has frantalkism at all in this kind of family? On Tuesday, 27 April 2010 at 12 minutes past midnight, Momany wrote to the Fon that it is:

Good to hear from you. Good also to know that you have made up your mind about what you want to do with your life. On this matter, of course, others can only suggest this or that to you but what is important is *what you yourself want to do*. I can only be happy that *you know what you exactly want and what you are getting into*. All is well that ends well. Dr NPAF (original emphasis).

The 8th Fon of Nwangong is quite right in seeking to keep his legacy. The rightness becomes questionable though when viewed in relation to his declaration that provoked the Belgium-Malta initiatives: his life being more important than the crown. I say he is correct in terms of his legacy because of what *Ahlahkem* requires. Ahlahkem was explained by Ndi Peter Asahtanyi on 8 December 2007 to be "the initiation period and [it] demands that the new Fon be there for nine weeks during which time he has to be brought up, given traditional rites, be briefed morally on how he has to behave in society; until after those nine weeks when he comes out, and there will be another big celebration. *Ahlahkem* is, therefore, very important to any Fon because it is meant to prepare him on how he is going to rule the Fondom."

Asked about what the exact duration of *Ahlahkem* is, Asahtanyi theorised on 8 December 2007 that "the initiation period takes nine weeks and during those nine weeks he [the new Fon] has to get married to a wife with whom he spends those weeks. For our Fon, he is billed to be out on Saturday, February 8, 2008." That period too is when the new Fon's own successor is expected to be born. In view of these requirements, the Fon, as earlier indicated, was right in sticking it out to preserve his legacy. What puzzles the mind has to do with what was in his mind when he declared that his life was more important than the throne that he now ardently wants to preserve? If one couples this with the reaction to the identity argument, could the conclusion lead one

165

anywhere than that he never really wanted to get out of Cameroon as such but was just trying to employ that talk of danger to his life as a technique to suck money out of Momany?

For your further response, you could also use the issue of Fondom integrity and development. I am particularly referring to the same Fon's reaction to the reaction of those (like Marie-Claire Afueh) purportedly questioning people (like Scholastica Asahchop) they consider as having ridiculed the Fon and Nwangong Fondom. I wouldn't want to layout all what the latter wrote for readers to comprehend the former's theorization already encountered in the first footnote of this book. The essential point is that Marie-Claire Afueh was dishing out the lessons (as I have also already evoked several times in my other works) on one 'only getting into discussing about something one is well aware of'. It is, however, the homework-doing part of her deceptionist lecture that is of concern right now. I am referring to her 4th (and concluding) paragraph:

Regarding matters of development in that village, you can write whatever colour of email you wish and do development, it is your village. But, when it comes to his [the Fon's] CHARACTER AND INTEGRITY, Please don't even Mess with it. For your information, his representatives in US and Canada are: Chief Forfah – USA; Dr. Nkemtaleh Fossungu – Canada. Give my kiss to the children and do your homework [paragraphing altered, original capitals].

Some crisebacologists even have the feeling that this is not even the correct approach to handle the Fon's Integrity issue. "Rather than work together to ameliorate the situation, the central figures of this family only exhibit their centrality in dragging the family and fondom down in moves that show clearly that they just want to be the 'only eye' around the place. They then go about writing silly emails to those they consider as having insulted the Fon. Do I hear you well, Marie-Claire Afueh? That is surely not the correct way to defend the family's INTEGRITY or HONOUR!" (Fossungu, 2016: 160 n.50). Having said that, her home-work instruction must push one to further wonder if Marie-Claire does her own homework well enough to know that one must not burn the bridge after crossing it, so as not to hinder crossing by those following behind. I will

166

not detain you any further with that but instead examine the reaction of the Fon to her reaction to Scholastica's write-up. No one (except, perhaps, the Fon himself) would here be entirely disagreeing with Marie-Claire's take on the issue. Not as yet and not on what subject she was talking because in Momany's own exceptional "Fw: Re: Ghent University" email of 10 April 2010 to Marie-Claire (said email is to be discussed shortly), Momany added this concurring message to "Chief Fofa'ah" (Marie-Claire), stating in regard of the email Marie-Claire was talking about (in her write-up in question) that "Wonders shall indeed never end. I have just read your email and the Fon's reaction as well. I can't say that you could have been more correct in reacting as you have. Well, I don't know what else to say than to let you read this confidential email that I had sent to the Fon. God bless. PAF."

The Fon's reaction to Marie-Claire's concerns appears to be solely motivated by moneyintriguism rather than by concerns of his integrity or honour. Here then is Fon NN Fossungu's Reaction (being his reply to the forwarded 'confidential email' that was sent to him in the wake of the email provoking the Integrity outburst) which came in on 9 April 2010 at 4.04 PM and addressed to Momany:

Good day,

Well, I never meant to hurt you people or to condescend in the name of having favours or promises. One thing is clear about my present status. I am facing the challenge of pulling the village ahead and there is much to do with money and people to work with them are supposed to be of a giving class besides dealing with our delicate family. Much has been said to me (negatively) about you people at the Diaspora that you are passive in the issues of development back home.

What I suggest we do is that the problem raised by Sister Schola should not result in conflicts as Chief Fofaah's mail is depicting. All I require from you and Chief Fofaah is that we should communicate regularly. I need more of moral support than anything, for my dignity and integrity lie on what I do rather than what I am. All I pray for is to move out of this financial dependency and be myself.

I still beg that we should avoid problems at this stage and work in collaboration

Greetings to mum and the baby

That was in response to the email message below which, to reiterate, was directed to the Fon in the wake of the controversial Scholastica write-up. Said 'confidential email' enormously fortifies understanding of not only the poverty situation of the Nwangong Royal House but also both the *Ghent University Dossier* and the Nwangong Succession Palaver; being one of the numerous responses to the important email (Re: Ghent University) that Momany wrote to HRM Fon NN Fossungu on Saturday, 3 April 2010 in which he extensively theorized as follows:

HRM Fon Fossungu,

The late Fon, your father, once said this (and I have it all on video tape): "If people are minimizing you, don't you ever minimize yourself." He was referring to Nwangong generally but more precisely to the Royal Family that you now head. This was in 2004 on the occasion of the generator, etc. that I had just surprised the village with. Late Fon D.F. Fossungu also noted on the same event: "One thing I like about Dr. Nkemtale'eh is that he does not make promises before doing anything, which is quite good because you could promise someone a thing and later find out that you cannot do it, and thus become a liar." My loose translation of our language through which the message came. The late Fon is quite right.

I am not the type that would go about boasting regarding whatever I have done, or will do, to help anyone. I am also not of the type that would make promises they cannot keep. Not the kind that would give people false hope. I am simply a person who will just do a thing when I can do it, without all the fuss.

Not claiming to be a prophet, I am also someone that has this nag of looking ahead and seeing some things (that are not very clearly defined) coming before they actually happen. I am confident that at this point you can see clearly that it is never wise to put all your eggs in one basket; and that *all that glitters is not gold*; that not everyone smiling in front of you is really your friend; that only the Fossungus can actually resolve the numerous problems (all resulting from the financial especially) that the Fon of Nwangong is facing, with the Fon still riding with head high up. And that in this important resolution, those who matter are **Formbuehndia of South Africa, Fofa'ah of Maryland**, (Frederick and Ignatius of Maryland,) and **Nkemtale'eh of Canada**. I am not going to speak for the others though because I am not competent to know what exactly they are going through and exactly how they can or cannot aid. In view of the position I have been put into here by the woman you know I brought into this country, I cannot do anything directly. It is a very long story that I hate to get into here. But you will not believe that, as we speak, I cannot even travel out of Canada, thanks to her. I am not telling you this so that you should go about spreading the news. It is only to cement the point made earlier that not everyone that is singing to you about what they want to do for you will actually do it. Sometimes the real idea or purpose is just to mock. Ask yourself, for instance, how many of the Asahchops are now out of Cameroon through her and how many Fossungus are out of the country through me, and you might comprehend what I am saying. I do not want to get into all that here.

Now, **this is what you have to do**. Concentrate on the Belgium mission and obtain your admission and then leave the rest to me. ***Do this in absolute confidentiality and do not, in any way, close the other doors that people are claiming they would open for you.***** Your current level of education makes your getting admitted in Belgium a matter of course. You are not going to Belgium to study as such but we are merely using it as a bridge to join me here (**on a basis that would enable you to travel back and forth as you desire**). I do not have the money on hand but, as you rightly said, I have contacts and other means that can help me accomplish the task of getting you out of Cameroon. To me money is not the amount that has been stacked in a bank account. Money, as I see it, is what money can do. Just obtain your admission letter and I will take it from there. I am ready to go, are you? Nkemtale'eh [bold & italics are original].

The imperative question remains: After all the steps taken because of the Fon's intimation of grave danger to his life if he does not leave

169

Cameroon, what was actually behind that talk of danger, other than moneyintriguism, now that he is sticking it out to keep his legacy? What can also be leant from the other family in North America called the CGAM?

Not properly grasping the "behaving sciences" properly accounts for African children being the leaders of *a tomorrow* that is never ever coming, but instead remaining yesterday forever: since the entrenched motto is *Children, Do As I Say* rather than *Do As I Do*. The CGAM and its presidents do appear to provide enough support to the "do-as-I-do" (and not "do-as-I-say") theory. These concrete illustrations are required to better tar the hypocritical Tomorrow Highway to Yesterday. Viewing the CGAM's objectives (which are both inward-looking and outward-looking), it is not then surprising for CGAM presidents particularly to be constantly reminding CGAMers to be active in the community. While striving to support the larger community, the CGAM does not forget to position itself well in said community. That explains why its administration encourages CGAMers to support other CGAMers who are vying for positions within the larger community like the Association of Cameroonians in Canada (ACC). Thus, on 25 May 2006, for instance, CGAM President Paul Takha Ayah's *'Elections – Let's Support our Goodwillers'* called on all CGAMers:

To show up massively to support two of our members who are running on the same [ACC] team – Fidelis Folifac as Treasurer and Berri Nsame as Vice-president in charge of Social and Community Affairs. To support them, please show up on time and bring along an ID. Also remember to come ready to purchase an ACC membership card ($10) which gives you the right to vote. There will be lots of food and drinks after the elections. Having two Goodwillers on the ACC executive will give us a very high profile in the community, so please come out in great numbers (CGAM Forun, 26 May 2006, altered paragraphing).

But there is also the inward-looking perspective of the objectives, the absence of which would be 'a mere slap on our own faces', as the Goodwill Projects Committee (GPC) would put it (see Fossungu, 2018: 126). The call to action was also the case with CGAM President Fidelis

170

Folefac (in Figure #52) whose "belie[f] in breaking down barriers and building bridges between communities" (LaSalle, 2010) earned him the 2010 Moulin d'Or Community Award. On 29 October 2009 President Folefac was also urging CGAM members to attend the LaSalle Forum in order "to foster changes you will like to see in LaSalle." Folefac would not just be practising the 'Do as I say' thing but doing it himself, explaining why

Fidelis Folefac has therefore endeavoured to develop projects that bring people together – projects that facilitate immigrants' integration and create ties among the various communities. His first initiative was to train an adult soccer team in order to participate in tournaments both in Montreal and outside the city. As sports are a good way of socializing and bringing people together, he met with immediate success (LaSalle, 2010).

Figure #52: Nkem Dr Fidelis Folefac giving speech in the capacity of CGAM President in May 2009 during the Flavie-Momany traditional marriage in Montreal
Source: MJR Production, Montréal

The adult soccer club mentioned is called Goodwill Football Club. Also important for mention is the 2013 Volunteer Committee chair, Paul Wanka Abongwa, who on Tuesday, 7 May 2013 made the following call on Goodwillers (another way of calling CGAMers):

Based on the responsibility assigned to me by the President of Cameroon Goodwill, and the chair of the 10th Anniversary Committee, I am touching base with you as the Head of the Volunteer Sub-committee, being part of the activities leading to our 10th Anniversary.

The Cameroon Goodwill Association is co-organizing a volunteer campaign with TDS, as part of their activities for the Earth's Day. The campaign is scheduled for this Saturday, 11th of May 2013, from 9 AM to Noon, and lunch will follow thereafter. Activities include cleanup campaign around Rue Airlie, 80th and 90th Avenues, LaSalle.

Due to the request for a definite number of participants, we are therefore soliciting for members to indicate their availability ASAP. Please let's remind ourselves that this is an opportunity for us to give a little back to the LaSalle community for all what they have been doing for us all these years. The LaSalle Community is highly assisting Goodwill in most of the activities leading to our 10th Anniversary, thus, the President of Goodwill, Mme Caren Ayah, is pleading with us all to be part of this campaign. All participants will be issued a certificate.

Your humble servant (CGAM Forum, 7 May 2013, bold has been taken off)

Here is the list of those who answered the call to volunteerism, as Paul Abongwa told CGAMers on 11 May 2013: "On behalf of the President of Cameroon Goodwill, Mme Caren Ayah, and myself, I would like to thank the following members: Paul Abongwa, Pascaline Abongwa, Walter Tita, Acheng Thomas, Rosaline Takang, Micheline Acheah, Ekwe Enongene, Magnus Ajong, Paul Ayah, Yvette Fuh-Cham and daughter, and Roger Ekuh-Ngwese, for their volunteer services this morning." Readers can thus see that, in these CGAM cases or examples, the ones calling for participation were themselves participating very actively. This pithy exposition of the question of walking the talk is vital in the Immaculate Freedom, Unity and Development Theory whose handmaiden, Crisebacology, would also be telling us that we must not only smile when praises are objectively heaped on us and then turn around and frown when objective condemnation comes, like the architects of *takebackism* appear to be well noted for doing. The next Chapter fortifies the numerous biological and other educational theories while discussing some family moneyintriguists and nonoselfists who are promoting African underdevelopment.

CHAPTER 4

THE BRIDGE-BUILDERS' HERCULES IN FOSTERING UNITY AND DEVELOPMENT IN AFRICA: SCHOLASTICALIZING AND EVALUATING THE FAMILY CANADA EDUCATION AND POVERTY ERADICATION PROJECTS

This Chapter brings something of a rethinking in the circles of unity conversation, poverty and illiteracy elimination discourses, and development communication. The poor of the South are often pointing accusing fingers at the rich of the North for their backward situation. No one doubts that the latter cannot be completely exonerated (see Mhango, 2018), but I seriously think the poor really have to step back and genuinely soul-search to discover just how they themselves contribute to (if not actually creating) their predicament. This contribution comes to help in the much needed re-direction while also greatly enhancing our comprehension of the ineffectiveness of the illiteracy and poverty eradication programmes that are hinged on the Nwangon Royal Family

173

to demonstrate how substituting *Africa* in place of *family* in it can give one a near perfect explanation of why the continent (like the studied Fondom) remains behind the others. According to some researchers of poverty, vulnerability, and disaster risk management, "many have always been wondering why the number of poor people in Africa keeps on increasing day-by-day when Africa's economies are reportedly said to be growing. There is a dissonance between Africa's growth performance and its poverty numbers" (Mawere, 2018: 13). You are invited to read on and discover for yourself how the exposition in this book (which is largely anchored on Momany, the bridge-builder) can generally help in explaining the growth in the number of poor people in Africa and the said dissonance.

The concept of family has also been easily extended to other groupings Momany has been involved in, such as the Black community in Aménagement MYR Inc. (MYR) in Dolbeau-Mistassini (Québec, Canada) and the CGAM, with his lifelong objective of "making things better for the greatest number of persons possible" (see Fossungu, 2013: ix) being seen there as well in both his pioneering role in creating the CGAM in July 2003 and in directing and shaping it (see Fossungu, 2015a) and in the car-owning revolution in MYR. But the discussion of that 'life-bettering ideal' of his in this Chapter principally focuses on the eradication of illiteracy and poverty in the Nwangong Royal Family. It is reflected here in its members' dishonourable bridge-burning comportment, moneyintriguism and nonoselfism; all of which further expose the manner Momany (as one of the prominent bridge-builders of said family) has been attempting to do (to no avail) both what the unknown Will of Chief Formbuehndia Nguajong demanded and what the current Fon of Nwangong would also be demanding of him (as the newly crowned Chief Fotale'eh) – all predicated on the eradication of poverty and illiteracy in the Nwangong Royal Family and Fondom: "Let Chief Fotale'eh take all the Chiefs to Canada! Let him take all the Mekem to Canada! Let him take the whole of Nwangong to Canada! Let him not take this as a joke!" (Fon N.N. Fossungu, private communication, 19 July 2014).

Fon Nicasius Nguazong Fossungu's instruction to the newly crowned Chief Fotale'eh to populate Canada with Nwangong inhabitants has always been top on Momany's agenda. This Chapter is out to further detail out information on both the Canada College Files and the Invitations Palaver that are all parts of the illiteracy and poverty eradication schemes. At their dad's tomb in October 2002, and without having seen or even heard anything about the contents of the deceased's Will, Momany had made a promise to see to it that his junior siblings that their father left behind never feel their father's absence too much. This same issue came up for further reiteration when the cameraman (Benjamin of Benji Photo-Video) posed this question to Momany on 19 October 2002: "You have lost your dad. What do you foresee doing so as to mitigate his absence to your siblings?" Momany's response was as follows:

That is a very essential question and it has been worrying me a lot since, and even before, the death of our father. I think I will do my best to see to it that the entire family and especially my younger siblings do not feel this absence a lot. They must not be left on their own and I am convinced that I will do the best I can to be there always for all of them, just as I have just told them while we were at papa's tomb together (Momany Fossungu, private communication, 19 October 2002).

Figure #53: (Left) leaving father's grave after 'farewell talk' & promise behind the house; & (right) at mother's grave in front
Source: Benji Photo-Video, Dschang

175

Readers must be told also that at the graves-gathering that Figure #53 evidences Bernard Mbancho Fosungu of South Africa had then also talked of the following of their dad's instructions to the letter. It is amazing though that no one, but especially the next of kin (Bernard), bothered at all to let Momany know what those instructions consisted of. Rather, the very next morning everyone was hurrying out of the village to the coast. A *Coastman* indeed as Bernard is called! But would a coast person also be ignorant of the importance of filming or video-taping an event like the one that took place in the village? Would some of them even be able to know what they looked like some years ago without the few pictures (some of which are provided in this book) that Momany took of them then? Many, many, and many questions! What this boils down to, for example, is that what was expected of Bernard in October 2002 was a sound debriefing/briefing of the lone sibling (out of three) from North America during or after the occasion and also to seek to see how a follow-up to/on the promise made at the graves of both their dad and mum could be organised and coordinated. That was just not the case at all since the following day (Sunday, 20 October 2002) everybody was on the road heading to the coast, as clearly indicated even in the burial-and-funeral programme!

That was not the only perplexing thing. None of Momany's junior sisters ever presented their so-called husbands (who are said to have been at the event) to him during or after the ceremony. I have to be calling them *so-called* because, in their place, I would personally have insisted on my wife formally presenting me to her brother from abroad that I had never formally met till then. That is the normal thing for any right-thinking married person to do. Of course, Momany had the intention of still going to their various homes during that trip to Cameroon. But he had other pressing issues that unexpectedly came up on his biological father's side which urgently demanded settling (within the short period he then had) before returning to Canada. It was during said issues settlement that his own troublesome 'Asoba' title metamorphosised into Nkemtale'eh (see Fossungu, 2013: 17–19). Yet, despite all the family issues and dragdownist obstacles in his own Household in Canada,

176

Momany steadfastly began trying to realise the projects he had long set out in regard of his siblings and other extended family members, as championed by the Canada College Enterprise, whose brief survey in this Chapter will further groom your comprehension of the moneyintriguism that is so rife in modern Africans' relationships; not being particularly conducive to freedom, unity and development. The issues of the Chapter are handled under three principal heads: (1) Revisiting the Philosophy of the Canada Fossungunization Project and Godparenting Canada, (2) the Regina-Bridget-Queenta disconnection and the Bridget-Kelie Invitations Marvels, and (3) the duelling between Pan-African Institute and Canada College because of no Scholasticalisation.

Revisiting the Philosophy of the Canada Fossungunization and Poverty Eradication Policies while Godparenting Canada

Momany's ideals for the family were significantly influenced and reinforced by his tragedy-loaded 2007 trip to Cameroon, a journey that was largely meant to (1) formally assume lectureship at the Université de Douala, (2) marry his beloved fiancée called Queenta Ngum Afanwi who you saw in Figure #41, and (3) set something up for Richard Ngufor Fossungu (see Fossungu, 2016: chapter 2). Two months after his abrupt return to Canada, Momany dispatched the following missive to his friends in Edmonton, in response to their enquiries as to what his new plans consisted of. It told them that:

I am sure everyone at home is doing fine. Well, I have been doing a lot of thinking about my Cameroon Mission. The [Douala] University is out not only because of the death of the Head of Department but mostly because I have come to realize that my immediate family (children, parents, & siblings) would have to come before the larger community. I therefore have to make sure that these people are sufficiently comfortable before embarking on the comfort of the larger community; and not the other way round.

Quite apart from my mother, I was not happy at all seeing my daughter in Douala. She is not as healthy as she should be. And I could not get any convincing explanation for her bony appearance from her mother. My direct follower (only brother from same mum) left a note behind and disappeared and no one until now knows to where. In the note he said he has already suffered too much in this world and that we shall only meet in Heaven. My junior half-sister already looks about one-and-the-half times my age, and my junior half-brother looks even worse. It is now clear to me that, in my bid to take on the bigger picture, I have inadvertently neglected these very close family members of mine. It is time to take a different approach.

You would not believe that Scholastica called here on 1 March 2007 demanding money! I simply shut out the phone and refused to pick it up again despite her repeated rings. Extend my greetings (Momany Fossungu, private communication, 8 March 2007).[9]

---

[9] Nancy Whistance-Smith appears again to capture well the vexing bridge-builder herculean issues when she wrote back to Momany as follows:

What a difficult situation you continue to find yourself
in! With half of your family on one side of the Atlantic and
half on the other side, you are torn in many
directions. And, with your level of education, I would hope
that you could find more permanent work that reflects your
intelligence and expertise. Maybe now that it is clear the
time is not to return to Cameroon, other opportunities will
present themselves in Canada. Please continue to be alert
in case a door opens for new employment. (Nancy
Whistance-Smith, private communication, March 2007)

Nancy was quite right because on 22 March 2007 Momany also informed them of the following:

Greetings to everyone at home. I came back from London
on Saturday 17 March 2007. I do not have any decision yet
but I can simply say that the end is at hand. She may get the
money that she's after but I'll certainly get her off my back
real soon because the divorce question was brought in this
time. You wouldn't believe what she told the court but any

Proceeding with the Programmes, with or without the Hercules and Biology

'Godparenting Canada' has to do with the *Maurinkemanang* (Maurine-Nkemanang) *File*, a dossier which is very interesting in many senses. One of which being that it cuts across all the Poverty-Eradication and Education Projects and can be better placed within this interwoven space by the philosophy driving the Canada Fossungunization Project, as also enumerated in Momany's distinguished email of 1 July 2008 to Bernard Mbancho Fossungu (see Fossungu, 2016: 137–39) to which Bernard will be replying below. That answer from Bernard would be better appreciated when an earlier letter from him is first studied. I am here talking about Bernard's first letter to Momany sent from South Africa. With address in Johannesburg, it told "Hi Guy" that:

You will certainly be surprised to read from me from this end. After all the problems that I had, coupled with my mum's death (I didn't call you because your wife told me you people were already informed), I decided to move here to battle it with life.

I arrived here last Thursday at about 11:30 PM and unfortunately I fell in the hands of thieves who robbed me in the taxi I boarded of all my money except that which I had put in my socks which of course was negligible. That notwithstanding, I am battling it out. I am still looking for a job and I have barely a month of legal stay after which I will have to report to the immigration office. Guy, what makes life very difficult here is their immigration policy and the hostility of the native blacks towards foreign blacks. They discriminate in employment. This of course is understood, the only thing which can make things easier for me to pick up a job is my knowledge of French and Spanish. I have not yet had one.

---

right-thinking person sitting in that court house and listening to her would not need to be told that she is just out to tear me apart at all levels: especially financially and professionally. I will keep you posted on the final decision. I did not get to see the children (Momany Fossungu, private communication, 22 March 2007).

179

Once you can't speak their native language you are discriminated upon and considered a second class citizen.

Guy, in the face of all these problems, I am begging you to send me some money as soon as possible to enable me survive this difficult beginning and to regularise my stay by the 15 of September else I run the risk of being repatriated.

Daddy says he did not receive the cheque you sent to him after the death of mum, this was due to the unreliability of the address. Before leaving the country last week, he asked me to inform you, Marie-Claire and if possible Joe (with him, Joe, we have lost contact for over 3 years, do you hear from him?) to use this address when writing to him: C/O Mr. Emmanuel Njanjo, Service de Sécurité, SONARA, P.O. Box 363 Limbe, Cameroon. NB: He is Anna's husband. You can phone me through this number 27114528913, we are one hour ahead of Cameroon Time. If you're phoning, call after 7 pm Cameroon time. I am desperately counting on you. The best way to send the money is through WESTERN UNION.

I wish you the best. Bye (B.M. Fosungu, private communication, 24 August 1998).

Of course, what Bernard narrated in 1998 in the first three paragraphs has been heavily vouched for even as recently as in 2018 by some researchers of poverty, vulnerability, and disaster risk management (see Duri and Chikonyora, 2018). Momany is certainly the last of the persons that would not rush to the assistance of someone (brother or not) who is in dire need of help. Not especially someone who has taken the initiative to battle it out by himself/herself rather than be contented in the notorious 'dependency syndrome' created and perpetuated in Africa by 'Colonial Education' (Gwaravanda, 2018: 258–60). Bernard's letter does not only make the point before it. It is also important because of its 4th paragraph that would sort of bring home the fact that it is not just an issue of biology (as some might be pushed to think) which is at the root of the discord in the Nwangong Royal Family. It is rather more of the propensity to think family only when we can take from the other side, never when that need is not there – *onesidetakism* being the new terminology to capture it. Joseph Njumo Fosungu was constantly in touch with the base when he just got to the USA, always demanding for money in the millions in similar terms with repatriation menaces and the like. It just did not matter to Joseph that his junior sisters and brothers also needed to be in school, etc. But once Joseph was well seated in the place and doing fine no one (biological to him or not) would seem to be hearing a thing from him; just as Momany would be after Bernard's regularisation of his stay in the Republic of South Africa (RSA) despite Momany's unending advice for Bernard to cross over to Canada and join him.

Well, Bernard still did not see with the point of immigrating to Canada, although this time in 2008 he gave his reasons that also let Momany, for the first time ever, to know what he was doing in the RSA. On Thursday, 3 July 2008, his response to 'Dear Nkem' was:

Thanks so much for your mail and the proposals made therein. I wish to inform you first of all that I was successful in the recruitment test into the African Union to be redeployed at the Pan-African Parliament here in Johannesburg. You remember when you phoned me in November last year I told you I was preparing for a recruitment exam into the African Union. That notwithstanding, I will check on www.cic.gc.ca and fill in the immigration form while waiting to be called up to assume duty at the African Parliament.

I will also urge Maureen, Justine, and Quinta [Lonche Fosungu in Figure 54] to react to your request. Please, can you send me Marie-Claire's e-mail address and phone number?

I phoned my wife a couple of minutes ago and they were busy making preparations for our three-month old baby girl, Anangfac, to be baptised on Saturday.

The Fon sent me a mail requesting assistance to buy his way into ENAM or École Normale. He also mentioned talking to you and Marie-Claire on the issue. I will do my best when ready.

Wishing you the best. Chief [this paragraph altered] (B.M. Fosungu, private communication, 3 July 2008).

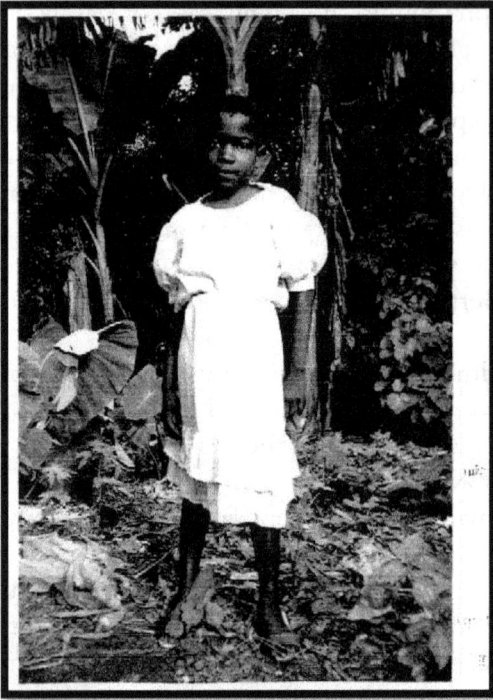

Figure #54: Quinta Lonche Fosungu in the 80s
Source: Photo taken by Momany Fossungu

On the same day Momany responded to Chief Formbuehndia Mbancho, indicating that "this is a lot of great news. Keep it up. Marie's phone numbers are (301) XXX-XXXX (home) and (240) XXX-XXXX (cell). The best of luck. PAF" But Momany never stopped trying to make Bernard see reason in relation to the Canada Question. Almost a year later, in his "Professional Prospects Here" email Momany wrote to 'Hello Chief', stating:

I hope you do quickly get your family down there as you wish to do. As for the professional prospects for you here, I would not hesitate to say they are very high. It is the more reason why I have long been suggesting that you migrate here. If I, for one, am not as yet professionally in place as I should be, it is simply because of the doings of the woman I brought from Cameroon to this country. But things are beginning to take shape, albeit sluggishly, since I met Flavie late last year. I was going to invite you to my marriage on Saturday, the 30th of May this year. The invitations would be ready by mid-April but let me take this opportunity to find out if you could make it here then. I have attached a photo of the bride and groom. Flavie is Bassa from Centre Province in Cameroon.

Please, if you take the Canadian permanent residence application seriously, let me know. You are very qualified for it.

Mafor is supposed to send the CAQ materials directly to the Québec Ministère, not to me. Their address is indicated in the forms. Stay blessed [paragraph altered] (Momany Fosungu, private communication, 23 March 2009).

Still on the Canadian permanent residence question, Fabian Zifack Fotabong of New York City recently wrote to Momany: "Hey doctor, Greetings! I am still researching on the information you requested from me last time. Once I receive any I will let you know. My wife was wondering if you could help her with the filing process of the Canadian professional immigration. She will like to migrate to Canada through the said process. Your contribution will be appreciated. Thanks. Zifack Fabian" (F. Zifack, private communication, 12 May 2016). In response to Fabian, Momany wrote: "Hi Mr Fabian: This is a programme I have myself encouraged many of the Fossungus, including the Fon and Chief Formbuehndia of South Africa, to embark on. They have shown no interest. Well, as you must know, it is not something someone else can do for another; otherwise, I would have gladly done so for the persons mentioned above. Madam should just go to the website (www.cic.gc.ca) and get all the necessary information and steps to follow in applying. It is called the 'Skilled Workers' category. Extend greetings. PAF" (Momany Fossungu, private communication, 13 May 2016). Talking of the possibility of inviting Chief Formbuehndia Mbancho to Canada takes us to the vexatious file in the bunch whose principal actors are in Figure #55.

Figure #55: Nkemanang Calestus Fossungu & Mme Fosang (aka Maurine N. Fosungu)
Source: Fon Nicasius Nguazong Fossungu

Ndemazalism and the Maurinkemanang Godparenting Dossier

Talking invitation to Canada obviously brings the discussion full circle to the non-scholars of the Canada Fossungunization Project in whose arena we actually are in this part of the Chapter. You have just noted the host of others who do not take things seriously being mentioned in the foregoing Nkem-Chief communications. One of them shares the same God-Parents dossier with Calestus Nkemanang Fossungu. I am talking about Maurine Nkengafac Fosungu whose invitation as godmother, Document B, would considerably shorten the narration.

Document B: Maurine Nkengafac Fosungu's Invitation

TO WHOM IT MAY CONCERN

I, the undersigned, **DR. PETER ATEH-AFAC FOSSUNGU**, a permanent resident of Canada currently residing at 8-879 Boulevard Bishop Power in LaSalle, Quebec, Canada, telephone (514) 366-3077 (home), (514) 298-4523 (cell.), born on 15 August 1960 at Fossungu-Fontem, Cameroon, hereby invite **MRS. FOSANG née MAURINE NKENGAFAC FOSSUNGU**, born on 1 August 1979 at Victoria (Limbe), Cameroon and who is currently residing in Yaounde, Cameroon, to the **BAPTISM CEREMONY** of my son, **NGUAJONG FORBEHNDIA FOSSUNGU** (born on 1 April 2003 at LaSalle Hospital Center). MRS. FOSANG née MAURINE NKENGAFAC FOSSUNGU is to be the **GODMOTHER** of NGUAJONG F. FOSSUNGU during his baptism that is scheduled for Sunday August 17, 2003 at St. John Brébeuf Parish (7777 George Street, LaSalle, Quebec, Canada) at 1.p.m.

I hereby undertake not only to provide her with round trip tickets but also to lodge Mrs. FOSANG née MAURINE NKENGAFAC FOSSUNGU, the Godmother, at my residence (879 Boulevard Bishop Power #8) during the one or two weeks surrounding the baptism date.

The present invitation/undertaking has been issued to be used only for the purposes it can serve such as securing leave of absence, travel documentation, etc.

Done at LASALLE, QUEBEC, CANADA

11 June 2003

PETER ATEH-AFAC FOSSUNGU, LL.D.

...me in LaSalle this
11th day of June 2003

LOUISE
POUPARD
195 553

Commissioner of oath

Source: Momany Fossungu's Documents

Nkemanang was billed for the godfather position but could not be reached at the time Momany called him through George Ndemaza's phone that was then their only contact point. The phone problem in Cameroon at the time needs no further embellishment here except to note this fact. That it would explain why, for a start and to facilitate easy and direct communication with targets in the main Poverty Eradication Programme, there was a mini-phones project which quickly culminated in the idea of effectively distributing money (50,000 FCFA each), during the disastrous January 2007 Cameroon visit, for phone purchase to the following persons: Calestus Tenangmock Fossungu (Nkemanang), Dieudonné Asongu Fossungu, Vincent Awandem Fossungu, Esther Asongnkeng Fossungu, and Richard Ngufor Fossungu. That mini project never happened, of course, for moneyintriguist reasons that are already well known but which are largely tied to the intervening death of Fon David Foncha Fossungu, plus all what radiated out of it (see Fossungu, 2016, chapter 2). The importance of this mini-project had been brought home not only by ineffective communication like Richard Ngufor Fossungu's (see Fossungu 2016, chapter 3) but also by the Calestus Nkemanang Narrative going on right here and now.

George Ndemaza had then informed Momany in the 2003 case that Nkemanang was not in Douala and could not be reached in Munyenge (suburb of Muyuka) where he then was carrying out a building contract. Explaining how important it was that he must get into contact with Nkemanang meant also telling George what was actually involved. It must be realised that some of these things are very time-conscious and the baptism cannot just be moved because your godparents coming from abroad cannot make it on time. Anyway, it was impracticable to get hold of the intended godfather. The conversation ended. But a few minutes later Momany's phone rang and it was George Ndemaza who explained to Momany how the last-mentioned phone call to him might just have been God's blessing sent from above. Because he (George) had everything of his ready for travelling to Canada except for an invitation! That was just what had been holding him down till then, George explained; pleading if Momany could help him with loosening that hitch? So, explain this to the crisebacologists: if a person can be so keen on taking all the time in the world to guide people who don't even care to be asking to be helped, what else would such a person be saying to a person

186

(like George Ndemaza) who has already done all the groundwork by himself or herself and needs just a simple invitation that you were about to send out to someone anyway? Why not, Momany had told George Ndemaza in answer and, with his essential information made handy, Momany immediately went and signed a different invitation, replacing unavailable Nkemanang's name with available George's as the godfather, as you can also see in his invitation, Document C.

Document C: George Ndemaza's Invitation

TO WHOM IT MAY CONCERN

I, the undersigned, **DR. PETER ATEH-AFAC FOSSUNGU**, a permanent resident of Canada currently residing at 8-879 Boulevard Bishop Power in LaSalle, Quebec, Canada, tel.: (514) 366-3077 (home), (514) 298-4523 (cell.), born on 15 August 1960 at Fossungu-Fontem, Cameroon, hereby invite **MR. GEORGE NDEMAZA,** born on 5 May1970 at Nwametaw in the Lebialem Division of Cameroon and who is currently residing in Limbe, Cameroon, to the **BAPTISM CEREMONY** of my son, **NGUAJONG FORBEHNDIA FOSSUNGU** (born on 1 April 2003 at LaSalle Hospital Center). Mr. GEORGE NDEMAZA is to be the **GODFATHER** of NGUAJONG F. FOSSUNGU during his baptism that is scheduled for Sunday August 17, 2003 at St. John Brébeuf Parish (7777 George Street, LaSalle, Quebec, Canada) at 1.p.m.

I hereby undertake not only to provide him with round trip tickets but also to lodge Mr. GEORGE NDEMAZA, the Godfather, at my residence (879 Boulevard Bishop Power #8) during the one or two weeks surrounding the baptism date.

The present invitation/undertaking has been issued to be used only for the purposes it can serve such as securing leave of absence, travel documentation, etc.

Done at LASALLE, QUEBEC, CANADA

11 June 2003

PETER ATEH-AFAC FOSSUNGU, LL.D.

Declared before me in LaSalle this ___ day of _____ 2003

LOUISE POUPARD # 138 553

Commissioner of oath

Source: Momany Fossungu's Documents

What is necessary to highlight here is that Momany had never before this time actually met George in person even if the latter knew/knows Momany well; just knowing that his phone number had been indicated as one through which Momany could then reach the Nkemanangs. Momany has admitted that George was very good in performing that duty and nice also talking to for the long period that he acted as contact point. Secondly, and this is where the Fossungu-Family incomprehensibility comes in again and again, George would take all the initiatives to arrive in Yaoundé and go looking for the Yaoundé-based godmother so that they both could go requesting for their visas together, and other such things. But what does Momany's sister do? Maurine Nkengafac Fosungu does not do as advised. George goes alone, after realising just how uninterested the woman is, and he is given his visa like ABC or, as the Bangwa like to put it, *meghteh schighteh njeghm* (without any hesitation). Asked later why she never went applying for the visa, Maurine said: "Brother, I thought you were to invite but my husband and I." *Sans commentaire*, except to again pose the same question that was posed to her in response: "Why didn't you then say so as soon as you got the invitation alone?" Besides, just hear who is talking 'husband' to the brother to whom that so-called husband could not even be presented during the event in Nwangong a year before! These family members would even have all the silly guts to sit around and talk about Momany not doing so and so. What a shameful shame! Some disgraces are not as shameful, you know!

Figure #56: Scholastica Achankeng Asahchop on Matriculation Day at
the University of Buea (Cameroon) in 1995
Source: Scholastica Achankeng Asahchop

In fact, let's all rise again and again and sonorously say thank you so very
much, Scholastica Achankeng Asahchop! Yes, this woman who you first
saw in Figure #23 (and who must be seen here again in Figure #56)
deserves that standing ovation for not similarly wasting the efforts of the
man who is bent on eradicating poverty and illiteracy around him. But
the only question to ask Momany's motivated darling Scholastica is: Why
have you thereafter been so keen on destroying the bridge-builder to
make sure that no other person (like you, not the sitting-on-their-ass
Fossungus) can also be provided a bridge of some sort? But is Momany's
dear moneyintrigust-dragdownist Scholastica even wholly responsible for

no other Fossungu being in Canada today? If Maurine Nkengafac Fosungu and Bernard Mbancho Fosungu do not answer NO to the question, then who else also should? Enter the Manifeut *complexing* files whose architect you can see *complexingly* reflecting in Figure #57.

Figure #57: Bridget Manifeut Fossungu in 2015
Source: Photo taken by Momany Fossungu

Regibriqueentism: The Lying Nonoselfistic Regina-Bridget-Queenta Disconnection and the Brikelie Invitations

Still about invitations on similar lines, let's now appropriately bring in Bridget Manifeut, Calestus Nkemanang's wife. Her case is different from Maurine's in that Bridget was very keen on going to Yaoundé for the necessary visa formalities; but similar, because she and her husband neglected a thing that was just not to be neglected and, in addition, even told an ugly big-fat clumsy lie about it. Making a mistake (like Fon NN Fossungu and others did) is one thing that can be tolerated but lying about something like they did, would just put Momany off just like the nonoselfist attitude that is found in his well known "Be Serious and Let's Know What You Really Want to Do" advice to Mafor Justine (see Fossungu, 2016: 120–121), an email of 1 October 2008 that was duly copied to both sister in Yaoundé (Maurine) and brother in Johannesburg (Chief Formbuehndia Mbancho). There was no response from Maurine at all but Chief Formbuehndia Mbancho (as already seen above) made some efforts to bring the young girl and the others to order and communicated same to Momany. So, what was it too that the Nkemanangs neglected that is so similar to Maurine's visa abandonment and Mafor Justine's blunder?

I am talking precisely about the prior insistence from Momany that they do formalise their marital union: by having an official marriage certificate, if they did not have one as yet. The constant response from both of them was that they did have it. When Bridget Manifeut eventually presented herself requesting for a visa with the two documents (Documents D1-2), on the spot she was told to just present a copy of her marriage certificate and obtain her visa immediately. Did she then have that marriage certificate to present? NO! Anyone can just clearly see how her case was compelling from the mentioned two documents bearing her names as well as the reason for her trip. That is precisely why the visa agent just needed a copy of her marriage certificate to issue her visa without much ado or *meghteh schighteh njeghm*. Their lie to Momany about that marriage certificate was thus very expensive because, in addition, Momany had to then cut off work for the period she was supposed to be there helping out. Let's not even go to be mentioning the children's grandmother (in Figures #8 & #34) who could then not get to ever meet her Canadian grandchildren in Figure #32 until her death in June 2014! What a disgraceful *Nkemanifeutizing* shame!

Document D1: Regina Akiefac Fossungu's &
Bridget Manifeut Fossungu's 2011 Invitation

INVITATION

I, the undersigned, Peter Ateh-Afac Fossungu, hereby invite Regina Akiefa
(my mother,) to Montreal, Canada. The purpose of his visit here is for her
with her three grand children (Peter ateh-Afac Fossungu, Jr., Nguajong
Forbehndia Fossungu, and Ngunyi Ateh-Afac Fossungu), my spouse, Henr
Flavie Bayiha, and her grand son who is due to be delivered in August 201
St. Mary's Hospital Center (3830, avenue Lacombe, Montreal, Quebec, H:
tel. 514-345-3511).

I reside in Montreal (5085, rue Sax #101, Montreal, Quebec, H4P 1C7, tel.
418-3639, 514-573-5509) but now work between the months of April anc
November in Dolbeau-Mistassini for Amenagement M.Y.R. Inc. (385, rue
Boulianne, Dolbeau-Mistassini, Quebec, G8L 6B5; tel. 418-276-3089). In v
her age and the fact that she does not speak English or French, I would lik
mother to travel together with Manifuet Bridget with whom she lives, and
have also invited here for the purpose of assisting Henriette Flavie Bahiya
my absence from Montreal.

I will be responsible for Regina Akiefac Fonge's flight ticket (Douala-Mont
Douala) and, of course, boarding and accommodation while she is here in
Montreal.

Signed:... at Montreal on 4 April 201

CHRISTINE CLARK
16B 247

192

Document D2: Doctor's Support to Bridget Manifeut's 2011
Invitation

Dr. Robert Pilorgé
5450 Cote des Neiges suite 302
Montréal, Québec
H3T 1Y6
Tel. (514) 739 7555
Fax. (514) 739 5599

Montréal, May 04 2011

To whom it may concern,

Madame Henriette Flavi Bayiha is presently 25 weeks pregnant. She will give birth around august 14 2011 at St-Mary's Hospital. She is requesting the presence of Ms. Briget Manifuet.

Sincerely,

Dr. Robert Pilorgé

DR. ROBERT PILORGÉ
5450 CÔTE DES NEIGES
B. 302, MONTRÉAL, PQ
H3T 1Y6

Source: Momany Fossungu's Documents

The London Court-Queenta Disconnecting Effect and the Dieudonné Syndrome

Still in attempt to realise the grandparent/grandchildren meeting, a similar undertaking in 2007 for Mamie Regina to travel with Queenta Ngum Afanwi (see Document E) failed to even take off the ground because of all what followed in the London Courthouse in Ontario on Momany's unexpected return to Canada after the intervening death of Fon DF Fossungu in January same year, coupled largely also with Queenta's own nonoselfistic impatience that is already well covered (see Fossungu, 2014: 128–29). As anyone can easily see, that invitation (Document E), coupled with the contract of employment that Momany already had with Queenta since June 2004 (Document F) would have produced the same effects (like in Bridget's 2011 case) of instant visa grant *meghteh schighteh njeghm.*

Document E: 2007 Invitation of Regina Akiefac Fossungu & Queenta Ngum Afanwi

TO WHOM IT MAY CONCERN

INVITATION AND UNDERTAKING

I, the undersigned, **DR. PETER ATEH-AFAC FOSSUNGU**, am a Canadian citizen currently residing at 7660A Rue Chouinard in LaSalle (Montreal), Quebec, H8N 2E3 Canada. Telephone (514) 364-3272, (514) 686-7660 & (514) 573-5509; Email fossungupa@yahoo.ca .

I am hereby inviting two persons to come to Canada in order to permit my mother to meet her two grand-children – **NGUNYI ATEH-AFAC FOSSUNGU** (daughter), born on 2 March 2000 at St. Mary's Hospital Center, Montreal and **NGUAJONG FORBEHNDIA FOSSUNGU** (son), born on 1 April 2003 at LaSalle Hospital Center – both of whom I have not been able to bring to the large family back there in Cameroon. The invited persons are:

- My mother, nee **REGINA AKIEFAC FONGE** now residing in Bafut, Mezam Division, and
- My mother's caregiver (since June 2004), **MS. QUEENTA NGUM AFUNWI** of Bafut, Mezam Division.

I do hereby undertake to provide the invited persons with round trip air tickets and also to lodge them during their stay in Montreal, Canada.

The present invitation/undertaking has been issued to be used only for the purposes it can serve such as securing leave of absence, travel documentation, etc.

Done at LASALLE, QUEBEC, CANADA on 22 January 2007

PETER ATEH-AFAC FOSSUNGU, LL.D.

DOCUMENTS ATTACHED TO THIS INVITATION/UNDERTAKING
1) Copy of my Canadian Citizenship Certificate
2) Copy of my Birth Certificate
3) Copy of Ngunyi's Birth Certificate
4) Copy of Nguajong's Birth Certificate
5) Copy of my Tax Return Notice of Assessment for 2005
6) Copy of Contact Information of my employer, La Brea Int'l Inc.
7) Copy of pay slips from Premiere Personnel (my other employer)
8) Copy of Contract of employment between Ms. Queenta Ngum & Dr. P. Fossungu
9) Copy of Court Order giving Custody of the two Children to their Mother who now lives in London, Ontario
10) Copy of my Hydro-Quebec Electricity Bill
11) Copy of my Bell Canada Telephone Bill

Source: Momany Fossungu's Documents

195

Document F: Employment Contract with Queenta

CONTRACT OF EMPLOYMENT

BETWEEN
Dr. Peter A. Fossungu (The Employer)
AND
Ms. Queenta Ngum Afunwi (The Employee)

I, **Dr. P. A. Fossungu**, a native of Bangwa – currently residing in Montreal (Canada) – do hereby undertake to pay Ms. Ngum Afunwi a basic monthly sum of fifty thousand francs (50,000 Frs.CFA) for taking general care of my mother (Mrs. Regina Akiefac Fossungu) while I am out of Cameroon.

I, **Ms. Queenta Ngum Afunwi**, a native of Bafut – currently residing and working in Nwangong (Lebialem Division) – do hereby undertake (in view of the monetary consideration from Dr. Fossungu to me) to generally take care of his mother, Mrs. Regina Akiefac Fossungu, just as I would do to my own mother.

Signed at Bamenda this Wednesday the 21st Day of June 2004:

....
The Employer   The Employee

Momany Fossungu's Documents

None of the foregoing instances would be the first time of trying to get Mamie Regina abroad though, because Momany's June 2004 trip to Cameroon (during which he met and fell in love with Queenta) had been solely meant to do just that as shown in the mother's 2004 Invitation (Document G). Mamie Regina was then living with Mamie Lucia Zinzi (who is seen in Figure #58) in the village and there was no one then to have been able to get her a passport beforehand (like Queenta easily did afterwards with her in Bafut in 2007). I am talking of no one being available until Queenta, of course, viewing the irresponsibility of Dieudonné Asongu Fossungu (who you saw in Figure #12) which is highly on top of the chart. This is especially so if you know a little bit more about this *bobby*-interested or *woman-wrapper* brother of mine who thinks that the mere fact that I am in Canada entitles him to be there too. You just need to hear him telling women in bars how he is going to take them to Canada! Call that his clever cocklering strategy, if you like. But just come to imagine that he would be doing so while soya-drinking the money meant to make his passport! You are surely wondering if people still can (like during the *known* slave trade) travel these days from Cameroon to Canada without passports. You are not wrong to conjecture (Fossungu, 2015a: 42–43, original emphasis but note omitted).

TO WHOM IT MAY CONCERN

I, the undersigned, **DR. PETER ATEH-AFAC FOSSUNGU**, a permanent resident of Canada currently residing at 8-879 Boulevard Bishop Power in LaSalle, Quebec, Canada, tel.: (514) 366-3077 (home), (514) 298-4523 (cell.), born on 15 August 1960 at Fossungu-Fontem, Cameroon, hereby invite my mother, **MRS. REGINA AKIEFAC FOSSUNGU**, born in 1931 at Nwangong in the Lebialem Division of Cameroon and who is currently residing in Nwangong, Cameroon, to Montreal, Canada. The purpose of her visit here is for her to meet and see, for the very first time, her grand children – **NGUNYI ATEH-AFAC FOSSUNGU** (born on 2 March 2000 at St. Justine Hospital in Montreal), **NGUAJONG FORBEHNDIA FOSSUNGU** (born on 1 April 2003 at LaSalle Hospital Center), and **REGINALDIE AKIEFAC FOSSUNGU** (expected in February 2005).

I hereby undertake not only to provide her with round trip tickets but also to lodge Mrs. REGINA AKIEFAC FOSSUNGU, my mother, at my residence (879 Boulevard Bishop Power #8) during her stay in Canada.

The present invitation/undertaking has been issued to be used only for the purposes it can serve such as securing travel documentation, etc.

Done at LASALLE, QUEBEC, CANADA

31 May 2004

PETER ATEH-AFAC FOSSUNGU, LL.D.

...me in LaSalle this
...2004
...re *Lepage*
of oath

SYLVIE LEPAGE
151 619

Document G: 2004 Invitation of Regina Akiefac Fossungu

Source: Momany Fossungu's Documents

198

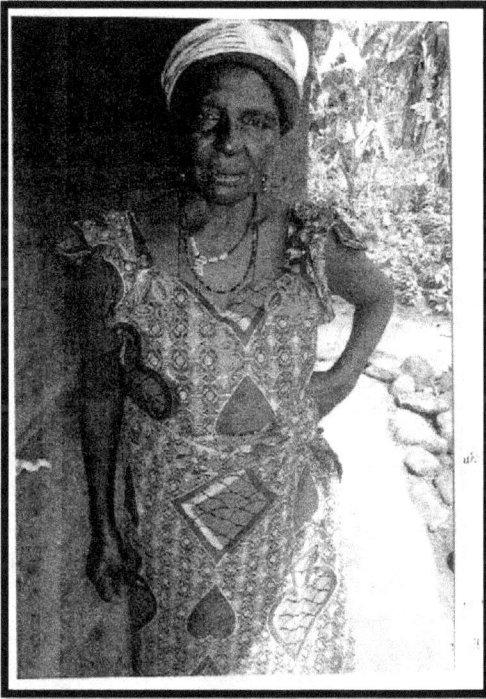

Figure #58: Mamie Lucia Zinzi in July 2014
Source: Photo taken by Momany Fossungu

There was, therefore, just no way Momany could have procured this vital travel document for his mother within the short period he had to be there; thus turning that 2004 trip also into an abortive Canada-going attempt for his mother until the 2011 frustrating 'clean-and-clear' Bridget-Nkemanang blunder. But that is not all there is to the lying nonoselfism of the Manifeut Folder because it extends *emailly* into Kelie's as well.

Emailing and Maforjustinising the Brikelie Invitations Marvels

This is where the discussion of this Chapter really exposes the unholy marriage between nonoselfism and moneyintriguism within the Nwangong Royal Family. The insistence of direct dealing so far has been predicated on phones but it is not the only thing that causes moneyintriguing problems. Having one's email too is also important and to understand this aspect, use will be made of Bridget's and Kelie's situations – the Brikelie Invitations. For donkey years, Momany has been insisting that at least one of the Nkemanangs should have an operational email address. At one point, Bridget talked of having created one which was going. The marriage certificate thing again! One message was sent through it but she was not the one who even wrote that email or received the response. It is just so hard to know what she and the actual operator (Fon Nicasius Nguazong Fossungu) of that email address in her name were thinking in doing what they did. But Momany has since stopped sending any mail there as she was always not aware (during phone conversation) of whatever email that had been sent. Whatever the case, let us see what the result of not having your own email is.

When Bridget's next invitation (Document H) had to be sent to her in 2014, Bridget indicated that Chief Blaise Tendongmo Fosanoh should receive it for her. Just as Momany had told Chief Formbuehndia Mbancho in the course of the Canada College File of Mafor Formbuehndia Justine who you saw in Figure #17, some of these things are loaded with sensitive information and have to be handled directly by the one concerned. You should listen to the Chief-Nkem conversation a little bit to properly grasp the importance of email communication as well as the moneyintriguist shadow that would soon be lurking behind the nonoselfistic scene. Chief Formbuehndia Mbancho asked Momany to provide a fax number to which documents were to be sent to him, telling "Dear Nkem" that:

I got your message on my answering machine last Saturday and read your mail this morning.

Given that the deadline for the interview is very close, I will prefer to send the requested documents to Mafor by fax latest Thursday. This delay is due to the fact that at the moment, the 10th Ordinary Session of the African Parliament is underway and I have very little time at my disposal to run my errands like going to the notary to have the affidavit notarised.

To this end, I would very much appreciate if you can also send me your fax number. I have sent an sms to Mafor requesting same.

Please give me a feedback.

Formbuehndia (B.M. Fosungu, private communication, 3 November 2008).

In "Re: Your Fax Number" Momany wrote to Chief Formbuehndia Mbancho (copying Justine) as follows:

Chief, I can imagine just how tight your day is at the moment. At this moment, I do not have a fax number. As you are aware, I have already filled the forms as much as I could with whatever information that I had and already sent them to Mafor Justine. You need to send the documents straight to her, assuming that she can have a fax number through which to receive them. Even if you fax them to her on Thursday she will eventually still be required to present the originals. Scanning and sending as email attachments could be better since a good scan will be identical to the original. For example, if not of the photo requirement, I would have asked her to complete and sign the forms remaining to complete her CAQ application, then scan them and send to me through email and I print and mail them from here. Maybe you should consider this scan and email option, especially in view of the limited time available until the visa application deadline.

Wishing you the best. PAF (Momany Fossungu, private communication, 3 November 2008).

Chief Formbuehndia wrote back (in "The Major Question: Please Reply ASAP"), stating to "Dear Nkem" that:

I spoke to Mafor Justine about an hour ago and she accepted sending me a fax number. However, I am also considering the scanning option. The major question is: will they accept faxed or scanned copies just for submission? The originals will arrive in Cameroon on Sunday because there are translators/interpreters from Cameroon who are here for the Parliamentary session and will be returning to Cameroon on Saturday night. I will send the originals through one of them. So, will the faxed or scanned copies be enough just for submission on Friday while she picks up the originals on Sunday? Please reply ASAP (B.M. Fosungu, private communication, 3 November 2008).

Of course, Momany does not joke with these matters and speedily wrote back as soon as he saw the mail, telling Chief Formbuehndia Mbancho that:

I have been out all day and have just returned now (5 PM local time). Well, I think you could use both methods since she now has avenues of both. But I think a faxed copy might delay a decision on her file unlike the scan copy which may not be easily deciphered as not being the original. Second, logistically, the scan is advantageous in that she gets it directly from her email without any third-party(ies) being involved. That is just my concern not only for delay in her application decision but also regarding the sensitivity of the information you are transmitting. Good thing that the originals will be arriving on Sunday. With the scan copy sent in before then, she can always present the original if need be and she is contacted for this purpose (very unlikely though). To be on the safe side do send them through both media.

The problem I am having though is that I don't see her as motivated concerning this process as she should be. I sent an important email to her (copying both you and Maurine) and called her to inform her and two days or a day later I called to talk about the contents of the email only to hear that she hasn't yet checked it. It is so discouraging. I know internet cafés are kind of costly back there and that is why I keep sending her some money in the hope that she can easily spend time using these facilities in order to go through this process hitch-free. Some others in her position would be those always reminding us about this or that and asking a lot of questions about this or that document that she or he has just received, etc. As we speak, I am not aware that she has the application forms already filled out and ready and only waiting for the documents from your end. Please, try to call and inform her as soon as you have faxed/emailed the documents. Bye now (Momany Fossungu, private communication, 3 November 2008).

Talking about money regularly sent to her could invite mentioning some instances here. In relation to just the first episode of the Canada College Dossier, (1) the sum of 200,000 FCFA was sent to Maurine Fosungu on 9 October 2008 (Western Union # 943-218-8405); and Justine Fosungu received, as part of the regular sums sent to keep her busy with her internet and other needs, (2) 50,000 FCFA on 4 October 2008 (Western Union # 459-117-6167), (3) 100,000 FCFA sent to Justine on 31 October 2008 (Western Union #158-345-6366), and (4) 100,000 FCFA sent to Justine on 4 November 2008 (Western Union #065-923-1045). Who is that person (knowing the sorrowful state of what late Chief Formbuehndia Nguajong left behind as family) that would not be shedding a river of tears knowing that Momany has been doing all this and more but nothing really has changed for good in this family? At this stage, of course, sensible readers would not even need that I state it again in black and white for them to know that, despite that up to two different smooth attempts (2008 & 2010) have been made with the Canada College Dossier, they have not been enough to get Mafor Justine to Canada. She thus competes in the numbers of enterprises in her regard with only Bridget Manifeut's invitations, because Bridget and her husband, too, would not pay attention to sane advice.

Document H: Bridget Manifeut Fossungu's 2014 Invitation

TO MRS. FOSSUNGU, NÉE BRIDGET MANIFUET

INVITATION

I have planned to have all my five children spend Christmas 2014 and New Year 2015 together for the very first time. It is also to be their first union under the same roof for the duration of said festive period. First time too that a majority of them will be meeting one another.

I badly need another adult in the house to aid in coordinating events and in other essential functions since, as you know, none of their mothers is still with me.

I am hoping that you and your husband can come to terms on alternative arrangements in your own household so that I can be privileged to have the same invaluable assistance of yours here during this historic reunion of my children just like I had during my mother's funeral back there in July 2014.

This invitation is issued to serve the purpose for which it may be required, such as acquisition of travelling documentation and permission from employer (if applicable).

Thank you

DR. PETER ATEH-AFAC FOSSUNGU

104-815 University Avenue West

Windsor, Ontario NA9 5S1 Canada

fossungupa@yahoo.ca

514-418-3639

SWORN Before me in the City of Windsor,)
In the County of (sic)Province of Ontario,)
This 22 day of October 20 14

A Commissioner, etc.,

Giovanna D'Agnolo, a Commissioner, etc.,
Province of Ontario, for Community Legal Aid
Expires May 17, 2016.

COMMUNITY LEGAL AID
2475 University
University of
Windsor, O...
N9B 3P4

Source: Momany Fossungu's Documents

Hence, despite all the explanation that some of these things were better handled directly, Bridget Manifeut (who stands a better chance than her husband) would not open her own email, nor would the husband. Bridget's chances are better since, not only did she (unlike the husband) attend secondary school; but it would also be unheard of to be inviting another man to help you with the lady's tasks at home like her 2014 invitation (Document H) indicates. Her 2014 invitation was thus sent through Chief Blaise Tendongmo Fosanoh in Figure #59, the recipient she had indicated.

Figure #59: Chief Blaise Tendongmo Fosanoh
Source: Fon Nicasius Nguazong Fossungu

By the way (as a big footnote), a lot of these things are usually kept private because of the way even some family members become unnecessarily jealous and sometimes find ways to destroy others' chances of progress. As I have expibasketically realized, 'If not me, no one else' appears to be *modern* Africans' reasoning and could largely account for some cautious people who succeed in the visa thing actually leaving the country before the news is spread. To better grasp the issue, you should hear, for instance, Scholastica's aunt, Mrs. Asaah Justine, in her letter to Scholastica:

Hello Schola, Sorry for having stayed for a long time before writing to you since you left Cameroon. I was first blaming you for leaving the country without informing me. I, as your grandmother, you left without telling that who should pray for your safe journey and your good staying? Anyway, I have forgotten about it. If a child excretes on your lap, you throw only the excreta and not your child. I was very happy when my sister told me you had left.

How are you enjoying your marital life? Stay well and be happy always with your partner.

Mr. Peter, your father, was sick and admitted in the hospital but now he is well and strong. Happy Christmas and New Year in advance! Extend greetings to your husband.

Your aunt, Asaah Justine (J. Asaah, private communication, 26 November 1999).

Mrs. Asaah's referring to herself as Scholastica's "grandmother" is better explained by the intriguing children-naming theory in Chapter 2 known as *Elizachoppism*. But readers should now just hear what then happened to the 2014 Manifeut File to believe in the theory of direct dealing. Chief Fosanoh got Bridget's 2014 invitation and all the supporting financial and other documentation and then played his game on the ignorant invitee. Chief Fosanoh told Bridget that he knew people who could furnish her with very good papers that would guarantee her being given a visa. Money, and I mean a lot of it (as Momany later heard), changed hands. Bridget probably went to the Canadian Embassy in Yaoundé with all the fabricated papers and was not given a visa after all. Some Questions Are: Why do some of these people believe so much in bend-bend or crooked things when the authentic documents are right there? Did Bridget ever get to obtain the exact documents sent together with the invitation? Why would they involve themselves with shady dealers without finding out what to do from the one inviting them? All these queries and many more are posed not only because Chief Fosanoh shortly thereafter travelled to the USA but especially because, after the refusal of visa to Bridget, Momany has tried until today to get the reason of the rejection, to no avail. Bridget Manifeut will even be *fully* shameless enough to say that she was not the person who went to the embassy to collect her own rejected documents! What do they often think when the one who invited them or sponsored their intended voyage insists on knowing why they were rejected?

This story is not new. After the rejection of a visa to Mafor Justine's 2008 Canada College bid, to be able to ask for and obtain a refund of the complete programme payment that Momany had made, the school needed a copy of the visa refusal. To just obtain this piece of document from Maurine Nkengafac Fosungu, who was then based in Yaoundé, became something else. In a communication titled 'The Letter', Momany had written, stating to "Hi Maurine" that "I hope you have not forgotten about the letter you are to send to me. I am waiting for it and, please, try to let me have the letter quickly. My home phone number is the other number below [in signature line]. Flavie can be reached through it. Greet everyone for me and bye now. PAF" (Momany Fossungu, private communication, 14 August 2009). Still not having any action taken, Momany then wrote to her in 'The Decision Letter from the Embassy' (copying Bernard and Justine) as follows:

Hi Maurine, I wonder what is so hard for you to send to me the decision letter from the Canadian Embassy regarding Mafor's visa refusal. We talked on the phone and I explained to you why Canada College here wanted to have the letter. You said you were going to send it as an email attachment the next day. But it is almost one week now and nothing has been done. This is the second letter I am sending to remind you. What is the problem? What should I tell the school that is the reason why a copy of the letter has not been forthcoming until now? Have a nice day. PAF (Momany Fossungu, private communication, 16 August 2009).

How maddening it can be to work with nonoselfists! Or, should I rather correctly say with moneyintriguists?

Does the fact that you send large sums of money to them in order to facilitate the process of going through the complicated visa processing steps hitch-free just mean to them that you just have to send more money (that you have nothing else to do with, according to their calculations) to them before they can release basic things like that letter to you? The money cases already mentioned are just a few examples, not the entire Money-Show for that particular file; not even to begin going near everlasting expenses relating to countless DHL packages sent and re-sent and re-re-sent....: just because someone cannot or chooses not to grasp simple and clear instructions or requests. Exemplification needed again? Then let's get a few more from the same Canada-going continuing mess.

No Scholasticalisation: *Duelling Between Pan-African Institute and Canada College*

You must be told again and again that Frederickeugeneckism or Takebackism is another form of moneyintriguism in the Nwangong Royal Family; a royal house so full of intrigues that are highly punctuated by 'rosy brother only' (*onesidetakism*, akin to the Police-Family Thesis) and never 'all-weather brother' (*giveantakism*, akin to Frantalkism). You can carry this to the Chief Formbuehndia Mbancho bank and still be very sure of easily cashing your cheque there too. It would not bounce. You thus would read Bernard's letter of 28 January 1998 to Momany, stating:

Hi Cinq, Happy New Year 1998! I hope it began on a good note. As for me, the status quo continues despite the enormous physical, mental and financial efforts and resources made and spent. Last March, I embarked on another venture: picking up a job with the CRTV [Cameroon Radio & Television]. So far I have spent close to 230,000 francs in the venture but it has not yet materialised. I am still following it up.

With regard to the admission into the University of Montreal, I barely received the enclosed acknowledgement of receipt from the Registrar but not the admission letter. I waited for it till the start of the academic year. I don't actually know what happened. Please, kindly check at the Registrar's office and see whether they can send me the admission letter for the autumn session. I wrote and sent certified copies of my certificates at the same time with those of Canada to Sweden but received no reply. Please note the change of address, Carol Takwi is in school in Yaoundé. Extend greetings to all. Ben.

Nonoselfists, Where Is the Scholasticalisation and Commitment? The question is quite apt, especially in the context of the self-help philosophy. If anyone is serious on getting the admission that someone else has initiated for him/her until a certain point, is it not that person's responsibility to communicate with said academic institution in case anything is not smoothly progressing? If Bernard changed address, as is obviously the case here, and never kept the institutions informed, what was Momany to do about that by then going to the Registrar's office? On the other hand, just finding someone as motivated in doing things to improve her own situation in life, like Scholastica was, would just fascinate Momany to the point where he wouldn't mind putting every other thing aside to push such a person forward. To better grasp the issue, let me use her entire letter of 12 May 1998 (same year as Bernard's) in which she is anxiously finding a way to get over her TOEFL problem and other hurdles:

Hi Dear! How are things moving on presently? I really felt disturbed when you told me that you do not have money to pay your bills (telephone). This TOEFL issue has really disturbed us. I don't know if it is because those people never sent my number? Presently one is not even sure if they will mark my answer sheet without a number on it. I don't know if we can only write a letter to them explaining it? Since calling is very expensive, one is not even sure to get them. My centre number is A305, Room Number 1 and desk number 119. Please can you use that information in writing to inform them that I never had a registration number?

Dear, I am too busy now in school. We are writing our projects, and school work is not easy, coupled with my many activities this semester. I keep imagining that, if we were together, I wouldn't have been doing many things alone like this.

Please, I wouldn't be able to send my project so that you should read and correct it as we planned. I shall only send one copy to you when I am through with everything, so that you can correct and send to the University of Alberta. I could have loved you to read and correct the English but time is against me and my supervisor is not always in school. The only good you can do to me is to send me money to type and bind it. They need three copies in school, and I need my own copy and a copy to send to you. My supervisor has asked me to make a draft and bring so that she can read and be sure before I do the final copy. I also need maps. I have already advanced money for the maps.

Dear, I am very grateful for the help you have been giving me. I keep asking myself this question, that, if you were not sending money regularly, I could have been doing how with all the problems facing me (us). Imagine that this semester I have gone to Yaounde several times! (Scholastica Asahchop, private communication, 12 May 1998)

Because of Scholastica's motivation and enthusiasm, Momany was actually initiating and doing all her admissions applications by himself, not to even mention all of them like the numerous applications and payments for GMAT and TOEFL testing. For an illustration, on 11 February 1998 he also made out a Royal Bank of Canada money order of CAD $60.00 (#97092608-044) to the University of Alberta, being application fee for Scholastica's bid for admission into the Department of Sociology of that institution.

Despite the confounding lack of such inspiration and gusto, Momany did the same (if not actually more) to the Canada College project that effectively began on Thursday, 4 September 2008 at 11.31 AM, when he had received an email correspondence (titled "Greetings") from his sister, Justine Mamefat Fosungu (aka Mafor Formbuehndia). It was obviously a belated response to his earlier enquiries as to what her plans for further studies were and read:

Dear brother: How are you and your work? Hope fine. I wish to greet you and to inform you about my new address so that we can be communicating. I am sorry for not writing to you, please forgive me for that. I wish to ask about the document and the school year over there so that I can be preparing for the year ahead of me. Brother, I wish to come over there so that I can get something better doing than in Cameroon.

Brother, please, I need a reply from you. Brother, I wanted to go to the PAN-AFRICAN INSTITUTE in Buea which has a programme of 12 months in order to come out with an HND (Higher National Diploma) so that after that I can apply in the higher institute over there which will be easier and economical. The fee for the first six months is 578,000 francs. Five hundred and seventy eight thousand francs and after that you will write an examination for the first degree and the next six months I need to pay another 578,000 francs for the HND. Brother, if I start it this October, I will end it next year October 2009, so that things will be easy for us.

Bye for now. May god bless you [paragraphing has been greatly altered].

Is this not just the kind of attitude that Momany has long been trying to instil in his siblings? Wouldn't this be such an exciting outing from the ghetto that he has for so long been working and looking for? Momany replied to his sister two days later, in his own message titled "PANAFRICAN INSTITUTE" on 6 September 2008. He wrote to Mafor Justine (copying both Maurine Fosungu and Chief Formbuehndia Bernard Mbancho) as follows:

Dear Mafor Justine,

It was nice reading from you after this long while. The idea of studying for the HND (Higher National Diploma) at the Pan-African Institute is quite a good one. It will not only be advancing you in the field but will also keep you busy during which time the alternative Canada-plan here matures. The main question is: Have you been offered admission there already? What do you need to do to be admitted there? As for the cost of studying there for twelve months (about a million francs CFA), I am going to gladly assume that. Just let me have all the details and other modalities. I am very happy that you are taking some of these initiatives. Extend greetings. PAF [paragraphing altered].

Because Mafor Justine had not been admitted in Buea at all and had not even sought admission there, Momany thus began doing all what needed to be done to secure her admission in a school in Canada (so that the academic year is not wasted) and on 8 October 2008, his email titled "Your Admission Letter" informed "Mafor Justine" that:

I have some good news for you. Your admission letter will be on its way soon. But you have to do some homework and familiarize yourself with your new school, program of studies and country (Canada). The school is called CANADA COLLEGE, and your program is OFFICE AUTOMATION. The school is in Downtown MONTREAL in the province of QUEBEC in CANADA. Since I cannot print out everything and send to you in time, I would like you to visit the following website where you will be able to print out as much information as you can and prepare yourself for the eventual and inevitable Visa interview at the Canadian Embassy: www.collegecanada.com.

While on the website, just follow the links and get as much information on your school and program as you can. I have already paid for your entire program that is to last for three months. It is your field and I am confident that you will enjoy this program better than the Buea course at PANAFRICAN INSTITUTE. I will be talking to you on a regular basis but don't hesitate to contact me any time that you have any questions that require some explication. Good luck with your preparation and hope to pick you up at the Airport here in Montreal soon. Bye now. Bro. Peter

On 18 October 2008 Momany's email was captioned "Your Admission Letter and Finances" and told "Dear Mafor Justine" that:

I have called several times today to talk to you but, strangely, your phone was always unavailable. Maurine's phone too was always busy.

Attached you will find your admission letter (JMF) and finances meant to cover the program (JUSTIN MAMEFAT FOSUNGU). You can print these out and get ready to commence the visa application as from Tuesday next week. On Monday (20 October) I will be getting another very important document (LODGING SUPPORT UNDERTAKING) certified and sworn before sending to you. You cannot go and apply for the visa without this third document from me, please. As you can see from the letter from Canada College, there is not much time left before your program begins. It is time therefore for serious and swift-moving business.

As you can also see, your greatest task (at a visa interview) will only most probably be to convince the visa officer (1) as to the necessity of your embarking on this program in Quebec, Canada (and not in Cameroon) and (2) that you will be returning home after you finish studying here. To contribute to point #2, make sure to include your child's birth certificate in your application (or, if there is no reason to do so at that time, have it handy when you go for the interview, if one is required). I don't know how serious your relationship with the child's father is; this too could also help depending on its seriousness, that is, if you decide to look at it as being a couple (no marriage certificate may be needed to prove this at this time). On top of that, remember that you are Mafor Formbuehndia and that, by our tradition and commonsense, you (the Mafor), Chief Formbuehndia (Ben, in Johannesburg, South Africa), Nkem Formbuehndia (Peter, in Montreal, Quebec, Canada), Nkwetta Formbuehndia (late Joe, in Dallas, Texas, USA) cannot all be based overseas or abroad. That at the time of dad's death, all the other members of this cabinet (except you) were already and are still based abroad. It is now not traditionally permissible for you too to be based abroad. This is a very formidable argument to show why you must return to Cameroon: provided you can present it well and back it up. I will include photos of the ceremony during dad's burial and the enthronement of the said cabinet in 2002 in the village when I send the full package through DHL courier. Make sure you also have Papa's will, Anna's death certificate, and other papers handy to show that you are now the sole person responsible for managing dad's estate since Anna's death. But (and this brings us straight on to point #1) you don't just want to stay home and manage your late father's estate without a job of your own in the Cameroon public service, especially now that you have a child of your own to raise. To be able to get the type of job in the civil service in Cameroon for which you have amply trained (Office Staff or Secretary), your job-seeking experience has shown that you need to be able to function well especially in French. This is why you want to pursue

213

this intensive 5-month FSL [French as Second Language] program at Canada College. (As to why it is here in Quebec and not there in Cameroon, see my earlier email to you.) Frankly, coupled with all the other documents sent to you from Canada, I don't see any visa official refusing to grant your visa for your intended program if you develop and present these arguments with confidence and clarity. Make it a habit to always look straight into his or her eyes as you speak to the visa official.

There is a lot to discuss but I just want you to print out these documents and get yourself prepared to start the remaining processes toward the journey to Canada College here in Montreal.

I would have liked that when all the required documentation get there you and Maurine visit the village (probably next weekend) to inform both your mum and dad of the steps we are taking and also ask for their blessings and guidance before you go and apply, say, in the week beginning 27 October. I do not know what both of you think about this suggested trip to the village. Have a nice day. PAF.

You would realize that when you are doing things with people who are not as motivated as they should be, you often end up doing the same things over and over whereas that shouldn't be the case. This exasperating attitude reminds me of this friend of mine who was so frustrated with what she was getting from a family member that she was similarly trying to help that she just wished "I could be capable of just smuggling this idiot of a brother into the country to let him go through what I go through here to be able to even do what I am doing to aid the fool!" It is truly "hell fire" from "Holy Ghost Fire" (to adopt from the Nigerian movie industry) what some of these people can put one through. There is just no need to prolong the demonstrations but anyone who is motivated to succeed in life must really be wondering here why Momany had to be literally doing everything for Justine. And that person must be very right in puzzling over the matter because, notwithstanding their educational levels, Scholastica never had anything as detailed as this, but she very successfully went through a more complicated visa process with what the "wingless flying *Etough*" from Nwangong aptly described

214

(on 19 October 2002) as "those visa-crazy Americans in Yaounde", and on very short notice too! And not even for school purposes but just to attend a conference! It is not for nothing that I keep going back to her as a reference point. I am here *expibasketizing* the bridge-builders' Hercules in illiteracy and poverty eradication in the family and Africa and would have failed in the job if I don't make it extremely clear that Canada would already have been fully Fossungunized had the Fossungus exhibited just a tenth of Scholastica's determination and motivation to follow up on the slightest opportunity that was/is made available to her. I have congratulated her for that a million times and would never stop doing so. How else is anyone going to reasonably put such a person in the same 'Basket of Progress' with someone who would be busy shamelessly drinking away money meant to make his own passport in the same bars where he is telling the same women helping him in the money-eating show how he is going to take them along to Canada? That was Dieudonné Asongu Fossungu, of course, who you have met above. But let's leave that and other similar cases for later and stay on with our unscholasticalized Canada College candidate.

You can clearly see the Scholasticalizing trait in Momany's response to Justine's pledge of seriousness. After shocking his lackadaisical sister with his famous 'Be Serious' email (see Fossungu, 2016: 120-21), Mafor Justine Formbuehndia would recover from it with her reply that came on the same Saturday, 11 October 2008, telling "dear Pa" that:

I am very sorry. I thought you had not seen that mail so that is why I forwarded it to you. I wanted to write at the end but internet services in Cameroon disturb a lot, the lines are always going off and on. So I only struggled that it should come to you, thinking that it will surprise you.

Concerning the email account you created in my name, I don't have the password so I cannot get into it. So if you can please send it to me, I will be grateful. Pa you cannot think that I will prefer to study at PANAFRICAN Institute here in Buea when you are doing everything that I should come over. I promise you I will double my effort so that the interest will be seen. Once more, I am sorry and I hope you are no longer angry with me.

I have printed that programme and am studying it, and I already know that we are going in for a student visa, what more Pa? I am waiting to hear or read from you. Thank you for everything that you have done so far. God bless you. Mafor.

Here is where the scholasticalization that I have been talking about really takes its effect and comes into play. On the same day Saturday, 11 October 2008 Momany told Mafor Justine that:

I do understand you now. Thanks for the undertaking of seriousness you have pledged. I am suspending every other thing I was about to do to anyone else to see that you get here first. Tell Quinta that I could not call her over the weekend as promised because Ngunyi and Nguajong were here and did occupy the entire weekend trying to catch up in enjoying their father. They will be leaving for London, Ontario, today. I will be getting back to Quinta later, let her know that ... [omitted] is the password. Within the coming week you will be getting the admission letter and other documents from here. I have added French language studies to make it have more weight and easier for you to justify why studying here is better for you than doing the same there in Buea. Mafor, try to be sharp and smart in convincing the visa officer that you will be returning home after your programme is terminated. For example, I made the school here understand that you want to study here in Quebec (the only purely French-speaking province in Canada) because you very much want to be able to work and communicate in French since you are looking forward to seeking employment at the presidency or some other government bureau there in Cameroon. And that doing the Office Automation course abroad gives you a lot of added advantage because, in your job-searching experience, you have realised that people with some foreign certification are usually preferred to those with only local diplomas.

Make sure you are in Yaoundé by this weekend because the documents will be reaching Sister Maurine inside next week. I have just talked to her and she is aware of it. Hoping to hear from you and, once more, good luck! Bro. PAF

216

What Is Driving the Option of Studies in the Republic of South Africa?

It is needless saying here again that Justine failed to obtain her visa; and not even after the whole process was again repeated in 2010. It was so very frustrating not only to Justine. What was really awkward with Mafor Justine's further education palaver would be in regard of what happened after the second failure of her Canada College bid. Chief Formbuehndia Mbancho then come up with the idea of getting Justine to school in the Republic of South Africa (RSA) which was a perfect idea, the worrisome timing notwithstanding. In his "Financial Assistance for Mafor" email of Wednesday, 24 November 2010 the Chief wrote:

Dear Nkem, Hope you and the entire family are okay. Following the second refusal by the Canadian Embassy in Yaoundé to grant Mafor visa and in light of the intense frustration she is certainly experiencing, I am proposing that, together, we can bring her down here to South Africa for further studies. South Africa is also a developed country with renowned universities like those of Cape Town, UNISA and Wits, among others. In this regard, I would like to know if you are ready to support me with US $2000 (two thousand US dollars) so that I can initiate the process. Please let me know as soon as possible if you can so that I start charting the way forward. Best Regards. Formbuehndia

Momany wrote back to Chief Formbuehndia Mbancho in his "Re: Financial Assistance for Mafor" of 26 November 2010, stating as follows:

I am only reading your mail now. Since Mafor announced the bad news, I have been down and really wondering what to do next. That is why I am only able to consult my inbox now, intending to ask you what you think we could next do. And BINGO! Your idea is perfect and I think it is very sensible that we do not let the accumulated frustration take hold of the better half of her.

Only issue is that right now I don't think I can afford a lump sum of about two thousand five hundred Canadian dollars.

Last time [in 2008] I asked you to furnish her with sponsorship documents because I was not then working, though I had enough money

217

then to cover her programme here. During that period however child support arrears were still accumulating. Now that I am seasonally unemployed, all my employment insurance payments are being retained by the Justice Department to make up for those arrears which, I have been made to understand, now total around thirteen thousand dollars. We are talking about the arrears only, because I have since resumed regular monthly payments from when I got a job. It's quite a hell here with some of these "sisters" of ours, if you're not lucky to have one of the very few that would work hand in hand with you.

But that retention (garnishing) of monies only holds for the monies one is entitled to from the government, only extending to the employment income and other financial institutions in cases of refusal to pay. As soon as I get back to work by May next year, everything will return to normal. So, please, if it is possible for you to proceed with getting her admission there, I am undertaking to foot all the expenses, with your aid being optional. I was even planning to try sending her next academic year to Malta since Belgium that was first in the plan does not offer undergraduate studies in English. I believe, as you say, that the RSA would not only be cheaper financially but also very convenient for her since she had even expressed concerns of not knowing anybody in Europe.

Thanks for the fast thinking and hoping to hear from you soon. Extend greetings to the entire family. Nkem.

It looks as if the financial-assistance tango that had begun was not going to end until moneyintriguism had scored a bend-bend goal like the notorious onesidetakist Taxi one of Inspector Elias Akendung. But let me first make a related point. Mafor Justine's expression of concern is also clear indication of nonoselfism and the lack of motivation to succeed, capped by her funny attitude (as seen below) after the failed episodes of her Canada College bids. Must one always know someone there before going there for studies? Who did Momany know in Alberta before his first trip to Canada in 1991 for further studies? And who (other than himself) even secured admission for him there? It appears as if the distrust built into the household they were brought up in makes most of its members to think of only always sucking from the other side, for family to be family. Thus, in his reply of Saturday, 27 November 2010 Chief Formbuehndia Mbancho wrote to Momany, in relation to Mafor Justine's education on the table:

Thanks so much for buying into my proposal. The earlier we avoid her from sinking into frustration the better. My situation is a bit tough now because my wife and kid joined me here just about eight months ago and God willing, we shall have a baby boy by the end of next month or latest mid January 2011.

So I am fighting a battle on two fronts; making her papers and preparing for the baby. In light of the fact that your situation has not yet stabilised, you do not need to send the money in a lump sum; you can be transferring about five hundred dollars into my account installmentally at your convenience. What is important is for us to kick-start the registration process and visa formalities will come later. The academic year here runs from January to December with the second semester beginning in June. Your opinion is awaited. Stay blessed. Formbuehndia

In his response of 28 November 2010, Momany wrote: "Chief, Let me first congratulate you for the pieces of good news: The family reunion and the expected boy. Hopefully the papers will work out. As for Mafor's case, I don't know what to say right now because, like you, I am myself very deep into the papers stuff for my wife here and her two kids back there in Douala. But I will need some days to look around and see if anyone can be of help and get back to you. Extend greetings. Nkem." There was no one with a helping hand found and Momany communicated that finding. Thereafter, he never again heard either from the candidate herself (Justine) or from Chief Formbuehndia Mbancho, despite numerous emails to them! What a family!

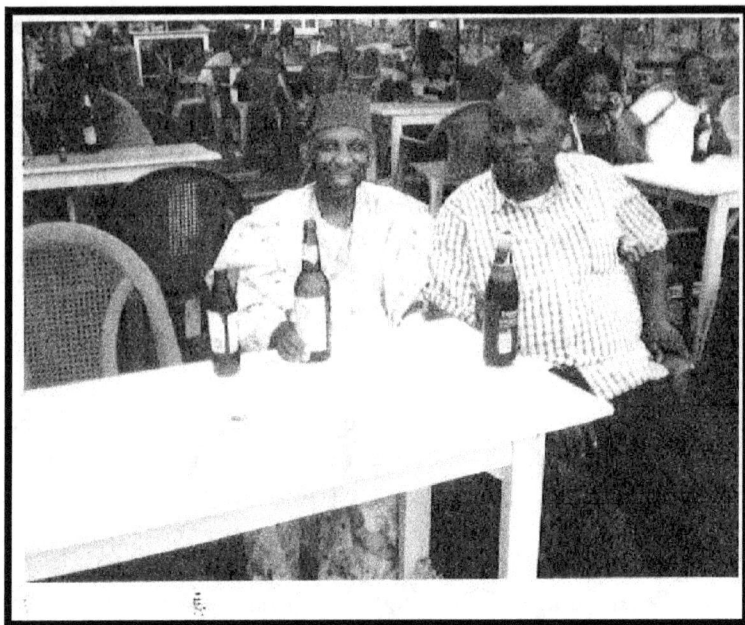

Figure #60: Chief Fotale'eh (Momany) of Canada & Chief Formbuehndia Bernard Mbancho of South Africa socializing in Limbe (Cameroon) in January 2016
Source: Kelie Tsopzem Fossungu

It was only about four years later, with the June 2014 death of Momany's birth mother that Bernard sent financial aid through the Fon of Nwangong as you hear from Momany's "Thanks" email of Monday 28 July 2014 to "Hi Chief Formbuehndia" in which he would "Thank you for the fifty thousand francs (50,000 CFA francs) you sent to me through Fon N.N. Fossungu of Nwangong on the occasion of the burial and funeral of Mama Regina Akiefac Fossungu. Everything went well and I have now returned to Canada. Once more, thanks." Chief Formbuehndia Mbancho on Tuesday, 29 July 2014 wrote back, stating: "Dear Nkem: Thank God that all went well as planned and especially that Mama was laid to rest with all the respect and dignity befitting her status. May the good Lord continue to bless us and, above all, protect us from our enemies. Stay well and God bless." Momany also briefly met Justine and Maurine (aka Mme Fosang) in Nwangong during same death celebration. Maurine, particularly, 'threw' a crate of beer at him, on her way to the coast on the same day of the funeral. What type of family would you think this one should be classified into: Rosy family only or all-weather family? What was actually behind the suggestion of further studies in the RSA then? Could the Ghent University palaver too (in the previous Chapter) not also better school you in the never-ending moneyintriguism matter in this 'Nwangong First Family'?

Viewing all the energy and expenses put into the two fruitless Canada College endeavours, I would want to think the Pan-African Institute option would have been very useful indeed. But you have seen that she had not even obtained admission there too. What then actually went wrong with this Canada College case, if not the candidate's frustrating disregard of simple instructions? Talking of money sent and spent in the foregoing exasperating manner plus the resulting frustration would bring in another similar case. *Enter the Kelie Case* with an invitation (Document I) that was to go together with Bridget's invitation of 2014. But let me commence it with a Western Union money issue since we are also still talking moneyintriguism. While trying to make the various sponsorship applications of Kelie Fossungu Tsopzem who you saw in Figure #22, money to the tune of 200,000 FCFA (reflected in Table 1) was sent on 15 March 2014 to her half-brother, Eclador Tsackeng in Figure #61, through Western Union #103-446-4406, for purposes of a medical examination that was to be speedily done and the attesting document sent back to Canada by express mail. But no matter how many email reminders were sent stressing the urgency, nothing was done: despite that the money was duly cashed on 20 March 2014 at 10 AM. The medicals were eventually done at the convenience of the one who received the money, and not the handiness of the sender of it or even its beneficiary. That case had to go the way it went mostly because Kelie herself then had neither phone nor email of her own.

Figure #61: Eclador Tsackeng & his two sisters in May 2014
Source: Photo taken by Momany Fossungu

A KELIE FOSSUNGU TSOPZEM

INVITATION

RE FILLE:

IIS QU'A CET MOMENT NOUS DEVIONS DEJA EU LA SUITE DE
SSIER A L'IMMIGRATION ET CITOYENNETE CANADA (ICC) EN
UE TU SOIS ICI POUR LES FETES DE NOEL 2014 ET NOUVEL
COMME NOUS AVONS PREVUE DURANT MA DERNIERE VISITE
EROUN LE MOIS DE JUILLET DERNIER.

E LE DOSSIER TRAINE ENCORE, JE T'INVITE DONC DE VENIR
QU'UNE VISITEURE POUR FETER ICI AVEC TES TROIS PETITS
ET PETITE SOEUR QUI SONT ICI AU CANADA AVANT DE TE
ICI DEFINITIVEMENT APRES LE CHEMINEMENT DE TON
A L'ICC.

VITATION EST DELIVRE POUR SERVIR DES DROITS.

ER ATEH-AFAC FOSSUNGU

niversity Avenue West

Ontario NA9 5S1 Canada

a@yahoo.ca

639

SWORN before me at the City of Windsor,)
In the County of Essex, Province of Ontario,)
This 22 day of October, 20 14)

A Commissioner, etc.,

Giovanna D'Agnolo, a Commissioner, etc.,
Province of Ontario, for Community Legal Aid.
Expires May 17, 2016.

COMMUNITY LEGAL AID
2475 University Ave West
University of Windsor
Windsor, Ontario
N9B 3P4

Source: Momany Fossungu's Document

Again, until her acquisition of her own email with which she sent the
'spirit-uplifting message' to her father on 10 December 2014 (see

Fossungu, 2015d: x), Kelie's invitation (Document I) was also sent by email through the same brother on 22 October 2014. But Kelie never had an idea of it until when Momany mentioned it to her in January 2016 while in Cameroon and then forwarded the said email to which the invitation was attached to her email that she has since created. These things are different now because the girl currently has direct dealings and contact with her father and can personally receive and manage any money or other information that is sent to her from Canada. But, even with direct phone and email communication, nonoselfism and moneyintriguism have also not spared Kelie's case. In other words, one would be interested in knowing why Kelie is still not in Canada despite Momany's unwavering determination to still bring her over even after the DNA fiasco discussed in Chapter 1?

It is a long and heartbreaking tale of lies and nonoselfism that can only be summarised here. First, Momany initiated admission for her into LaSalle College in Montreal (on similar lines with the Canada College case) for her to continue her schooling in Fashion Design. Kelie never made the necessary response and follow-ups, not only to LaSalle College but also to other similar institutions in bilingual New Brunswick province. Momany then asked her to get enrolled in any study programme of her choice at the Université de Douala while he is finding another way for her to get to Canada. That, too, she never did; but instead began bringing up talk of *une formation* (training) that she wanted to pursue there in Douala which costs three million francs CFA! When asked if the said amount was not far beyond what her schooling out of Cameroon would even cost, she quickly changed the figure to three hundred thousand francs CFA. At this point, it was very clear to Momany that Kelie was being coached and pushed by someone to simply suck him dry (most probably before the news of her until then undisclosed pregnancy could reach Momany).

The next step Momany took was to embark on sponsoring her as a child-to-be-adopted-in-Canada. Since she was then no longer a minor, she had to sign sections of the papers too. The documents were therefore sent to her by email so that she could quickly print the pages needing her signature, sign and date them before speedily sending said pages back to Canada for the Application to be filed. She never did so. No explanation was forthcoming thereafter except her unconvincing talk of not having seen the documents because she was so seriously sick that she could not even go to internet cafés. All these lies notwithstanding that she had been duly called and instructed on the issue during which conversation she never mentioned any sickness! Like mother like daughter? What else then was still remaining to a man who was hell-bent on seeing her cross the Atlantic than the marriage option? Even the strong arguments favouring marriage as the last way out of the DNA deadlock then barring her (and her unborn baby's) passage to Canada never appealed to heavily pregnant and lying Kelie who, seemingly, was then interested in nothing else than the money flow from Canada, a country which Fon NN Fossungu would be there in July 2014 asking Momany, the newly crowned Chief Fotale'eh, to Nwangongerise or fill with people from Nwangong. How else could that task be performed? Is it by chasing away the moneyintriguists and nonoselfists or what?

Concluding Observations

The demonstration of the perplexing general Nwangong-Royal-Family minimisation of Momany's clairvoyance in this Chapter must have greatly schooled readers in moneyintriguism, onesidetakism, nonoselfism, distrust, and disunity within the said family, a fact that is obviously dragging down its progress and multiplying its financial poverty and consequent marginalisation and misery. It is certain that many people would be enormously surprised to find out that Momany (one of 'the biological outsiders' of the Chief Formbuehndia Household) could even have done a lot of the things they read in this book. All that is understandable because Momany is not only non-discriminatory but is also not good at showing off what he does or has done in the field of ameliorating the lives of people generally.

This Chapter particularly also aids in a way in reversing the mistaken perspective that holds that Momany has not done enough to strengthen the Nwangong Royal Family financially and economically, to leave out many other aspects. The true theory is the reverse because Momany's efforts to generally improve children's education and welfare are simply astounding. Anyone who has read up to this point would hardly need any specific indication again that it is largely the other members of his complex family that have, in the foremost cases, frustrated his praiseworthy efforts to improve on the education and welfare of the Royal Family especially, either through the predominating moneyintriguism and/or their nonoselfism or mamiteelization (defining the division and distrust planted in the minds of children relating to who is biological to them and who is not): all combined into onesidetakism and the dependency syndrome from the colonial education that is still prevailing unperturbed in modern Africa. Those are some of the giant Hercules to family and African development that bridge-builders confront daily. Advanced, as diagnosis, is the Immaculate Freedom, Unity and Development Theory, a premise which is anchored heavily on the three notions of Frantalkism, Giveantakism and Crisebacology.

CONCLUSION

A lot of conclusions are normally to be drawn from this book, an exercise that I humbly beg to leave to readers. In other words, I am saying that the appropriate conclusion to this book is that there is no conclusion, but conclusions because (1) every reader is entitled to draw their own conclusions and (2) the closing of the chapters would also have to be part of the conclusion. Nevertheless, I cannot close the book without emphasising that the family is regarded as the best institution for the socialization of children. You can obviously agree that the Fossungus are supposed to be one of the most significantly powerful and respected families of the entire Lebialem or Bangwaland. But that is not the case since they are not only not remarkable in Bangwaland as a whole but, even paradoxically still, in the Fondom of Nwangong that the family heads 'with its foot'. The marginalisation of this family even in the Fondom results from its financial poverty, a trait that is the direct consequence of the astounding distrust and disunity between its members who, normally, should have been working hand in hand to maintain the integrity of the exalted 'First Family' position in the Fondom. As exposed in this contribution and other works (notably *The Expibasketics and Intrigues of Love*: Fossungu, 2016), this working together has not been the case solely because of the moneyintriguing comportment of the central figures, the bulk of who have actually been central only in fanning and promoting the marginalisation of the family and Fondom. Substitute 'Fondom' with 'Africa' and you see clearly just how African unity and development always ends up being without Africa. That is what properly explains the fact that, "generally, when one talks about African development, it ends up being a talk about Africa's underdevelopment" (Nwosu, 2015: 297). Dr Patrick Nwosu is right on top of the issues; and it means that what is presently being practised does not streamline with the Immaculate Freedom, Unity and Development Theory herein advanced as what is necessary to advance the wellbeing of Africans generally but particularly of children worldwide, the much-sung-about 'leaders of tomorrow'. It is time to vehemently condemn the biological justification that seems to be behind the short-ranged moneyintriguist and takebackist heads of biological parents, guiding all their anti-development reflection that hides behind that cliché of vaguely regarding 'children as leaders of tomorrow'. If not using children as the new excuse for everything as some experts have aptly theorised, what tomorrow are they actually talking about when the majority of these parents would never want to even pass the torch?

An important underlying theory of this book is that, to correctly chart its own development path (that is, Getting Africa into Africa), Africa needs people who (with or without the Whiteman's colonial educational certifications) can see into the future and decipher the supposed charity that is in fact a dangerous trap for Africans; those who can save Africa from the wolves in sheep skins and the redundant calamities that have befallen this continent. People clairvoyant enough to know (like Fon DF Fossungu) when 'the other side' has 'stolen our culture'; to perceive the interminable war that has not yet even begun; to give our children meaningful names that would shape their lives for the better for the community; people who understand that at no price would they sell their conscience or betray the community for their own self-aggrandisement. The book has thus significantly advocated for Africa's dire need for political leadership which, as Frank Bruni (2016) capably tells us, is ideally about representing kin and stranger alike, casting the widest possible net of compassion and letting common values, not personal interests, be the compass.

This stance also seems to be the underlying philosophy of Momany's objective if we duly understand that "the amelioration of living conditions for the 'greatest number of persons possible' net does not distinguish the people to be captured by it. Moneyintriguists or not, family members or not, his birth children or not, friends or foes, the important thing is that life is made more convenient for the greatest number of people possible" (Fossungu, 2016: 219).

228

REFERENCES

Alamu, Akiti Glory (2015) "Exploring Indigenous Religious Tenets for Democratic Sustainability in Contemporary Nigerian Society", in Munyaradzi Mawere and Tendai Rinos Mwanaka (eds.), *Democracy, Good Governance and Development in Africa* (Bamenda: Langaa RPCIG), 213-32.

Asa'na, Akoh (2015) "What Indian Independence Leader Thought about Black People" @ https://www.washingtonpost.com/news/worldviews/wp/2015/09/03/what-did-mahatma-gandhi-think-of-black-people/ [as sent to SobaAmerica@yahoogroups.com by Akoh Asa'na on September 26, 2015 at 9.26 AM].

Berry, Mary Frances and John W. Blassingame (1982) *Long Memory: The Black Experience in America* (New York: Oxford University Press).

Bruckner, Pascal (2011) "Making War, Not Love: A French View on Sex in America - From Abu Ghraib To DSK" @ http://www.worldcrunch.com/making-war-not-love-french-view-sex-america-abu-ghraib-dsk/eyes-on-the-u.s./making-war-not-love-a-french-view-on-sex-in-america-from-abu-ghraib-to-dsk-/c5s3642/

Bruni, Frank (2016) "Daughters and Trumps" @ http://www.nytimes.com/column/frank-bruni/2016/10/12/

Coding, Rosetta (2013) "Fossungu's *Africans in Canada: Blending Canadian and African Lifestyles?*" @ http://www. examiner. com/review/fossungu-s-africans-canada-blending-canadian-and-african-lifestyles?cid=rss (last visited on 24 September 2013).

Dowd, Maureen (2016) "Solving the Riddle of the Slovenian Sphinx and the Pussy Bow" @ http://www.nytimes.com/column/maureen-dowd/2016/10/11/

Duri, Fidelis Peter Thomas and Eussbiah Chikonyora (2015) "Seeing Beyond National Borders: Impoverished Visually-impaired Zimbabwean Beggars in Johannesburg, South Africa", in Munyaradzi Mawere (ed.), *The Political Economy of Poverty, Vulnerability and Disaster Risk Management:*

Building Bridges of Resilience, Entrepreneurship and Development in Africa's 21st Century (Bamenda: Langaa RPCIG), 333-59.

Fossungu, Peter Ateh-Afac (2019) *Getting Africa Out of the Dungeon: Human Rights, Federalism, and Judicial Politics in Cameroon* (Masvingo, Zimbabwe: Africa Talent Publishers).

_____ (2018) *Historical and Partyological Postponement of Democracy in Canada: Elongating the Business Pleasure War in Africa?* (Saarbrucken, Germany: LAP Lambert Academic Publishers).

_____ (2016) *The Expibasketics and Intrigues of Love* (Bamenda: Langaa RPCIG).

_____ (2016a) "Freedom is Free: Liberating Cameroonians (Africans) with the Trilogy of Good Governance – Multiculturalism, Federalism, and Fossungupalogy" @ http://bamendaonline.net/blog/freedom-is-free-liberating-cameroonians-africans-with-the-trilogy-of-good-governance-multiculturalism-federalism-and-fossungupalogy/ (May 6).

_____ (2015) *Family Politics and Deception in Northern North America and West-Central Africa: Litigating God's Marriage Intention?* (Bamenda: Langaa RPCIG).

_____ (2015a) *The HISOFE Dictionary of Midnight Politics: Expibasketical Theories on Afrikentication and African Unity* (Bamenda: Langaa RPCIG).

_____ (2015b) *Africans and Negative Competition in Canadian Factories: Revamping Canada's Immigration, Employment and Welfare Policies?* (Bamenda: Langaa RPCIG).

_____ (2015c) "African Democracy vis-a-vis Western Democracy: Afrikenticating, Follyfying, Expibasketizing, and Reversing the 'African Democracy' Debate", in Munyaradzi Mawere and Tendai Rinos Mwanaka (eds.), *Democracy, Good Governance and Development in Africa* (Bamenda: Langaa RPCIG), 71-124.

_____ (2015d) *Canadian Institutions and Children's Best Interests: Henriflavipeterism as the Quebec 'Money-Only' Sole Custody Case Meant for the Hall of Shame?* (Bamenda: Langaa RPCIG).

_____ (2014) *Africa's Anthropological Dictionary on Love and Understanding: Marriage and the Tensions of Belonging in Cameroon* (Bamenda: Langaa RPCIG).

_____ (2013) *Africans in Canada: Blending Canadian and African Lifestyles?* (Bamenda: Langaa RPCIG).

_____ (2013a) *Understanding Confusion in Africa: The Politics of Multiculturalism and Nation-building in Cameroon* (Bamenda: Langaa RPCIG).

_____ (2013b) *Democracy and Human Rights in Africa: The Politics of Collective Participation and Governance in Cameroon* (Bamenda: Langaa RPCIG).

_____ (1998) "Challenging Intellectuals in Politics: The Village Experience" *The Herald* N° 598 (Yaoundé, 22-23 April), 10.

_____ (1998a) "Intellectuals in Politics: Essential Education from the Villages?" *The Herald* N° 604 (Yaoundé, 6-7 May), 10.

Furlong, Paul and David Marsh (2010) "A Skin Not a Sweater: Ontology and Epistemology in Political Science", in David Marsh and Gerry Stoker (eds.), *Theory and Methods in Political Science* 3rd edition (London: Palgrave Macmillan), 184-211.

Goell, Yosef Israel (1978) *Bi-Nationalism and Bi-Lingualism in Three Modernized States: A Comparative Study of Canada, Belgium, and White South Africa* (PhD Dissertation, Columbia University, University Microfilms International).

Gwaravanda, Ephraim Taurai (2018) "The Impoverished African and the Poverty of Colonially Inherited Education in Africa", in Munyaradzi Mawere (ed.), *The Political Economy of Poverty, Vulnerability and Disaster Risk Management: Building Bridges of Resilience, Entrepreneurship and Development in Africa's 21st Century* (Bamenda: Langaa RPCIG), 255-77.

Hay, Collin (2007) "Controversy: Does Ontology Trump Epistemology? Notes on the Directional Dependence of Ontology and Epistemology in Political Analysis" 27(2) *Politics*: 115-118.

Hindmoor, Andrew (2010) "Rational Choice", in David Marsh and Gerry Stoker (eds.), *Theory and Methods in Political Science* 3rd edition (London: Palgrave Macmillan), 42-59.

Kinni, Fongot Kini-Yen (2015) *Pan-Africanism – Political Philosophy and Socio-Economic Anthropology for African Liberation and Governance: Caribbean and African-American Contributions (Volume One)* (Bamenda: Langaa RPCIG).

LaSalle (2010) "2010 Moulins d'Or Community Award: Fidelis Folifac" @ www.http.ville.montreal.qu.ca/pls/portal/docs/page/arrond_1st_en/me dia/document/folefac.

Magaisa, Alex (2015) "Global Political Agreement and the Government of National Unity in Zimbabwe: Legal and Political Reflections", in Munyaradzi Mawere and Tendal Rinos Mwanaka (eds.), *Democracy, Good Governance and Development in Africa* (Bamenda: Langaa RPCIG), 233-67.

Marongwe, Ngonidzashe and Tinashe Mawere (2015) "Mandela and Coloniality in South Africa", in Munyaradzi Mawere and Tendal Rinos Mwanaka (eds.), *Democracy, Good Governance and Development in Africa* (Bamenda: Langaa RPCIG), 125-55.

Mawere, Munyaradzi (2018) "The Political Economy of Poverty and Vulnerability: How Africa Can Break the Cycle of Poverty to Unlock its Underdevelopment Jam?", in Munyaradzi Mawere (ed.), *The Political Economy of Poverty, Vulnerability and Disaster Risk Management: Building Bridges of Resilience, Entrepreneurship and Development in Africa's 21st Century* (Bamenda: Langaa RPCIG), 11-37.

Mawere, Munyaradzi, Annastasia M. Mawere and Pedro Celso Jovo (2015) "Culture, Ethics and Politics for a Better and Sustainable Africa: The Mozambican Experience", in Munyaradzi Mawere and Tendai Rinos Mwanaka (eds.), *Democracy, Good Governance and Development in Africa* (Bamenda: Langaa RPCIG), 269-95.

Mawere, Munyaradzi and Gertjan van Stam (2015) "Paradigm Clash, Imperial Methodological Epistemologies and Development in Africa: Observations from rural Zimbabwe and Zambia", in Munyaradzi Mawere and Tendai Rinos Mwanaka (eds.), *Democracy, Good Governance and Development in Africa* (Bamenda: Langaa RPCIG), 183-211.

Mbipgo, Ngah Christian (1997) "Hairdressing Is Not a Profession for School Drop-Outs – Mokom Anna" *The Herald* N° 541 (Yaoundé, 1-2 December), 10.

Mhango, Nkwazi (2018) "Poverty and the Discourse about the Global North's Playing of the Global South", in Munyaradzi Mawere (ed.), *The Political Economy of Poverty, Vulnerability and Disaster Risk Management: Building Bridges of Resilience, Entrepreneurship and Development in Africa's 21st Century* (Bamenda: Langaa RPCIG), 39-61.

Mubaya, Tapuwa Raymond, Munyaradzi Mawere and Joshua Chikozho (2015) "The Unsung Dimension of Great Zimbabwe National Monument: A Critique", in Munyaradzi Mawere and Tendal Rinos Mwanaka (eds.), *Democracy, Good Governance and Development in Africa* (Bamenda: Langaa RPCIG), 315-41.

Nhemachena, Artwell (2018) "World Not Humanistic Enough to Listen to Afrikan Voices" @ https://www.unisa.ac.za/sites/corporate/default/Colleges/Human-Sciences/News-&-events/Articles/World-not-humanistic-enough-to-listen-to-Afrikan-voices.

Nwosu, Patrick U. (2015) "Education for Sustainable Development in Africa: An Appraisal with Focus on Nigerian Experience", in Munyaradzi Mawere and Tendal Rinos Mwanaka (eds.), *Democracy, Good Governance and Development in Africa* (Bamenda: Langaa RPCIG), 297-314.

Reaves, Celia S. (1992) *Quantitative Research for the Behavioral Sciences* (Washington, D.C: John Willey & Sons).

Rush, Rep. Bobby (2011) "The Maid and the Millionaire" @ http://www.huffingtonpost.com/rep-bobby-rush/the-maid-and-the-milliona_b_918560.html.

Sa'ah, Randy Joe (1997) "Judo Does Not Affect a Lady's Beauty – Awa Marceline" *The Herald* N°541 (Yaoundé, 1-2 December), 11.

Sanders, David (2010) "Behavioural Analysis", in David Marsh and Gerry Stoker (eds.), *Theory and Methods in Political Science* 3rd edition (London: Palgrave Macmillan), 23-41.

Selick, Karen (1996a) "Children: The New Excuse for Everything" *Canadian Lawyer* (January), 46.

233

_____ (1996b) "Child Support – The View from Mars" *Canadian Lawyer* (July/August), 46.

Stanley, Liam (2012) "Research and Analysis: Rethinking the Definition and Role of Ontology in Political Science" 32(2) *Politics* 93-99.

Yinusa, Muhammed A., Joseph A. Oluyemi and Raji Abdullateef (2018) "Children, Women, Development and Fundamental Human Rights in Some African Societies", in Munyaradzi Mawere (ed.), *The Political Economy of Poverty, Vulnerability and Disaster Risk Management: Building Bridges of Resilience, Entrepreneurship and Development in Africa's 21st Century* (Bamenda: Langaa RPCIG), 279-308.

Mmap Nonfiction and Academic books

If you have enjoyed **FAMILY LAW AND POLITICS WITH BIOLOGY AND ROYALTY IN AFRICA AND NORTH AMERICA,** consider these other fine *Nonfiction and Academic* books from **Mwanaka Media and Publishing:**

Cultural Hybridity and Fixity by Andrew Nyongesa
Tintinnabulation of Literary Theory by Andrew Nyongesa
South Africa and United Nations Peacekeeping Offensive Operations by Antonio Garcia
A Case of Love and Hate by Chenjerai Mhondera
A Cat and Mouse Affair by Bruno Shora
The Scholarship Girl by Abigail George
The Gods Sleep Through It All by Wonder Guchu
PHENOMENOLOGY OF DECOLONIZING THE UNIVERSITY: *Essays in the Contemporary Thoughts of Afrikology by Zvikomborero Kapuya*
Africanization and Americanization Anthology Volume 1, Searching for Interracial, Interstitial, Intersectional and Interstates Meeting Spaces, Africa Vs North America by Tendai R Mwanaka
Africa, UK and Ireland: Writing Politics and Knowledge Production Vol 1 by Tendai R Mwanaka
Writing Language, Culture and Development, Africa Vs Asia Vol 1 by Tendai R Mwanaka, Wanjohi wa Makokha and Upal Deb
Zimbolicious: An Anthology of Zimbabwean Literature and Arts, Vol 3 by Tendai Mwanaka
Drawing Without Licence by Tendai R Mwanaka
Writing Grandmothers/ Escribiendo sobre nuestras raíces: Africa Vs Latin America Vol 2 by Tendai R Mwanaka and Felix Rodriguez
Nationalism: (Mis)Understanding Donald Trump's Capitalism, Racism, Global Politics, International Trade and Media Wars, Africa Vs North America Vol 2 by Tendai R Mwanaka
It Is Not About Me: Diaries 2010-2011 by Tendai Rinos Mwanaka

Chitungwiza Mushamukuru: An Anthology from Zimbabwe's Biggest Ghetto Town by Tendai Rinos Mwanaka
The Day and the Dweller: A Study of the Emerald Tablets by Jonathan Thompson
Zimbolicious Anthology Vol 4: An Anthology of Zimbabwean Literature and Arts by Tendai Rinos Mwanaka and Jabulani Mzinyathi
Parks and Recreation by Abigail George

Soon to be released

Writing Robotics, Africa Vs Asia, Vol 2 by Tendai Rinos Mwanaka
Zimbolicious Anthology Vol 5: An Anthology of Zimbabwean Literature and Arts by Tendai R. Mwanaka and Tembi Charles

https://facebook.com/MwanakaMediaAndPublishing/